Savvy in the City:

NEW YORK CITY

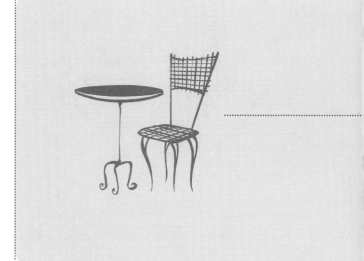

Jayne Young

and

Sheridan Becker

St. Martin's Griffin ✼ New York

Savvy in the City:

NEW YORK CITY

A "See Jane Go" Guide to City Living

For Mary Frances Young,

"The Original Jane Girl"

www.stmartins.com

BOOK DESIGN BY VICTORIA KUSKOWSKI

MAPS BY JEFFREY L. WARD
ARTWORK © 2001 BY JORDI LABANDA

Library of Congress Cataloging-in-Publication Data

Young, Jayne.
    Savvy in the city—New York : a "see Jane go" guide to city living / Jayne Young and Sheridan Becker.—1st ed.
      p. cm—(A "see Jane go" guide to city living)
    ISBN 0-312-25277-3
    1. New York (N.Y.)—Guidebooks. 2. Women—Travel—New York (State)—New York—Guidebooks. 3. City and town life—New York (State)—New York. I. Becker, Sheridan. II. Title.

F128.18. Y68 2001
917.47'10444—dc21   2001041949

10 9 8 7 6 5 4 3

Contents

Eats   1

The Five Food Groups: Beluga, Chardonnay, Truffles, French Fries, Pop-Tarts . . . Whether you are interested in nouvelle cuisine or scrumptious munchies, you can find the best of the best here.

Treats   49

For any pocketbook, everything fun and fabulous to pamper your every sense . . . Be kneaded like fresh baguette dough, be aromatically oiled like an Indian princess, be tattooed like a Hells Angel, and then be tightened and tucked like . . . Never mind, we'll drop names later!

Traumas   83

Nifty tips on where and how to solve girl traumas of all magnitudes (we know you're prone to hysteria) in case you ever leave home without whatever "it" is.

Anything and everything your heart, mind, body, soul and mother desire all over the city in every nook and cranny . . . Big or small, outrageous or simple, luxurious or bargain . . . If you can't find what you need, we suggest you contact NASA for a shuttle ticket.

Twilight 169

"Twinkle twinkle little star, how I wonder what cute boy we might trip over on our adventures into the night . . ." The Big Apple becomes even bigger— and more "poisonous"—as the sun goes down, so take advantage of all these opportunities for entertainment and wild abandon. Little black dress not provided!

Tripping 205

We're not talking acid, we're talking adventure. You've hit the Big Apple with a bang . . . What's fun, unique, free, freeing, shocking, educational, trendy, playful, creative, exotic, adventurous, athletic, and artistic this side of the Statue of Liberty (and beyond!)? Fasten your seat belts.

Acknowledgments

This book would not have been a reality without

Mary Dorrian
&
Whitney Daane

Extra special thanks to: William Clark, agent extraordinaire; Adam Robinson, a genius man with a plan; Jordi Labanda, for making "Jane" come alive; Kelley Ragland, for belief and motivation; Sally Carnes, truly a visionary graphic artist; W&R Group, for patience and understanding; James Young, for his unwavering positive attitude and "clippings"; and last but not least, my loving siblings: Gary, Linda, Gilbert, Brian, Mary Ann, and Larry.

Jayne would also like to thank: Stuart Allen, Siobhan Callahan, Stefano Eco, Amy Young, Parma Chaudhury, Pacy Wu, Claire Canavan, Michela Hill, Bob Doyle, Peter Imber, Pam Rousakis, Andy and Helga Fuhrmann, Alexandra Hannen Scott, Tracy Denton, Jennifer Paterino, Steve Prue, Ben Sevier, John Carley, the Dorrian family, Patrica Murphy, Dewey and Barbara "Bubbles" Daane, St. Martin's Press, Stephanie and the Art Department, and all of the cooperative estabishments listed (you know who you are!).

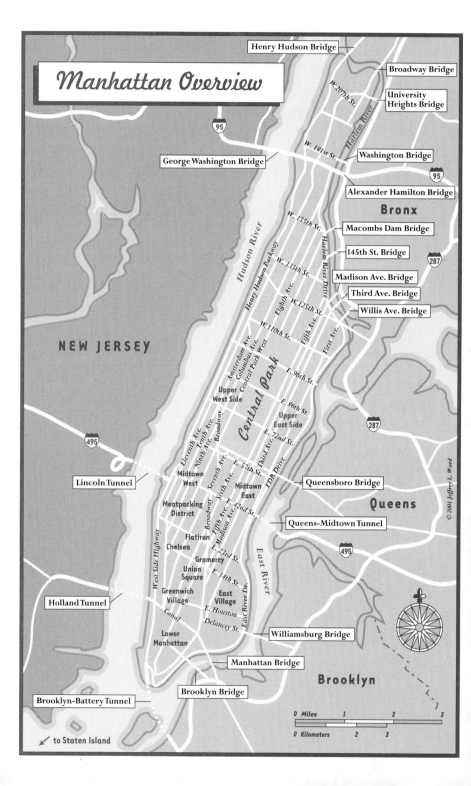

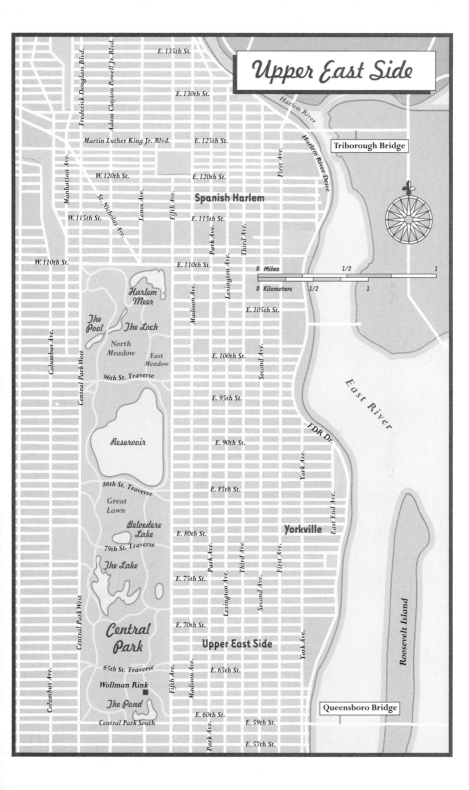

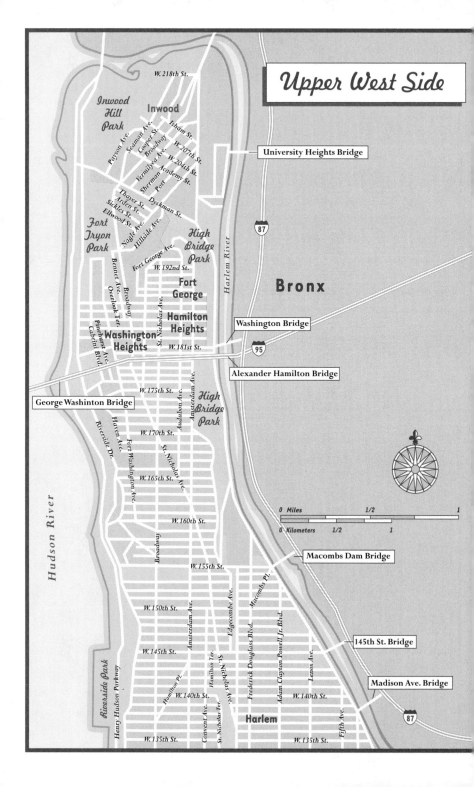

Bronx
Third Ave. Bridge
Harlem River
Willis Ave. Bridge
Harlem
Morningside Heights
Morningside Park
Columbia University
Hudson River
West Side Highway
Harlem Meer
The Pool
The Loch
North Meadow
East Meadow
96th St. Traverse
Reservoir
86th St. Traverse
Great Lawn
Belvedere Lake
79th St. Traverse
The Lake
Upper West Side
Central Park
65th St. Traverse
Wollman Rink
The Pond
Central Park South
W. 135th St.
E. 135th St.
E. 130th St.
W. 125th St.
La Salle St.
Martin Luther King Jr. Blvd.
E. 125th St.
W. 120th St.
E. 120th St.
W. 115th St.
E. 115th St.
W. 110th St.
E. 110th St.
Duke Ellington Blvd.
W. 105th St.
E. 105th St.
W. 100th St.
E. 100th St.
W. 95th St.
E. 95th St.
W. 90th St.
E. 90th St.
W. 85th St.
E. 85th St.
W. 80th St.
E. 80th St.
W. 75th St.
E. 75th St.
W. 70th St.
E. 70th St.
W. 65th St.
E. 65th St.
W. 60th St.
E. 60th St.
W. 59th St.
E. 59th St.
W. 57th St.
E. 57th St.
Broadway
Convent Ave.
St. Nicholas Ter.
Frederick Douglass Blvd.
Adam Clayton Powell Jr. Blvd.
Riverside Dr.
Claremont Ave.
Amsterdam Ave.
Morningside Dr.
Morningside Ave.
St. Nicholas Ave.
Lenox Ave.
Fifth Ave.
Park Ave.
Madison Ave.
Lexington Ave.
Manhattan Ave.
West End Ave.
Columbus Ave.
Central Park West
Third Ave.
First Ave.
Second Ave.
York Ave.
Eighth Ave.
Seventh Ave.

Midtown

Hudson River

East River

Roosevelt Island Tramway

Queensboro Bridge

Roosevelt Island

FDR Dr.

Sutton Pl. South

Mitchell Pl.

Beekman Pl.

Sutton

1st Ave.

2nd Ave.

3rd Ave.

Turtle Bay

Tudor City Pl.

E. 45th St.

E. 44th St.

E. 43rd St.

Queens-Midtown Tunnel

FDR Dr.

1st Ave.

2nd Ave.

3rd Ave.

E. 60th St.
E. 59th St.
E. 58th St.
E. 57th St.
E. 56th St.
E. 55th St.
E. 54th St.
E. 53rd St.
E. 52nd St.
E. 51st St.
E. 50th St.
E. 49th St.
E. 48th St.
E. 47th St.
E. 46th St.

Madison Ave.
Fifth Ave.
Park Ave.

Lexington Ave.

E. 42nd St.

E. 41st St.
E. 40th St.

E. 39th St.
E. 38th St.
E. 37th St.
E. 36th St.
E. 35th St.
E. 34th St.
E. 33th St.

Park Ave.
2nd Ave.
3rd Ave.

Murray Hill

Grand Central Terminal

Bryant Park

Midtown East

Rockefeller Plaza

Sixth Ave.

Seventh Ave.

Central Park

Central Park South

Columbus Circle

Eighth Ave.

Broadway

Times Square

Theater District

Broadway

Herald Square

Garment Center

Port Authority Bus Terminal

W. 60th St.
W. 59th St.
W. 58th St.
W. 57th St.
W. 56th St.
W. 55th St.
W. 54th St.
W. 53rd St.
W. 52nd St.
W. 51st St.
W. 49th St.
W. 48th St.
W. 47th St.
W. 46th St.
W. 45th St.
W. 44th St.
W. 43rd St.
W. 42nd St.
W. 41st St.
W. 40th St.
W. 39th St.
W. 37th St.
W. 36th St.
W. 35th St.
W. 34th St.
W. 33th St.

Ninth Ave.
Tenth Ave.
Tenth Ave.

Dyer Ave.

W. 38th St.

W. 41st St.

Eleventh Ave.

Twelfth Ave.

West Side Highway

Midtown West

Lincoln Tunnel

0 Miles   1/4   1/2
0 Kilometers   1/4   1/2   1/2

Greenwich Village

W. 21st St.
W. 20th St.
W. 19th St.
W. 18th St.
W. 17th St.
W. 16th St.
W. 15th St.
W. 14th St.
W. 13th St.
W. 12th St.
W. 11th St.
W. 10th St.
W. 9th St.
W. 8th St.

Broadway
Park Ave. South

Union
Square

Fifth Ave.
Sixth Ave.
Seventh Ave.
Eigth Ave.
Ninth Ave.
Tenth Ave.

W. 14th St.
W. 13th St.
Little W. 12th St.
Gansevoort St.
Horatio St.
Jane St.
W. 12th St.
Washington St.
Bethune St.
Bank St.
W. 11th St.
Perry St.
Charles St.
W. 10th St.
Barrow St.
Morton St.
Leroy St.
Clarkson St.
West St.
Hudson St.
Greenwich St.
Christopher St.
St. Luke's Pl.
W. Houston St.

Greenwich Ave.
Waverly Place
W. 4th St.
Eigth Ave.
Bleecker St.

Milligan Pl.
Patchin Pl.

University Place
Broadway

Christopher St.
Gay St.

MacDougal
Alley
Washington
Mews

Waverly Place

Washington
Square
Park
W. 4th St.

E. Washington Pl.

W. Washington Pl.
Grove St.
Barrow St.
Jones St.
Cornelia St.
Bleecker St.
Commerce St.
Bedford St.
Carmine St.
Downing St.
Seventh Ave. South
Sixth Ave.

W. 3rd St.
Minetta La.

Great Jones St.
Bond St.
Shinbone
Alley
Jones
Alley
Bleecker St.

MacDougal St.
Sullivan St.
Thompson St.
La Guardia Pl.
Broadway

W. Houston St.

Hudson River

West St.

0 Miles   1/4   1/2
0 Kilometers   1/4   1/2

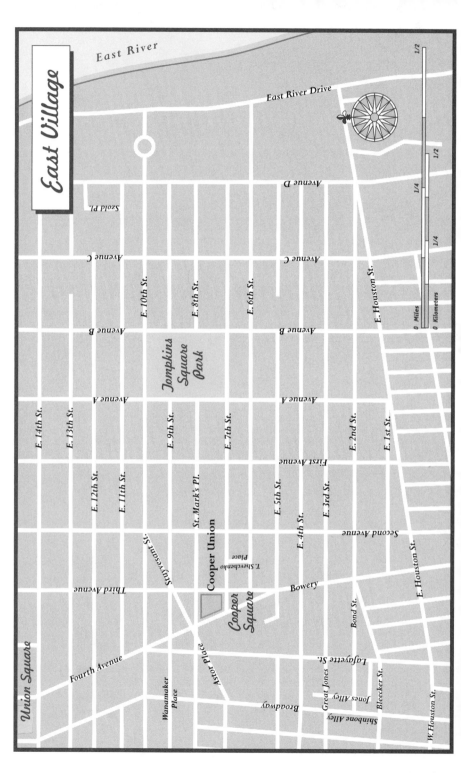

Chelsea/Gramercy/Flatiron/Meatpacking District/Union Square

East River

Hudson River

Stuyvesant

Gramercy

Union Square

Union Square Park

Flatiron

Chelsea

Meatpacking District

Madison Square Park

Empire State Building

Penn Station

Lincoln Tunnel Entrance/Exit

Penn Plaza Drive

West Side Highway

Eleventh Ave.

Twelfth Ave.

Tenth Ave.

Ninth Ave.

Eighth Ave.

Seventh Ave.

Sixth Ave.

Fifth Ave.

Broadway

Madison Ave.

Park Ave. South

Lexington Ave.

Third Ave.

Second Ave.

First Ave.

Gramercy Pk. W.

Gramercy Pk. E.

E. 34th St.
E. 33rd St.
E. 32nd St.
E. 31st St.
E. 30th St.
E. 29th St.
E. 28th St.
E. 27th St.
E. 26th St.
E. 25th St.
E. 24th St.
E. 23rd St.
E. 22nd St.
E. 21st St.
E. 20th St.
E. 19th St.
E. 18th St.
E. 17th St.
E. 16th St.
E. 15th St.
E. 14th St.

W. 34th St.
W. 33rd St.
W. 32nd St.
W. 31st St.
W. 30th St.
W. 29th St.
W. 28th St.
W. 27th St.
W. 26th St.
W. 25th St.
W. 24th St.
W. 23rd St.
W. 22nd St.
W. 21st St.
W. 20th St.
W. 19th St.
W. 18th St.
W. 17th St.
W. 16th St.
W. 15th St.
W. 14th St.

0 Miles   1/2
0 Kilometers   1/2

Lower Manhattan

Wash. Square Park

Seventh Ave. South

Hudson St.

MacDougal St.
Sullivan St.
Thompson St.
La Guardia Pl.

Broadway

W. Houston St.

Mercer St.

Greene St.

Crosby St.

Lafayette St.

Cleveland Pl.

King St.
Charlton St.
Vandam St.
Spring St.
Dominick St.

Sixth Ave.

Prince St.

Spring St.

Wooster St.

SoHo

Broome St

Broadway

Holland Tunnel Entrance

Holland Tunnel

Holland Tunnel Exit

Grand St.

Lafayette St.

Watts St.
Desbrosses St.
Vestry St.
Laight St.
Hubert St.

Hudson St.

Varick St.

Tribeca

Howard St.

Canal St.

Lispenard St.

West Side Highway (Joe DiMaggio Highway)

Beach St. Ericsson Pl.
N. Moore St.
Franklin Place

West Broadway

Walker St.
White St.
Franklin Place
Leonard St.

Centre St.

Harrison St.   Staple St.
Jay St.

West St.

North End Ave.

Worth St.
Thomas St.
Duane St.
Reade St.

Chambers St.

Federal Plaza

Elk St.

Greenwich St.

Warren St.
Murray St.
Park Pl.
Barclay St.

City Hall Park

Park Row

Beekman St.

Vesey St.

Church St.

Dey St.

Ann St.
Fulton St.

William St.

Maiden La.
Liberty St.
Cedar St.

Nassau St.

Pine St.

Trinity Pl.

Broadway

Wall St.

Hanover St.

South End Ave.

Albany St.
Rector St.

Greenwich St.

Thames St.

New St.

Exchange Pl.

Battery Park City

West Thames St.
3rd Pl.
2nd Pl.
1st Pl.

Washington St.

Morris St.

Beaver St.

S. Williams St.

Stone St.

Battery Pl. Bowling Green

Bridge St.

Whitehall St.

Broad St.

State St.

Battery Park

South St.

Hudson River

Holland Tunnel

0 Miles   1/2
0 Kilometers   1/2

Brooklyn-Battery Tunnel

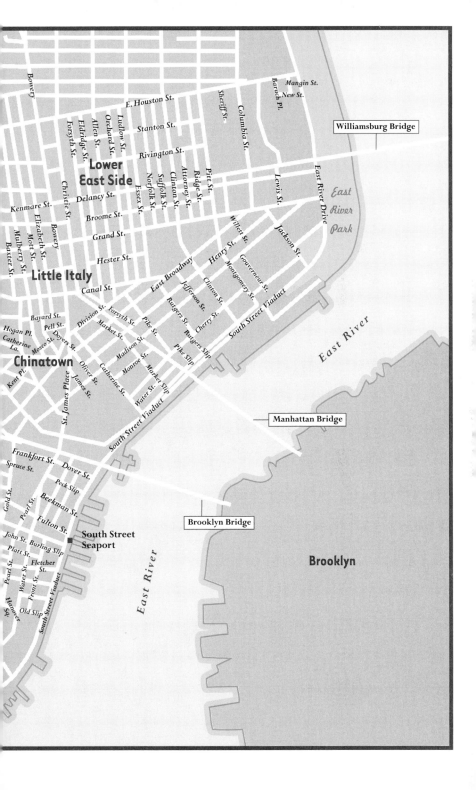

Eats

Avenue Bistro, 520 Columbus Ave. (@ 85th St.), (212) 579-3194, *Brunch Bistro*

If you are in search of an authentic bistro, try Scott Campbell's brunch for a true treat. This man wants you to eat well: he smokes his own salmon and stuffs his own sausages! What a way to enhance the flavor of your everyday eggs Benedict. Though, the service is spotty at best. Be sure to leave room to sample the ice cream and sorbet. *Psst. . . . if you have Baby in tow, sample Campbell's own line of organic baby food!*

Big Nick's Burgers and Pizza Joint Too, 70 West 71st St. (@ Columbus Ave.), (212) 799-4450, *Hangover Cure*

This 24-hour dive delivers until 5 A.M.! So when the bed is spinning or you're weaving up Columbus after a rollicking night out, these guys are a lifesaver. The giant succulent burgers are world-renowned for their curative properties after a night of trendy cocktails or fighting with your fiancée. (The pizza isn't bad either.)

Bodhi Organic Juice Bar, 473 Amsterdam Ave. (bet. 82nd & 83rd Sts.), (212) 362-1891, *Savory Slurpies*

If you jones for wheat grass, this is your destination. A liquid lunch haven for the healthy or crash-dieting debutante. The pear and grapefruit smoothies are groovy!

Café Lalo, 201 W. 83rd St. (bet. Broadway & Amsterdam Ave.), (212) 496-6031, *Dessert*

Like an adorable European movie set complete with romantic twinkling lights that make it perfect for a casual date, Café Lalo serves salads and sandwiches, but they're just an excuse to get to the fantastic array of desserts and coffee—oink, oink! Speaking of movie sets: Tom and Meg met here for their first date in *You've Got Mail*.

Columbus Bakery, 474 Columbus Ave. (bet. 82nd & 83rd Sts.), (212) 724-6880, *Morning Hang*

Newspaper, large coffee, even larger bagels and pastries get you on your way in this everyday destination for Upper Westsiders. See other locations in UES.

Gabriel's, 11 W. 60th St. (bet. Broadway & Columbus Ave.), (212) 956-4600, *Homey Upscale Italian*

Down-to-earth Northern Italian with formal flair but zero attitude, it's the perfect blend of casual mood and fancy surroundings. A bit steep in price for the single gal, but a delicious experience all the same. Great if your daddy (biological or sugar) is treating.

Gennaro, 665 Amsterdam Ave. (bet. 92nd & 93rd Sts.), (212) 665-5348, *Early Evening / Italian*

Amazing Italian with a bad attitude but reasonable prices. Check it out early in the evening before the fourteen tabletops are gobbled up by locals. Must bring cash and patience.

Good Enough to Eat, 483 Amsterdam Ave. (bet. 83rd & 84th Sts.), (212) 496-0163, *Breakfast / Brunch*

Our thoughts exactly! Cheap, good, go! Beware of careening strollers . . .

John's Pizzeria, 48 W. 65th St. (bet. Columbus Ave. & CPW), (212) 721-7001, *Traditional Pizzeria*

See details in GV, other locations in UES, MTW.

Josie's, 300 Amsterdam Ave. (@ 74th St.), (212) 769-1212, *Health Trend*

Yuppies and vegetables galore. The trendy tofu crowd waits for tables in this cacophonous health-food hot spot. Even a carnivore will find something tasty to try.

Levain Bakery, 167 W. 74th St. (bet. Amsterdam & Columbus Aves.), (212) 874-6080, *Cookie Break*

Giant, chunky, chocolate-chip cookies melt in your mouth in the shank of the afternoon—that is, if you can find them tucked away in the basement, so just follow your nose!

Le Monde, 2885 Broadway (bet. 112th & 113th Sts.), (212) 531-3939, *Hip Brasserie*

The unique bistro ambiance masks mediocre food, but the place is "hopping" and the waiters are cute Parisians, so if you're looking to date a waiter or Columbia University francophile, start practicing your French! You might even feel as if you're "downtown" . . . for a minute.

Picholine, 35 W. 65 St. (bet. Broadway & CPW), (212) 724-8585, *Fine Dining*

In the desert of excellent gourmand-style food known as the Upper West Side, this is an unpretentious oasis . . . especially if you have an expense account. Perfect for an impressive business lunch or romantic Mediterranean dinner. Among the best risotto anywhere in town, and save room for its noted cheese cart selection.

Popover Café, 551 Amsterdam Ave. (bet. 86th and 87th Sts.), (212) 595-8555, *Brunch*

Rendezvous with your girlfriends for gourmet homemade popovers in this quaint albeit "foo foo" café, complete with teddy bears. Go for jam and butter on the side or the more exotic and hearty combinations, like "The Butler Did It" and "Sweet William . . ."

Rosa Mexicana, 61 Columbus Ave. (@ 62rd St.), (212) 977-7700, *Neighborhood Newcomer*

This is the second brainchild of Rosa and she has outdone herself. New Yorkers have long been in love with this critically acclaimed authentic Mexican food dream. Beautifully designed by famed New Yorker David Rockwell, a grand wall of a million little divers greets you. The house specialty drink, pomegranate margaritas, should not be missed. If you are ambitious enough to want to re-create the magic in your own kitchen, pick up the Rosa Mexicana cookbook. See other location in MTE. *Psst . . . the bar is an inviting, casual yet elegant place to meet after work for a drink and some fresh guacamole.*

Ruby Foo's, 2182 Broadway (@ 77th St.), (212) 724-6700, *Sorta Sushi*

Brought to you by famed NYC restaurateur Steve Hanson, whose name will mean several things as you navigate your gastronomic way: great food, great prices, great crowds, and great fun. This latest endeavor is a happening spot for dim sum or sushi set in a "theme" room. It's pretty and always feels like a party. Order the pink drink "Ruby Foo" upon arrival and you too will be "fooed" in no time at all. See other location in UWS.

Sarabeth's Kitchen West, 423 Amsterdam Ave. (bet. 80th & 81st Sts.), (212) 496-6280, *Brunch*

Delicious destination for a rainy Sunday (perhaps with visiting relatives) where you can be soothed by homegrown yet inventive cuisine. Ignore the somewhat Laura Ashley decor and dive into such treats as pumpkin waffles that add a new dimension to brunch. *Psst . . . weekday high tea at its best—skip the weekend crowds and nosh on dainty sandwiches and scones in peace.* See other location in UES @ the Whitney Museum.

Shun Lee Café, 43 W. 65th St. (bet. Columbus Ave. & CPW), (212) 769-3888, *Dim Sum*
Casual little sister to the elegant Shun Lee and the UES Shun Lee Palace. Incredible dim sum this side of Beijing, and they deliver!

Spazzia, 66 Columbus Ave. (@ 77th St.), (212) 799-0150, *Innovative Nouvelle*
At the sister haunt to Tribeca's Spartina, expect excellent nouvelle Med cuisine with an exceptional wine list. Brunch is delightful—try the melt-in-your-mouth oatmeal cinnamon waffles. The decor suffers from a bit of identify crisis but do not let that deter you from enjoying a perfect culinary experience!

The Terrace, 400 W. 119th St. (Amsterdam Ave. & Morningside Dr.), (212) 666-9460, *Enchanted Dinner*
If your boy-toy has bucks this is a perfect destination for romance and in-credible French cuisine . . . It's rare to have delicous food equal such a stunning view, so if you can manage the price tag it's worth a look-see!

Tom's Restaurant, 2880 Broadway (@ 112th St.), (212) 864-6137, *Cheap Diner*
Seinfeld and Suzanne Vega tipped us off about this typical NYC hang . . . A 24-hour coffee shop with the basic diner fare, it boasts only the famous sitcom storefronts. But don't be too quick to judge—it's the perfect stake-out for snagging millionaires-in-the-making on the MBA track at nearby Columbia University. "Elaine" must not have been paying attention!

222, 222 W. 79th St. (bet. Broadway & Amsterdam Ave.), (212) 799-0400, *Intimate Affair*

Table for two, please! Think wood-paneled boudoir mixed with Ver-mont country inn. The food is hearty, like every good indulgence should be: escargot baked in butter, huge shrimps, and foie gras dripping in currants, in addition to simpler dishes. Nuzzle up to your honey over the Beluga caviar with crême fraiche and finish up with a chocolate dessert before you head over to Central Park for a stroll on a snowy night! *Psst . . . don't miss the collection of Barbie dolls in the corridor or the tableside snow globes in this adorable place.*

♦ *Not to Miss:*

Barney Greengrass, 541 Amsterdam Ave. (bet. 86th & 87th Sts.), (212) 724-4707, *Kosher Deli*

Café Luxembourg, 200 West 70th St. (bet. Amsterdam & West End Aves.), (212) 873-7411, *Neighborhood Favorite*

Gabriela's, 685 Amsterdam (@ 93rd Street), (212) 961-0574, *Cheap Mexican*

Isabella's, 359 Columbus Ave. (@ 77th St.), (212) 724-2100, *Neighborhood Favorite*

Vince and Eddie's, 70 W. 68th St. (bet. Columbus Ave. & CPW), (212) 721-0068, *PreTheatre Nibble*

♦ *Good to Know:*

Pickle-Licious 580 Amsterdam Ave. (bet. 88th & 89th Sts.), (212) 579-4924

Pickle-sicles to Go! If your passion is pickles, search no more! Barrels of sweet and sour in many varieties hold court with cucumbers, turnips, and celery . . . Country store feel with gourmet candy and nuts as well.

Upper East Side ....

Bella Donna, 307 E. 77th St. (bet. First & Second Aves.), (212) 535-2866, *Penny Pasta*

A là carte entrees for under ten dollars allow for a cheap and chic dining experience. Fun date destination if you go for the starving artist type! B.Y.O.B.

Bistro Du Nord, 1312 Madison Ave. (@ 93rd St.), (212) 289-0997, *Local Fave*

A charming Carnegie Hill oasis with Parisian style and attitude. Prix-fixe lunches & delicious dinners—a mellow neighborhood find with cozy seating and interesting art adorning the walls. Perfect for a little conversation over a steak frites and a bottle of Brunello di Montalcino.

Blanche's Organic Café and Juice Bar, 972 Lexington Ave. (bet. Fifth & Madison Aves.), (212) 717-1923, *Low Calorie*

Models hang where the steamed veggie platter and pita (both under 300 calories) are par for the course. No cellulite here, baby! See second location in UES on the second floor of the hip DKNY store (see Treasures). *Psst . . . It's the perfect place to start your new health regime in style.*

Candle Café, 1307 Third Ave. (bet. 74th & 75th Sts.), (212) 472-0970, *Healthy*

Organic and natural, you'll never miss what is *not* in this ultratasty UES mecca for health food. No animals allowed in this laid-back "California-esque" eatery—at least in the food. *Psst . . . granola moms delight in the selection of organic baby foods. You know what they say about getting them when they're young . . .*

Ciao Bella Café, 27 E. 92nd St. (bet. Fifth & Madison Aves.), (212) 831-5555/(800) 435-2863, *Dessert*

If ice cream merited five stars, this place would more than deserve the rating. Seasonal and personalized gelato masterpieces set this gourmet cove café apart. Try seasonal specialties like pumpkie pie gelato or order a custom-made dream blend concocted to your taste specifications. Anything goes, so dream away. The minimum order is five gallons at $35 per gallon. Maybe the perfect idea for a party!

Coffee Time @ Big Apple, 145 E. 62nd St. (bet. Lexington & Third Aves.), (212) 829-9595, *Stay or Go*

Take a coffee break at this adorable new spot that is even so gracious as to have water outside for Muffy the dog to enjoy. Specializing in Lavanzza coffee, sandwiches, and pastries to go or to eat in. You will feel truly re-laxed in this pretty place as you sip coffee and read the newspaper (finally!) at one of the few tables on hand.

Columbus Bakery, 957 First Ave. (bet 51st & 52nd Sts.), (212) 421-0334, *Morning Hang*

See details in EATS, UWS.

E.A.T., 1064 Madison Ave. (bet. 80th & 81st Sts.), (212) 772-0022, *Gourmet Diner*

E.A.T. is synonomous for more "bread" than brains. The food is delicious but ridiculously priced—for those who like million-dollar matzo ball alongside Woody Allen, Tom Wolfe, and Candace Bergen, it can't be beat. Unlike Café Bould in the neighborhood, this place is Prada Sport casual all day long. The take-out "deli" has gourmet salads and sandwiches as well as irresistible treats for that sugar craving, and they ship their fresh breads nationwide for the E.A.T. deprived!

Eli's Manhattan, 1411 Third Ave. (bet. 80th & 81st Sts.), (212) 717-8100, *Food Shop / Brunch*

A high-end food emporium developed by Eli Zabar of E.A.T. and Zabar's fame. Replete with 75 varieties of vinegar, it has gained the moniker "Vinegar Factory," also the name of the spacious restaurant downstairs. Gorgeous organic vegetables and the largest gourmet salad bar in the city (75 Mediterranean selections daily) attract higher palates from all neighborhoods . . . Don't miss the Parisian-style flower mart and newspaper kiosk. Brunch is excellent as are to-go sandwiches for gals on the go!

Etats-Unis, 242 E. 81st St. (bet Second & Third Aves.), (212) 517-8826, *First Date*

Don't let the name fool you. This tiny chic family-run restaurant is more innovative American with a French nouvelle cuisine twist. You'll have to dig to the bottom of your Kate Spade bag to pay the check, but the dazzling, innovative and eclectic menu is well worth it. The two-and-a-quarter-pound steak for two will set you back ($64) and really is to die for—reserve in advance. An "insider's" delight, you will be made to feel like one upon first visit. Excellent wine list rounds out the perfect secluded dinner.

Fred's @ Barneys NY, 10 E. 61 St. (bet. Fifth & Madison Aves.), (212) 833-2200, *Shopping Lunch Break*

After bingeing on Manolo Blahnik shoes upstairs, why not binge on the scrumptious truffle pizza . . . Tasty salads and lunch fare are highlighted by the "wine on tap" and coffee bar. Celeb sighting alert.

Glaser Bake Shop, 1670 First Ave. (bet. 87th & 88th Sts.), (212) 289-2562, *Bakery*

Family-run since 1902, this blast from the past is a must for elementary school celebrations and manic sugar binges . . . Closed July through first week of August.

John's Pizzeria, 408 E. 64th St. (bet. First & York Aves.), (212) 935-2895, *Traditional Pizzeria*

See details in GV, other locations in UWS, MTW.

King's Carriage, 251 E. 82nd St. (bet. Second & Third Aves.), (212) 734-5490, *Town House Dining*

Set in a lovely nineteenth-century carriage house with a private English dinner club ambiance. Enjoy continental cuisine at a bargain during lunch or impress your mother-in-law at teatime. Great for bridal luncheons or drinks on a rainy afternoon nestled among a stack of books at a tiny little bar near the entrance.

La Goulue, 746 Madison Ave. (bet. 66th & 67th Sts.), (212) 988-8169, *Euro French*

Don't be swept away by the dashing owner François . . . he's taken. You can, however, be swept away by the delicious French cuisine that has made this a destination for Upper Eastsiders for quite some time. A place to see (Goldie Hawn, George Clooney) and be seen (you!). La Goulue has graciously filled the partial gap in Madison Ave. sidewalk cafes since longtime favorite Le Relais exited the neighborhood.

Le Bilboquet, 25 E. 63rd St. (bet. Park & Madison Aves.), (212) 751-3036, *Euro French*

The food is sexy and delicious and so is the staff, straight from the fashionable streets of Paris . . . with attitude! This *tiny* yellow-walled hideout for the ultrachic doesn't always embrace "outsiders" with open arms (it is unmarked save for the green awning), but a great handbag and some attitude usually will land a table next to a model and the millionaire who supports her! Don't be surprised as the lights dim and the world music deafens as a few Brazilian "It" babes go tabletop for a little solo dancing!

Le Refuge, 166 E. 82nd St. (bet. Lexington & Third Aves.), (212) 861-4505, *Garden Dining*

Country French cozy atmosphere . . . A charming hideaway inside and out! The romantic garden and sumptuous cuisine makes for a deliciously private "pot au feu" evening. A great little find.

Lexington Ave. Candy Store Luncheonette, 1226 Lexington Ave. (@ 83rd St.), (212) 288-0057, *Counter Dining*

An old-fashioned soda fountain with homemade lemonade, malts and sandwiches. (You may recognize it from *The Sting*.) Delicious breakfast in an adorable setting makes up for slightly outrageous prices. Beware, my little caffeine junkies, they charge for refills and we found out the hard way . . . Ouch!

Maya 1191 First Ave. (bet. 64th & 65th Sts.), (212) 585-1818, *Gourmet Mexican*

Elegant and traditional Mexican cuisine for those in the know and diplomats from the Mexican Embassy. No Tex-Mex tacos here. Sip margaritas from beautiful handmade Mexican pitchers and splurge on delicious entrees. Pricey, but worth it, senorita! The small bar will accommodate a few who are looking to just "appetize" the night away!

Mitchell London Foods, 22 E. 65th St., #A (bet. Madison & Fifth Aves.), (212) 737-2850 *Gourmet To Go*

See details in MTW.

Payard Patisserie and Bistro, 1032 Lexington Ave. (bet. 73rd & 74th Sts.), (212) 717-5252, *Brunch/Desserts*

When you ask your friend what you can bring to the party and she says "dessert", don't think twice! Run, don't walk, to this Sugar Plum Fairy fantasy tearoom. Tiers of authentic French patisserie will entrance your sugar zombie, so beware, you may have to spend an hour or so nibbling scones at a side table. If the cake makes it to the party alive, you'll be crowned Dessert Queen of the Party.

Rao's, 455 E. 114th St. (@ Pleasant Ave.), (212) 722-6709, *Ethnic/Italian*

Rumor has it Frank Sinatra's standing reservation was part of his last will and testament. Need we say more? Head way uptown where this downhome ethnic Italian attracts celebs like music mogul Tommy Mottola and other modern-day gangsters with money and drivers. Speaking of drivers, this is not an easy place for gals to hail cabs in the dark—if you can get a reservation, then get a car service. Get it?

Sant Ambroeus, 1000 Madison Ave. (bet. 77th & 78th Sts.), (212) 570-3670, *European Coffee Bar*

Sister restaurant to the Milanese original, it's usually packed with neighborhood "regulars" who stop in for the best cappuccino and sandwiches

Stateside. A true European bar that serves coffee made to order while you stand and ponder why Americans can't make coffee this good? The decor is less than hip by some standards. (In fact it feels like an overdone Italian grandmother's home, but it grows on you.) The sandwiches are to die for and the gelato is worth the trek alone. Owners, take a hint: NYC could use a downtown Sant Ambroeus!

Serafina, 29 E. 61st St. (bet. Park & Madison Aves.), (212) 702-9898
1022 Madison Ave. (@ 79th St.), (212) 734-2676, *Euro Hang*

If you are planning to meet your someone at Serafina, know two things: they have three locations and they used to be called Sofia. The farther uptown location is best for its open-air terrace and tolerance for children; the 61st St. location is close to Barneys! Menus vary, but you can't go wrong with one of their wafer-thin crusted gourmet pizzas and a glass of Veuve Cliquot (see other location in TWILIGHT, LES). *Psst . . . heaven for "Modelizers," so don't bring your Gabrielle-obsessed boyfriend or you will wind up in a crunch! PS They deliver.*

Serendipity 3, 225 E. 60th St. (bet. Second & Third Aves.), (212) 838-3531, *For Kids (Of All Ages)*

Adults and children alike endure the horrendous wait because the frozen hot chocolate beats all . . . (Somehow we have justified the calories because it is not ice cream but "frozen milk"!) Take your inner child upstairs, our favorite space in the town house, for a burger, but don't forget that desserts matter more than dinner in this magical ode to the ice-cream parlor of yesteryear!

Sharz Café and Wine Bar, 177 E. 90th St. (@ Madison Ave.), (212) 876-7282, *Neighborhood Favorite*

Good things come in tiny packages describes this secret find of NYC wine aficionados. It's a good thing it is a secret because there's barely room for the wait staff in this precious Mediterranean-tinted hideaway.

Terramare, 22 E. 65th St. (bet. Fifth & Madison Aves.), (212) 717-5020
152 E. 79th St. (bet. Lexington & Third Aves.), (212) 585-2093, *Solo Lunch*

Authentic fresh ingredients with a nouvelle NYC twist make this Italian eatery perfect for a quick lunch break. Both locations are special but we prefer to sit outside at 65th St. and take in the fresh air. All you need is your Vespa to "when in Rome" the day away.

Toraya, 17 E. 71st Street (bet. Fifth & Madison Aves.), (212) 861-1700, *Tea Party*

Traditional Japanese tea ceremony in the heart of Museum Mile . . . Dare to spend a peaceful late afternoon tasting Koto-style delicacies and sipping exotic teas in this airy skylit room with natural wood walls and authentic décor. Sinfully Zen as delicious cakes and a myriad of teas help your troubles melt away in this truly relaxing setting. Closed Sunday.

Ulrika's, 115 E. 60th St. (bet. Lexington & Park Aves.), (212) 355-7069, *Nouvelle Swedish*

Girl power in full force! This adorable welcomed newcomer was opened by two Swedish women named Ulrika and Mimi in 1998. With a ton of experience under their belts and a lot of TLC, they have turned this charming space into a taste of Stockholm. There is no pretension here, baby. And best of all, the food is exceptional, a fun departure from the usual Continental fare and Euro dining . . . Prix-fixe lunch attracts professional women and models alike. The small portions assure that you fit into your little black dress.

Viand, 673 Madison Ave. (@ 61st St.), (212) 751-6622, *Cheap Diner*

"The original Viand" was established in 1976 and has been feeding the neighborhood the best fresh roast turkey sandwiches money can buy. Don't be bothered by the no-frill décor or lack of friendliness; nothing personal, they just have plenty of burgers and fries to get out! If you have blown all of your bucks at the makeup counters at Barney's (see Treasures, UES) this is the place to counteract your guilt!

Yura and Company, 1645 Third Ave. (@ 92nd St.), 1292 Madison Ave. (@ 92nd St.), (212) 860-1598, *Catering / To Go*

Café by day, caterer by night, the eclectic fare and full-service catering have a monopoly on the UES social calendar. Nibble on smoked turkey pinwheels in a light airy atmosphere; a seat by the window for lunch is a must.

◈ *Not to Miss:*

Café Boulud, 20 E. 76th St. (bet. Fifth & Madison Aves.), (212) 772-2600, *Ladies Who Brunch*
J.G. Melon, 1291 Third Ave. (@ 74th St.), (212) 650-1310, *Chili*

Jo Jo, 164 E. 64th St. (bet. Lexington & Third Aves.), (212) 223-5656, *Celebrity Chef*

Le Pain Quotidien, 1131 Madison Ave. (@ 84th St.), (212) 327-4900, *Solo Lunch*

Sylvia's, 328 Lexington Ave. (bet. 126th & 127th Sts.), (212) 996-0606, *Soul Food*

The Trustees Dining Room, The Metropolitan Museum of Art, 1000 Fifth Ave. (bet. 82nd & 83rd Sts.), (212) 535-7710, *Exclusive*

Via Quadrono, 25 E. 73rd St. (bet. Fifth & Madison Aves.), (212) 650-9880, *Solo Lunch*

✒ *Good to Know:*

Hosting a business gathering in your hotel suite and angling for a promotion? Call Feast & Fetes (20 E. 76th St. bet. Fifth & Madison Ave.), (212) 737-2224 . . . They'll do it up in style and make you look like a genius!

Best Salads . . .

California Pizza Kitchen, 201 E. 60th St. (bet. Second & Third Aves.), (212) 755-7773

Fresco Tortillas, *Mexican on the Go*
980 Second Ave. (bet. 51st & 52nd Sts.), (212) 688-0718
719 Second Ave. (bet. 38th & 39th Sts.), (212) 972-7648
546 Third Ave. (bet. 36th & 37th Sts.), (212) 685-3886

Best Spots for Tea:

Lowell Hotel, 28 E. 63rd St. (bet. Park & Madison Aves.), (212) 838-1400, *with your soul mate*

Heartbeat, The W Hotel Lobby, 149 E. 49th St. (bet. Lexington & Third Aves.), (212) 407-2900, *with hip friends*

The King's Carriage House, 251 E. 82nd St. (bet. Second & Third Aves.), (212) 734-5490, *with your lover*

The Pierre Hotel, 2 E. 61st St. (bet. Fifth & Madison Aves.), (212) 838-8000, *with your parents*

The Four Seasons Hotel, 57 E. 57th St. (bet. Park & Madison Aves.), (212) 758-5700, *with your sugar daddy*

The Carlyle Hotel, 35 E. 76th St. (bet. Park & Madison Aves.), (212) 744-1600, *with your daughter*

Did you know . . . the nighttime spot named **Big Sur,** 1406 Third Ave. (@ 80th St.), (212) 472-5009, is a cocktail lounge by night and a cool coffee bar by day. From 7 A.M. to 5 P.M. daily they serve yummy coffee, pastries, salads, and sandwiches. And when the sun sets, it's back to the bar you know and love.

𝓜𝓲𝓭𝓽𝓸𝔀𝓷 𝓦𝓮𝓼𝓽

Amy's Bread, 672 Ninth Ave. (bet. 46th & 47th Sts.), (212) 977-2670, *Bakery*

Located in the neighborhood formerly known as Hell's Kitchen, Amy Scherber's little treasure will send your taste buds to heaven in one bite. We are particularly fond of the olive twists that go so well with a gin martini on your friend's balcony at sunset—why else would you have ventured this far? Arrive early in the morning—they open at 8 A.M. for the sour-dough loaves that leave you anything but sour. *Psst . . . second location in the Chelsea Market. (see* Eats, *Chelsea)*

Biricchino Restaurant, 260 W. 29th St. (bet. Seventh & Eighth Aves.), (212) 695-6690, *Casual Italian*

A little find in the back of an Italian sausage shop (Salumeri Biellese), it's like stepping into a Northern Italian village café with polished granite tables and bar. Malfitti, tortellini, ravioli . . . simple butter sage sauce, really fresh tomato sauce . . . outrageous shrimp scampi . . . and we won't even go into the traditional tiramisu. Ask for the owner if you are a wine cono-scienta because better bottles lurk off-menu!

Chez Josephine, 414 W. 42nd St. (bet. Ninth & Tenth Aves.), (212) 594-1925, *Theater Favorite*

Owned by Jean Claude Baker (son of Josephine), this sleek, sultry red-velvet *bôite* is the complement to any theater experience. In fact, if you miss the show, you'll be sure to see something memorable here! FYI—This was perhaps Jacqueline Kennedy Onassis's favorite pretheater eatery. Happy, feel-good, full of memories and memorabilia.

Cupcake Cafe, 522 Ninth Ave. (@ 39th St.), (212) 925-2898, *Birthday Cakes*

The sweet-tooth girl's dream . . . You can order gorgeous cakes ($45 for a

9" standard floral cake); may we suggest the Kahlua Raspberry filling number that will make your hair extensions stand on end! This cake-o-rama can fulfill every fantasy or office birthday need. If you are in the neighborhood and just want to peak at the edible art (or use that as an excuse), pick up some delicious donuts, cookies or pies (don't stay too long, though, the place is a real dive).

Del Frisco's, 1221 Sixth Ave. (bet. 48th & 49th Sts.), (212) 575-5129, *Steak Brasserie*

The best steak we've ever had. (And the biggest check to match it.) A major "boys' club," this is sure to please male clients and beaus alike. Bankers, martinis, filets . . . happiness!

44@ The Royalton Hotel, 44 W. 44th St. (bet. Fifth & Sixth Aves.), (212) 944-8844, *Business Lunch*

The Conde Nast crowd arrives in spades in Kate Spade, along with their music and fashion compadres, to share nouvelle American cuisine. Feel free to powder your nose in their very mod "little girls' room." The ever-changing staff makes for quite a wait, so beware of low blood sugar.

Hour Glass Tavern, 373 W. 46th St. (bet. Eighth & Ninth Aves.), (212) 265-2060, *Fun Pretheater*

And you thought Cinderella had problems. They get you in and out for the theater by literally timing your meal with an hourglass! Reliable food in a setting beyond funky and ultracool. Not for a leisurely dining experience but a must if you're trying to make the show!

John's Pizzeria, 260 W. 44th St. (bet. Broadway & Eighth Ave.), (212) 391-7560, *Traditional Pizzeria*

See details in GV, other locations in UWS, UES.

La Vinera, 19 W. 55th St. (bet. Fifth & Sixth Aves.), (212) 247-3400, *Lunch*

Classic, moderately priced, yet light Italian fare sets the stage for a business or romantic lunch. Order off the unique menus sketched on wine crates . . . We recommend the brick oven pizzas. *Viva Italia!*

Little Pie Company, 424 W. 43rd St. (bet. Ninth & Tenth Aves.), (212) 736-4780, *Pie To Go*

See details in Chelsea/Meatpacking, or visit the satellite @ The Grand Central Terminal.

Mangia, 50 W. 57th St. (bet. Fifth & Sixth Aves.), (212) 582-5882, *Delivery/To Go*

See details in Lower Manhattan, other location in MTE.

Michael's, 24 W. 55th St. (bet. Fifth & Sixth Aves.), (212) 767-0555, *Power Lunch*

California chic rules in this NY satellite of a Santa Monica original. An ultrapower scene for local music execs and publishing moguls drawn to the cuisine and contemporary art on the walls. Expect to spend a couple of hours and many more bucks. *Psst . . . we heard that they have a great breakfast "scene" . . . not that any divas we know are up that early!*

Milos Estiatorio, 125 W. 55th St. (bet. Sixth & Seventh Aves.), (212) 245-7400, *High-End Greek*

"Greek Goddesses Who Lunch" . . . Ultrachic vaulted ceiling with canopies and fish by the pound that will send you floundering for your wallet. Order the entrée-sized Greek salad and appetizers if you must be budget-conscious. The ingredients are as fresh as if you were ordering from your yacht in the Greek isles. First-class service, food, and prices. Be sure to bring your corporate expense account or rich boss.

Mitchell London Foods, 542 Ninth Ave. (@ 40th St.), (212) 563-5969, *Gourmet To Go*

Catering and To Go galore. Reasonably priced for the gourmand gal on a budget. The soups are par excellence. See other location in UES.

New World Grill, Worldwide Plaza, 329 W. 49th St. (bet. Eighth & Ninth Aves.), (212) 957-4745, *Outdoor lunch*

This indoor/outdoor culinary haven overlooks the Worldwide Plaza's piazza, where entertainment biz locals can be seen noshing on chopped salads and veggie burgers and manning their cell phones by the fountain. Service can be slow so go on a day when the weather is nice and you are not expected back at the office.

Orso, 322 W. 46th St. (bet. Eighth & Ninth Aves.), (212) 489-7212, *Neighborhood Favorite*

A little taste of Tuscany tucked into the theater district. Impossible without reservations, seal a deal or grab a bite before heading to the theater. Don't fill up on the delicious white bean spread before you order!

Pitchers of house wine make for festive group dining. A definite "insider's" choice.

Osteria Al Doge, 142 W. 44th St. (bet. Broadway & Sixth Ave.), (212) 944-3643, *Business Lunch*

A midday sanctuary from the hustle bustle of Times Square, this slice of Tuscany is prime luncheon real estate for the nearby Conde Nast editor crowd. The antipasto platter will put you in the heart of Venice. Great for a quick pre-theater nibble sans gondola.

Pax's Deli, 736 Seventh Ave. (@ 49th St.), (212) 399-9100, *Tossed Salads*

Newly renovated and hands-down a step above most delis . . . Your salad is hand-tossed after your choice of ingredients . . . artichoke hearts, Cajun chicken, cherry tomatoes, chickpeas, yellow corn, feta cheese to name a few. No two salads are the same! Very chic for a deli if we do say so ourselves! Delivery available. The rest of the items are outrageously priced so opt for the salads only.

Soup Kitchen International, 259A W. 55th St. (bet. Broadway & Eighth Ave.), (212) 757-7730, *Seasonal To Go*

The Soup Nazi à la Seinfeld. Line up, your soup is personally scooped up by the man himself, but be prepared, stumbling and stuttering are not allowed. Don't miss the lobster bisque. Open seasonally during cooler months according to the whim of the Soup Nazi himself . . .

Town, 15 W. 56th St. (bet. Fifth & Sixth Aves.), (212) 685-4300, *Neighborhood Newcomer*

Dreaming of the perfect place to dine on sumptuous, innovative cuisine and lounge in an equally chic hangout afterwards? Tucked gracefully inside the oh-so-pretty Chambers Hotel, Town reeks of big city chic. Reservations are hard to come by, but The Balcony @ Town is a secluded spot one level above the eatery that offers delicious appetizers, desserts, and a wide selection of vodkas and champagne by the glass. Uptown sophistication with downtown attitude.

Ustav, 1185 Ave. of the Americas (bet. 46th & 47th Sts.), (212) 575-2525, *Festive Indian Lunch*

Suspended between two Midtown high-rises, Ustav gives the illusion that you are dining on a cliff above the rain forest or the Ganges. The downstairs houses a small bar that is a misleading entrée into what lies above. Upstairs past the tranquil glassed waterfall, enter a spacious, modern and elegant room hosting the feast of Babel. The shocker: $11.95 allows you to nibble or gorge your way through the vast array of delicacies from the fresh and appetizing daily buffet. Perfect wait staff: no hovering. Lunch/Dinner.

⊿ Not to Miss:

Alain Ducasse, 155 W. 58th St. (bet. Sixth & Seventh Aves.), (212) 265-7300, *Parisian Chef*

Aquavit, 13 W. 54th St. (bet. Fifth & Sixth Aves.), (212) 307-7311, *Celebrate Something*

Carnegie Deli, 854 Seventh Ave. (@ 55th St.), (212) 757-2245, *NYC Institution*

Firebird, 365 W. 46th St. (bet. Eighth & Ninth Aves.), (212) 586-0244, *Romantic Russian*

La Bernadin, 151 W. 51st. (Sixth & Seventh Aves.), *Fine Dining*

Petrossian, 182 W. 58th St. (Seventh Ave.), (212) 245-2214, *Caviar Dreams*

Trattoria Dell' Arte, 900 Seventh Ave., (@ 57th St.), (212) 245-9800, *Brunch/Lunch*

21 Club, 21 W. 52nd St. (bet. Fifth & Sixth Aves.), (212) 582-7200, *Power Girl*

Midtown East ··

Bice, 7 E. 54th St. (bet. Fifth & Madison Aves.), (212) 688-1999, *Euro Italian*

Grab your Vincent Longo Bronzer from Sephora and fake a tan on your way to this neighborhood mainstay that has thrived. A high-end Euro café with an airy feel and an overpriced Italian menu, single gals play emotional roulette at the bar that is a breeding ground for celebs and freaks of all flavors. If 20-dollar calamari doesn't frighten you, then come on down!

Blanche's Organic Café, 22 E. 44th St. (bet Fifth & Madison Aves.), (212) 599-3445, *Healthy*

See details in EATS, UES.

Brasserie 8½, 9 W. 57th St. (bet. Fifth & Sixth Aves.), (212) 829-0812, *Neighborhood Favorite*

Step down into the dramatic room and slink over to the Champagne bar to start your evening at this red-hot, renewed French brasserie. The food and wine is as chic as its clientele. And if you are looking to host a small semiprivate gathering (and spending a semismall fortune!), there is nice room adjacent to the bar that seats 50. Just make sure you bring your most fashionable friends. It seems casual but it is high-browed and high-tech in tone.

Dishes, 47 E. 44th St. (bet. Madison & Fifth Aves.), (212) 687-5511, *Solo Lunch*

Drown your diet counselor and head here for a gourmet twist on healthy lunch fare. A salad bar and tasty soups put this gourmet cafeteria-style eatery at the top of our list for workweek dining at our desk or on the spot. Grab a snack, then catch a train as Grand Central Station is but a hop, skip, and a jump away!

Genki Sushi, 9 E. 46th St. (bet. Madison & Fifth Aves.), (212) 983-5018, *Japanese*

Conveyor belt sushi that we first spied upstairs at Harrod's . . . Pick your poison or should we say *poisson*? And, if this means anything to you surroundings-conscious girls: Allison Spear décor.

Jubilee, 347 E. 54th St. (bet. First & Second Aves.), (212) 888-3569, *Bistro*

Sutton Place's answer to the French bistro. Some say they have the best fries in the City, and the mussels are also a favorite at this reasonably priced cozy neighborhood hang. Breathe in, breathe out . . . and go for it.

Mangia, 16 E. 48th St. (bet. Fifth & Sixth Aves.), (212) 754-7600, *Delivery / To Go*

See details in Lower Manhattan, other location in MTW.

Mavalli Palace, 46 E. 29th St. (bet. Madison & Park Aves.), (212) 679-5535, *Vegetarian Indian*

India's answer to vegetarian bliss! No more veggies buried deep in curry, this has spunk, flair, and taste galore. Simple, beautiful and economical among the sea of "Curry Hill" mediocrity! Mavalli stands in its own category.

Meltemi, 905 First Ave. (@ 51st St.), (212) 355-4040, *Greek Lunch*

This light and airy Greek taverna nestled in the heart of Sutton Place is a lovely upbeat alternative for business lunch. The bright dining room has a happy feel to it, and the food is authentic—complete with yummy spanakopita and ultrafresh fish. Indulge in some low-fat pita bread, baby!

Mr. Chow, 324 E. 57th St. (bet. First & Second Aves.), (212) 751-9030, *French Chinese*

Make a grand entrance here as the stage is set with a beautiful sunken art deco dining room and mezzanine bar for vigilant celebrity watching. Prepare to wait even if you manage to get a reservation. Chicken sate, fried seaweed, squab, and crispy beef are must-haves. Be at your festive best and don't stare if Stevie Wonder and Prince waltzes in with his late-night entourage!

Oscar's @ The Waldorf Astoria, 301 Park Ave. (bet. 49th & 50th Sts.), (212) 872-4920, *World-Famous Salad*

Oscar Tschirky, the maître d' of this venerable institution, invented the signature salad that launched a thousand lunches! Still the same, at six times the price . . . For health-conscious gals you can forgo the mayo and add turkey in its stead! The hotel itself has undergone a three-million-dollar renovation, and is still a destination lunch spot.

Patroon, 160 E. 46th St. (bet. Lex & Third Aves.), (212) 883-7373, *Power Screen*

Great place for a business lunch with boss or beau—the clubby intimate feel mixed with great American fare will leave even the suitiest suit satisfied. Testosterone alert: this celeb/exec-packed power place has a cigar bar too. But if you feel left out of the boys' club, ladies, ask about seating in the wine cellar.

Rosa Mexicana, 1063 First Ave. (@ 58th St.), (212) 753-7407, *Top Guacamole*

See details in MTW.

Serafina On The Run, 38 E. 58th Street (bet. Madison & Park Aves.), (212) 832-8888, *Breakfast On The Go*

All the greatness of Serafina without the stress of being cutting-edge coifed and attired. Grab it and go like the career "it girl" that you are! Trendy and delicious breakfast and lunch.

Teadora, 141 E. 57th St. (bet. Lexington & Third Aves.), (212) 826-7101, *Romantic/Italian*

The Stateside sister to Rome's famed La Rosetta, Teadora has that same magic touch tucked away under a small gold crown logo on bustling 57th St. Blink and you will miss this lace-curtained jewel evocative of a café on Lake Como . . . Hearty but not heavy, the traditional cuisine is unparalleled. Upstairs allows for some intimacy, but they can accommodate parties of six to eight as well for a little home-style levity around the table! Reservations suggested.

The Oyster Bar @ Grand Central Terminal, (Lower Level, 42nd St. & Vanderbilt), (212) 490-6650, *Neighborhood Treasure*

A fun diversion for those who eat out often and want to break out of their shell (literally!) . . . A classic jewel for those "in the know," the recent renovations, due to a fire, have only added to the sparkle of the magnificently cavernous inlaid tile ceiling. Can you say "Moët and Mollusks"? Award-winning wine list completes the experience.

✦ *Not to Miss:*

Ess-A-Bagel, 831 Third Ave. (bet. 50th & 51st Sts.), (212) 980-1010, *Authentic Bagels*

La Grenouille, 3 E. 52nd St. (bet. Fifth & Madison Aves.), (212) 752-1495, *Fine Dining/French*

Richart, 7 E. 55th St. (bet. Fifth & Madison Aves.), (212) 371-9369, *Indulgence*

The Tea Box Café at Takashimaya, 693 Fifth Ave. (bet. 54th & 55th Sts.), (212) 350-0180, *Formal Tea*

Vong, 200 E. 54th St. (@ Third Ave.), (212) 486-9592, *Chic Thai*

Bottino, 246 Tenth Ave. (bet. 24th & 25th Sts.), (212) 206-6766, *Garden / Italian*

The garden or the bar, nothing in between. The retro/modern orange cushions and streamlined décor cannot completely disguise the flaws in the menu or the service, but the sexy waiters do their best to cover any inconsistencies, and ultimately who cares when the vibe is so right. Swish through the door, order a Campari and soda, pout, and let the night unfold . . . *Psst . . . excellent takeout offered next door!* And don't miss their latest chic outpost, Bot, at 231 Mott St. (bet. Spring & Prince Sts.), (646) 613-1312, in Nolita.

Bright Food Shop, 216 Eighth Ave. (bet. 21st & 22nd Sts.), (212) 243-4433, *Cheap Brunch*

Dive into delicious fusion food (Asian meets Albuquerque) in the comfort of this 45-seat hole-in-the-wall with a sort of minimalist charm. Okay, charm is a stretch but cool feel is not! Bet on brunch. Prepare for spice. Bring cash.

Chelsea Market, 75 Ninth Ave. (bet. 15th & 16th Sts.), (212) 727-1111, *Food Shop*

An industrial gourmet gallery gives you one-stop access to many high-end boutique food emporiums under one roof! Browse or beeline it for your favorite shop. An event in itself, the nifty hostess could walk away with the makings for a great gift basket or banquet for 50.

Da Umberto, 107 W. 17th St. (bet. Sixth & Seventh Aves.), (212) 989-0303, *Tuscan Italian*

A somewhat formal but impressive neighborhood haunt, this Italian restaurant has sensational food. Great for those chic city girls needing to impress a client (or beau) and lucky enough to have the corporate Amex to flash after the delectable tiramisu!

Empire Diner, 210 Tenth Ave. (@ 22nd St.), (212) 243-2736, *Nighttime Institution*

Five in the morning. BLTs and shakes for late-night cravings. Post-cosmopolitan party crowd gathers to soak up the delicious diner fare. The sleek silver exterior of this deco landmark have made it the backdrop for many a movie set in Manhattan. Pass the fries, please!

Jerry's Bar and Grill, 470 W. 23rd St. (@ Tenth Ave.), (212) 989-8456, *Reliable Lunch*

Offering friendly, quick service and reliable eats, go for lunch. Be sure to have the mango chicken salad. Tell them we sent you! Just kidding . . . Open seven days a week, 10:30–5:00 for lunch and 5:30–11:30 in the evenings. Casual yet citified! See other location in SoHo.

Little Pie Company, 407 W. 14th St. (bet. Ninth & Tenth Aves.), (212) 414-2324, *Pie To Go*

So you just bought a fabulous dress at Jeffrey's (see Treasures) for the dinner party with your new "it" boy. Trot by and pick up a pie to make him think you spent the afternoon laboring instead of spending! You will surely impress him with sour cream walnut or summer specialties of peach and raspberry. Delish cookies and muffins as well, but we go for the round, crusty creations! Not for the budget-conscious, but well worth every penny. See other locations in MTE, @ The Grand Central Terminal, or MTW.

Pastis, 9 Ninth Ave. (@ Little W. 12th St.), (212) 929-4844, *Trendy French*

Restaurateur Keith McNally (of Balthazar, Lucky Strike, Café Luxembourg) has blasted into Chelsea with French flair . . . air kiss kiss! The summer terrace is lovely. The "scene" outweighs the menu but the spaciousness makes it accessible at most hours of the day and night. It's not nice to stare when you see Madonna at the next table for dinner with friends. *Psst . . . make sure you have round-trip transportation as the remote locale makes taxi hunting difficult at best in winter months.*

Rio Mar, 7 Ninth Ave. (@ Little W. 12th St.), (212) 242-1623, *Spanish Dive*

Have a taxi driver "in the know" seek out this Spanish dive that takes you to Madrid and back in one night. Tacky and wacky but fun—complete with jukebox and pitchers of sangria on the cheap! Slow New York at its best.

Wild Lily Tea Room, 511 W. 22nd St. (bet. Tenth & Eleventh Aves.), (212) 691-2258, *More Than Tea*

Can you really create food that is "emotional"? They claim it and after one visit, you will believe it. Serving over 40 different premier loose teas that match the yummy and ultimately feminine menu. You can't beat the Wild Lily Tea Box that includes Carrot Puree Soup, Apple Potato Salad, exotic entrée of choice like Mascarpone Cheese

Risotto, and a dessert of a green apple cooked in wine sauce. With tea too for $14.99. Serving lunch and dinner.

❧ Not to Miss:

Chinghalle, 50 Gansevoort (bet. Greenwich & Washington Sts.), (212) 242-3200, *Neighborhood Newcomer*
Markt, 401 W. 14th St. (@ Ninth Ave.), (212) 727-3314, *Belgian Trend*

Union Square/Gramercy/Flatiron

Chat'n'Chew, 10 E. 16th St. (bet. Fifth Ave. & Union Square West), (212) 243-1616, *Cheap Comfort Food*
   Funky antique garage sale meets down-home fern bar with big-city slant. This highly popular destination is perfect for group gatherings over delicious "comfort food." You'll literally chat and chew your way to the monstrously sinful desserts. Best bet for a hangover cure: tuna melt with sweet potato fries finished with red velvet cake . . . (And if you are on the Weight Watchers diet plan, you have just eaten your "points" for two days!)

City Bakery, 3 W. 18th St. (@ Fifth Ave.), (212) 366-1414, *Healthy Desserts*
   Maury Rubin has gained the esteemed title of "King of Tarts," so you little tarty travelers will feel right at home. But you may not know that this dessert maverick does a healthy lunch spread too. An exceptional minimalist salad bar is stocked with superior-quality exotic veggies from nearby Union Square Green Market. Be sure to call for the automated "blow-by-blow" of the daily delicacies at extension 1 . . . and to inquire about the all-natural cookie-dough, press 2!

Commune, 12 E. 22nd St. (bet. Park Ave. & Broadway), (212) 777-2600, *Neighborhood Newcomer*
   Could the *Sex and the City* gals lead us astray? Never! Ultra "in" Park Ave. South hot spot done in modern reds and oak. The food is seasonal American fare: pasta, steak, seafood. Boys will love the menu, you will love the walls. Outdoor seating in warmer months.

Eisenberg's Sandwich Shop, 174 Fifth Ave. (bet. 22nd & 23rd Sts.), (212) 675-5096, *Lunch To Go*

At this 1929 luncheon counter, you'll find Cagney throwbacks with attitude behind the counter. Don't miss the stellar tuna salad at this greasy spoon. (Maybe you'll be discovered on your stool!)

52 Irving Place, 125 E. 17th St. (bet. Irving Pl. & Third Ave.), (212) 995-5252, *Relax Over Coffee*

Perfect spot to sip and spy on the cute boy at the next table. Tucked into a side-street in Gramercy Park, one of the most beautiful spots in the city, nibble on a pastry and in iced latte or lemonade over the Sunday *Times*. If your little toes are aching from your four-inch Jimmy Choo's, the requisite line to order can be painful, but it's worth it to hang in the relaxed and cozy environment.

Food Works, 10 W. 19th St. (bet. Fifth & Sixth Aves.), (212) 352-9333, *Eat In Or Out*

This gourmet food shop lives up to its name: the food does work! We recommend the Rise & Shine breakfast for your prepresentation "boost." Or, impress your clients with more than your negotiation skills—order the meat and cheese platter as a midafternoon pick-me-up. Stop by and order a custom pizza, salad or sandwich to your liking. They aim to please your refined taste buds!

Lady Mendl's, The Inn at Irving Place @ 56 Irving Place (bet. 17th & 18th Sts.), (212) 533-4466, *Afternoon Tea*

Five-course tea for grannies and groovers. Celebrities and civilians rejoice in this Victorian tradition that adds civility to a city gone mad!

Les Halles, 411 Park Ave. (bet. 28th & 29th Sts.), (212) 679-4111, *Steak Frites*

Popular spot for a casual Saturday afternoon lunch with friends amidst the Toulouse-Lautrec vintage posters. You are greeted at the door by meat cabinets, so you can pick your own "pound of flesh." Order the steak frites and a delicious red wine. The waiters are pros with a bit of French attitude for good measure! Reservations requested, though walk-ins are welcome if you don't mind a wait.

Periyali, 35 W. 20th St. (bet. Fifth & Sixth Aves.), (212) 463-7890, *Greek*

Upscale Greek for the chic movers and shakers of the Flatiron area. In other words, no plate breaking allowed. If only hottie Michael Douglas hadn't snagged Catherine Zeta Jones, he might have brought you here for the fantastic fish and Aegean delicacies!

Picnic, 52 Irving Place (@ 17th St.), (212) 539-0240, *Lunch With Kids*

Home to Rosie O'Donnell's precious "ring dings" although they no longer are called that due to circumstances beyond their control. . . . Hmm . . . Casual country atmosphere and a giant picnic table proves their point—you may not be attacked by ants, but feel free to bring your own blanket.

Tabla, 11 Madison Ave. (@ 25th St.), (212) 889-0667, *Nouvelle Indian*

Danny Meyer's answer to Indian-inspired fusion . . . Have lunch with a client or boss in this impressively attractive and spacious setting overlooking Madison Park. Low-key with an outstanding menu upstairs or down at the Bread Bar for more casual dining. If you're under pressure to deliver a dining experience, you can't miss. Leave your sari at home! *Psst . . . Bread Bar's hearty homemade pizzas topped with Indian specialties add zing to the standard pie! Tandori ovens produce delicious flatbreads and mouth-watering specialties.*

Verbena, 54 Irving Place (bet. 17th & 18th Sts.), (212) 260-5454, *Garden Party*

The canopied garden delivers the utmost in tranquil elegant dining. Serene and sophisticated, it feels like a Mediterranean escape with a foundation in nouvelle American dishes. The rowdy need not apply as higher minds mingle over haute cuisine. Prepare to pontificate on the meaning of life and designer handbags at the same time.

Veritas, 43 E. 20th St. (bet. Broadway & Park Ave. South), (212) 353-3700, *Romantic*

Unbearable prices, unbelievable American food. Clean lines and indirect lighting will help you keep your cool when the bill arrives. The wine list rivals *Gone with the Wind* in length, complete with expensive wines by the glass. A newcomer par excellence. God willing, a date or your dad will pick up the tab! If not, you won't mind paying for such a graceful and elegant experience.

Yama, 122 E. 17th St. (@ Irving Place), (212) 475-0969, *Delish Sushi*
  "The Sushi Closet"—worth the wait, but you wait and wait for gigantic portions and an enviable assortment of Japanese beers. For raw fish it can't be topped. See other locations in WV and Soho. *Psst . . . put your name on the list and grab a cocktail around the corner at one of the cool neighborhood bars.*

✦ Not to Miss:

Eleven Madison Park, 11 Madison Ave. (@ 24th St.), (212) 889-0905, *Park View*

Gramercy Tavern, 42 E. 20th St. (bet. Broadway & Park Ave.), (212) 477-0777, *Fine Dining*

Patria, 250 Park Ave. South (@ 20th St.), (212) 777-6211, *Cuban Fusion*

Union Pacific, 111 E. 22nd St. (bet. Lexington & Park Aves.), (212) 995-8500, *Impress Your Client*

Union Square Café, 21 E. 16th St. (bet. Fifth Aves. & Union Square West), (212) 243-4020, *Neighborhood Favorite*

Greenwich Village ···

Aggie's, 146 W. Houston St. (@ MacDougal St.), (212) 673-8994, *Comfort Food*
  Could be the Big Apple's original "family-style diner" with home cooking beyond reproach. Don't miss the grilled pork chops and homemade applesauce. They take no shortcuts, including homemade "curly" fries. Maybe you're not in Kansas anymore, Dorothy, but you can feel like it at Aggie's!

Babbo, 110 Waverly Place (bet. McDougal St. & Sixth Ave.), (212) 777-0303, *Imaginative Italian*
  Good luck getting in after *Food & Wine* and *Wine Spectator* (2001) nailed this as tops in the Best Italian Wine List in the city. Incredible regional Italian cuisine at fairly reasonable prices, so you can blow it on the vino, baby!

  Menu changes frequently under the magic touch of Mario Batali, of Po fame. The tasting menus give you ample portions of their best delicacies (ie., fresh mint and duck ravioli), The bill is not for the faint of heart (even Garth Brooks's manager balked) after ordering wines with every course, but you only live once. . . . We would like to die here. *Psst . . . don't miss the scrumptious crostini snacks and Bombay martinis at the bar before dinner.*

Balducci's Café, 331 Sixth Ave. (@ 10th St.), (212) 673-6369, *Solo*

If you are not already clued in, Balducci's has cornered the market when it comes to fine foods to go. It's the place to get a quick, delicious nibble. Sandwiches, salads, pastries and great cappucino to top it off, all made with the freshest ingredients from the famous food store across the street.

Blue Ribbon Bakery, 33 Downing St. (@ Bedford St.), (212) 337-0404, *Neighborhood Favorite*

Bromberg brothers Bruce and Eric are at it again. And why not? Good things happen in threes: Blue Ribbon, Blue Ribbon Sushi, and now this. They spent one full year restoring the ancient (okay, it's only 120 years old) wood-burning oven, which they discovered by accident when renovating. We love the filet mignon with truffle sauce and the Caesar salad with house-baked croutons. Though with no reservations the rule of the house, you'll have plenty of time for anticipation.

Boughalem, 14 Bedford St. (bet. Downing & Houston Sts.), (212) 414-4764, *Romance & Garden*

A romantic hideaway on a sultry tree-lined street. Tuck yourselves away at the lovely bar or entwine your fingers over dinner in the garden. Reliable and ultratasty Franco-American fare. A real "jewel."

Café Loup, 105 W. 13th St. (bet. Sixth & Seventh Aves.), (212) 255-4746, *French Favorite*

Locals and artists keep this place alive, and we enjoy rubbing elbows with future Basquiats. Casual enough to lunch post flea market (see Treasures) but with enough panache to toast your three-month anniversary with a new beau. Simple food at a great price.

Café Mona Lisa, 282 Bleecker St. (bet. Jones St. & Seventh Ave.), (212) 929-1262, *Dessert & Coffee*

Join the locals nestled into one of the oversize armchairs in this antique-clad coffeehouse. No pressure to leave makes this a great place to read Sunday's *Times* from front to back. The treats are out of this world! If you must refrain, the salads aren't bad either.

Casa, 72 Bedford St. (@ Commerce St.), (212) 366-9410, *Brazilian*

This ethnic, enthusiastic Brazilian hosts many a model and the men who love them. Trendy yet tasty with a fun staff. Brunch is a blast with a group of friends on Sunday. Reservations recommended.

Colette's Cakes, 681 Washington St. (bet. 10th & Charles Sts.), (212) 366-6530, *Birthday Girls*

Colette started her cake-making career by turning a hobby into a real business. With a master's degree in painting from Pratt and experience designing for Tiffany, her fantastic designs impress anyone lucky enough to be the birthday recipient of a masterpiece. Starting at $250 per cake. Order far in advance, no request is too difficult. Just ask Al Pacino or Bette Midler.

Corner Bistro, 331 W. 4th St. (@ Jane St.), (212) 242-9502, *Hangover Cure / Late Night*

Best downtown burger! Greasy, dripping, succulent ground beef on paper plates. Pub atmosphere complete with cigarette smoke. Eat at the bar or wait for a table. Late night too.

EQ, 267 W. 4th St. (@ Perry St.), (212) 414-1961, *French delicacies*

Sunday night prix-fixe ($42—three courses) in a relaxed setting. Pricey but excellent French cuisine with delicious terrines and cassoulet.

Grange Hall, 50 Commerce St. (@ Barrow St.), (212) 924-5246, *Brunch / Hood Fave*

Thirties American deco with a lively bar. Classic American food with an occasional twist attracts a good-looking crowd from all walks of life. Rendezvous for a sexy late-night pork chop with your own little "tenderloin" . . . Nibble nibble!

Ice Cream Artisans, 272 Bleecker St. (bet. Sixth & Seventh Aves.), (212) 414-1795, *Exotic Cream*

They may have 32 flavors, but you won't mistake this for Baskin-Robbins! Two Argentinian brothers have cornered the specialty gelato market . . . one handles the exotic flavorful recipes, the other handles you with grace and charm. Canteloupe is our favorite.

John's Pizzeria, 278 Bleecker St. (bet. Sixth & Seventh Aves.), (212) 243-1680, *Traditional Pizzeria*

The original location for this city brick oven standard. Delectable thin-crust but prepare to buy the whole pie—no price by the slice. Go with appetite or friends. See other locations in UWS, UES, MTW.

Les Deux Gamins, 170 Waverly Place (bet. Grove St. & Seventh Ave.), (212) 807-7357, *Neighborhood Favorite*
Popular destination for Village "insiders" despite the insolent staff and inconsistent food. Perhaps the sidewalk seating, giant bowls of café au lait and the ability to linger all afternoon without hassle has us hooked. . . . Great brunch a là française, but arrive early or prepare to wait and wait some more!

Magnolia Bakery, 401 Bleecker St. (@ 11th St.), (212) 462-2572, *Cupcake Craving*
"June Cleaver's Cookie Kitchen" . . . Fifties retro linoleum tables amid lime green walls set the stage for Paper Doll Cupcakes and Hummingbird Cake that has patrons baring their fists for the last piece. "Eloise" would definitely hang here if she could ever find her way downtown from the Plaza!

Marquette Patisserie, 50 E. 12th St. (bet. University Pl. & Fifth Ave.), (212) 229-9313, *Pretty Lunch*
This yellow-walled, cozy bakery/café transports you to the Left Bank. There is always a "singleton," boys and girls, having lunch or dinner on their own over a book or paper. Proust would approve of the melt-in-your-mouth madeleines. Or pick up a roasted chicken for dinner at home. Too tired to take out? They have started serving dinner (B.Y.O.B.!) with enchanting live music. *Psst . . . close to our favorite alta-movie house, the Quad Cinema* (see Tripping).

Paris Commune, 411 Bleecker St. (bet. Bank & 11th Sts.), (212) 929-0509, *Cozy French Bistro*
Very arty crowd and ambiance. Translation? Cool people, lots of attitude. A Village hotspot during winter months thanks to the cozy fireplace . . . just beware of secondhand smoke. A good brunch makes for long waits on the weekends.

Peanut Butter and Company, 240 Sullivan St. (bet. Bleecker & West 3rd Sts.), (212) 677-3995, *Sugar Shock*
If you love this spreadable staple, you'll love these adult spins on the childhood classic. The most popular contender? The Elvis: PB with banana

and honey grilled on white bread, though the Original PB&J runs a close second to "The King." Believe it or not, they mail-order these puppies nationwide! And yes, they do "got milk"!

Pearl Oyster Bar, 18 Cornelia St. (bet. Bleecker & W. 4th Sts.), (212) 691-8211, *Neighborhood Treasure*

New England–style seafood at its best. Even those waiting outside for a table or stool smile in anticipation. Two tables, a marble counter and chowder, baby! Such a "find" you will feel like there's a pearl in *every* oyster!

Piadina, 57 W. 10th St. (bet. Fifth & Sixth Aves.), (212) 460-8017, *Romantic Italian*

Tuscan jewel. Don't go for the food (although it's good); go for the lighting, which yet again, girls, is exceptional for disguising the flaws of life in the career girl fast lane. *Molto italiana, bella!* Cash only and no reservations accepted so prepare for a wait on some nights.

Po, 31 Cornelia St. (bet. Bleecker & W. 4th Sts.), (212) 645-2189, *Celebrity Chef / Italian*

Chef Mario Batali's first endeavor, before Babbo (see Eats), we still love this tiny Village spot with siimple, modern Italian fare. The tasting menu is scrumptious and just the ticket when you can't make one more decision after a long day. Not for the girl who likes to be spontaneous, reservations are a must and harder to come by than that perfect black dress. . . .

Shopsin's General Store, 63 Bedford St. (@ Morton St.), (212) 924-5160, *Local Favorite*

Funky rustic. The menu is all over the place—literally, every ethnicity is represented—and the food is hearty. Great for hangovers, or perhaps just watching the eccentric owner give "'tude" to the customer sitting nearby. A feast for the eyes and the palate.

Tartine, 253 W. 11th St. (@ W. 4th St.), (212) 229-2611, *Cheap French*

Very very French. Great prices make for long lines of starving artists and students. So put your name on the list and go buy a bottle of red wine (B.Y.O.B.). *Psst . . . a class from Miette Cooking School takes over on Monday nights taught by the chef and his partner in crime from Titou down the street . . . Inquire about classes over dinner!*

Tea and Sympathy, 108 Greenwich Ave. (bet. 12th & 13th Sts.), (212) 807-8329, *English Tea*

English tea a là Notting Hill . . . Clotted cream et al on mismatched china. The owner has big plans to satisfy her Brit clientele: an English movie theater next door, an authentic London cab for deliveries, and a pub on the corner. A "food court" fit for the queen! Don't miss the take-away store next door.

The Adore, 17 E. 13th St. (bet. Fifth Ave. & University), (212) 243-8742, *Quaint Lunch Spot*

Rustic New England two-story café. Downstairs is take-out, upstairs has tasty sandwiches and overlooks the tree-lined street below. A charming luncheon spot that will leave you feeling rejuvenated for your trek back to the office, the gym, or Serena (see Twilight, Chelsea) for your late-night date!

Yama, 38–40 Carmine St., (bet. Bedford & Bleecker Sts.), (212) 989-9330, *Delish Sushi*

See details in Gramercy/Union Square; other location in SoHo.

✦ Not to Miss:

Auturo's Pizzaria, 106 W. Houston St. (@ Thompson St.), (212) 677-3820, *Classic Pizza*

Bar Pitti 268 Sixth Ave. (bet. Bleecker & Houston Sts.), (212) 982-3300 *Sidewalk Dining*

Café Dante's, 79 McDougal St., (bet. Bleecker St. & W. Houston St.), (212) 982-5275, *Desserts*

Cornelia St. Café, 29 Cornelia St. (bet. Bleecker & W. 4th Sts.), (212) 989-9319, *Upscale Bohemia*

Gotham Bar and Grill, 12 E. 12th St. (bet. Fifth Ave. & University Pl.), (212) 620-4020, *Prix-fixe Lunch*

Gourmet Garage, 117 Seventh Ave. (bet. 10th & Christopher Sts.), (212) 699-5980, *Food Shop*

Tomoe Sushi, 172 Thompson St., (bet. Bleecker & Houston Sts.), (212) 777-9346, *Tiny Sushi*

Ye Waverly Inn, 16 Bank St. (@ Waverly Place), (212) 929-4377, *Romantic*

James Beard House, 167 W. 12th St. (bet. Fifth & Sixth Aves.), (212) 675-4984, *Group Dining*

Julia Child's brainchild and tribute to her late friend/chef. Membership will gain entry to the Foundation's benefit dinners ("hosted" by famous chefs from around the world) that raise money for chef scholarships. A private and privileged dining experience.

East Village/Lower East Side

Angelica's Kitchen, 300 E. 12th St. (bet. First & Second Aves.), (212) 228-2909, *Healthy*

When you feel your arteries hardening, head here. You'll be back on the health track in no time at this peaceful organic vegetarian haven without pain to your palate. A bit pricey for steamed sprouts, but your heart is worth it! Now if only he felt the same way . . .

Café Habana, 17 Prince St. (@ Elizabeth St.), (212) 625-2001, *Trendy Cuban*

Fashionistas munch on plantain fritters, corn on the cob (150 cals, charred, sprinkled with cheese, chili powder, and a dash of lime) and caffe con leche at this Latin-flavored luncheonette that is less crowded for dinner. Open till midnight daily.

Cafe Pick-Me-Up, 145 Ave. A (@ 9th St.), (212) 673-7231, *Casual French*

Downtown Parisian café vibe, complete with accordion player and light opera on the weekends during brunch. You may want to sit at a sidewalk table to avoid contracting lung cancer from the heavy Gitane action inside, but that's to be expected, *n'est-ce pas?* Typical light cafe fare to be munched with the black-as-night coffee. You can almost see the Seine. . . .

Danal, 90 E. 10th St. (bet. Third & Fourth Aves.), (212) 982-6939, *Brunch With A Group*

Brunch or lunch with the gals . . . Shabby chic goes to Paris! Interesting art and ambiance keep Kate Moss coming back for more treacle pudding. Also great for a candlelit romantic dinner in the garden with "you know who."

Emerald Planet, 2 Great Jones St. (bet. Broadway & Lafayette St.), (212) 353-9727, *Lunch On The Go*
Quick lunch with a bit of celebrity splash. Grab a wrap and a Styrofoam cup . . . just don't trip over yourself stargazing.

Frank, 88 Second Ave. (bet. 5th & 6th Sts.), (212) 420-0202, *Hearty Italian*
Mozzarella imported weekly from Naples (where else?) and reasonably priced trattoria fare make up for mismatched silverware and cramped quarters. Rigatoni al Ragu is the house specialty. Our pick: the fresh-squeezed orange juice.

Holy Basil, 149 Second Ave. (bet. 9th & 10th Sts.), (212) 460-5557, *Nouvelle Thai*
"Nouvelle Thai" at its best. Chef/owner Lek plays hostess in this unique quasi-library setting complete with antique tables. The excellent wine list has been handpicked to enhance dishes like the delectable crispy duck and soft-shell crab (in season). Great place to take that boy you're eyeing for an intimate conversation in muted lighting that hides every wrinkle the Botox didn't cure . . . *Psst . . . don't let the low-key atmosphere fool you . . . Holy Basil got a papal nod from* Gourmet Magazine *for best Thai food in the city a few years ago. Sunday nights are the most intimate.*

Il Bagatto, 192 E. 2nd St. (bet. Aves. A & B), (212) 228-0977, *Cheap Italian*
"She wears an eenie weenie, itsy bitsy yellow polka dot bikini," smokes and dates Antonio Sabato, Jr., and loves traditional food like his Italian great-grandmother might have made. Think hearty dishes with the sweetest marinara that are shockingly cheap. About the size of Granny's kitchen, the homemade gnocchi is worth sitting on a stranger's lap! Let's just say that it is pretty much perfect Italian food. *Psst . . . stop by the adorable place next door, Il Posto Accanto (same owners), for a homey glass of Italian vino. Over 100 selections by the bottle, half carafe, and the quarter carafe for the solo adventure. Comfy and cozy, just like you picture your home in Tuscany!*

Il Buco, 47 Bond St. (bet. Bowery & Lafayette Sts.), (212) 533-1932, *Romantic Tapas*

Antique armoire vs. grilled squid? This neighborhood gem used to be an antique store by day and a tapas bar by night. Now they've grown into a full-blown restaurant filled with an eclectic mix of country tables, chairs and dimly lit chandeliers, setting the stage for a perfect first date. The food is Mediterranean and the menu changes every day. Leonardo and Brad love it here! Lunch M–S and dinner every day. Great wine list for lingering over your delish arugula and pear salad. *Psst . . . make plans to celebrate your birthday in the wine cellar ever-so-cool downstairs hideaway.*

Il Cantinori, 32 E. 10th St. (bet. Broadway & University Pl), (212) 673-6044, *Fine Dining / Italian*

Bottles of Bonoglio, the champagne of olive oils, are left on the tables of this elegant Village trattoria. Tom and Nicole (pre breakup, of course) have been spotted in the corner. Quite a celeb scene, but you will pay the piper for your stargazing at this pricey Italian *boite.*

Kossar's, 367 Grand St. (@ Essex St.), (212) 473-4810, *Bagels / Bialys*

Get a fresh bagel or bialy all night long at this Village staple. We recommend not eating carbs after 9 P.M., but do as we say, not as we do!

Life Café, 343 E. 10th St. (@ Ave. B), (212) 477-8791, *Cheap Neighborhood Hang*

Hassle-free dining among the bohemians and leftover grunge wannabes. Count on throngs of starving "artistic" ne'er-do-wells noshing on the cheap, somewhat uneventful food. Smoking is a must if you want to be a tortured artist or just part of the scene.

Lucien, 14 First Ave. (bet. 1st & 2nd Sts.), (212) 260-6481, *Smokey Bistro*

1940s Paris transported to the East Village. Berets, cigarettes, and francophiles vie for elbow room at this popular bistro that serves delicious food with no frills.

Miracle Grill, 112 First Ave. (bet. 6th & 7th Sts.), (212) 254-2353, *Southwestern / Garden*

Veer off the beaten path and into a magical garden the size of backyard suburbia! The scrumptious food is fresh and inventive, combining elements of Mexico and California with a mod twist . . . Mystical margaritas add the finishing touch to a delightful evening under the stars! When you crave vibe without 'tude!

Mugsy's Chow Chow, 31 Second Ave. (bet. 1st & 2nd Sts), (212) 460-9171, *Romantic Dive*

This hideaway is a one-man culinary "show." You could freeze to death waiting for a table and one of the pasta gems from his kitchen, but you can taste the chef/owner's personal effort in every dish. Dark, dingy, and darling!

Pomme Frites, 123 Second Ave. (bet. 7th & 8th Sts.), (212) 674-1234, *Snack On The Go*

A mini-Frenchie experience. Walk up to this one-table joint for a sinful paper cone of french fries done Belgian style, complete with a myriad of unique dipping sauces. You may need a 12-step program to get over the experience. Winner of the Walk, Talk, and Nibble Award, but don't sue us for your chubby thighs . . .

Radio Perfecto Rotisserie, 190 Ave. B (bet. 11th & 12th Sts.), (212) 477-3366, *Cheap Chicken*

Whimsical antique-radio-themed Alphabet City dinner spot. Their famous chicken and fries with special sauce is de rigueur. Cash only.

Roettele A. G., 126 E. 7th St. (bet. Ave. A & 1st St.), (212) 674-4140, *Garden/German-Swiss*

Fondue all over him in the adorable back garden of this Swiss-German restaurant where clusters of Concord grapes off the vine are served with dessert or added to tables for decoration. Beware: portions are enormous, and your eyes are bigger than your stomach!

Sammy's Roumanian Steak House, 157 Chrystie St. (@ Delancey St.), (212) 673-0330, *Hearty Kitsch*

Yiddish Disneyland with frozen vodka drinks. Bat Mitzvahs surround you, but it's all about partying at this genuinely hilarious, cholesterol-infused theme park pretending to be a restaurant . . .

71 Clinton Fresh Food, 71 Clinton St. (bet. Stanton & Rivington Sts.), (212) 614-6960, *Hot Chef*

He's all the rage among the foodies of this food-obsessed city. Wylie

Dufresne was a protégé of Jean-Georges Vongerichten (including a recent stint as a sous chef at Jean-George) whose influence is evident in the creative seasonal menu at this little Lower East Side outpost. You can tell Wylie actually loves what he does. The food has feeling but is not overdone. Simple yet richly complex flavors will leave you undaunted by the one-month wait list. *Psst . . . the James Beard Foundation has discovered his talents too!*

Stingy Lulu's, 129 St. Mark's Place (bet. Ave. A & First Ave.), (212) 674-3545, *Wacky*

A hoot a minute in this East Village meets Mel's Diner, more of a spectacle than a place to eat. Fifties-style "waiters" boogie your order to the DJ's beat and every other night appear in "drag." RuPaul meets Alice . . . Why not? Open seven days a week, call to check late hours.

Veniero's, 342 E. 11th St. (bet. First & Second Aves.), (212) 674-7264, *Italian Bakery*

Since 1894, New Yorkers have ventured here for special-order birthday cakes, cannoli, fruit tarts and cheesecakes par excellence. Stop in for a late-night pastry and decaf espresso before diving into your Pratesi sheets! Don't worry, we're sure you know how to work off that sugar buzz. . . .

✦ Not to Miss:

Katz's Delicatessen, 205 E. Houston St. (@ Ludlow St.), (212) 254-2246, *Institution/Deli*

Pisces, 95 Ave. A (@ 6th St.), (212) 260-6660, *Best Seafood*

Two Boots, 37 Ave. A (bet. 2nd & 3rd Sts.), (212) 505-2276, *Pizza With A Twist*

Veselka, 144 Second Ave. (@ 9th St.), (212) 228-9682, *Casual*

SoHo/Nolita/Little Italy/Chinatown

Angelo's of Mulberry Street, 146 Mulberry St. (bet. Grand & Hester Sts.), (212) 966-1277, *Viva Italia*

Touristas and "made" men intermingle in this pretty yet tiny place. A landmark for red sauce and red wine, don't be alarmed if you get caught in charming repartee with a mobster look-alike at the bar . . . or have one as your waiter. Ancient staff and outside seating make this a worthwhile destination for pasta lovers or just plain lovers, period. Closed on Monday.

Aqua Grill, 210 Spring St. (@ Sixth Ave.), (212) 274-0505, *Seafood Lovers*

It's impossible to get a reservation, so we serendipitously choose to swagger to the bar for an afternoon and evening of champagne and oysters . . .

Balthazar Bakery, 80 Spring St. (bet. Broadway & Crosby St.), (212) 965-1785, *French Bakery*

Odors sweet enough to make you moan waft from this Parisian transplant. Itsy bitsy with gargantuan price tags. Check out the Couronne de l'Advent, a delicious confection of dacquiose rings layered with chocolate mousse. Or make your life easy and pick up a box of cookies for $24 per pound. *Psst . . . if only getting a reservation at the sister restaurant next door were so convenient!*

Bistro Margot, 26 Prince St. (bet. Elizabeth & Mott Sts.), (212) 274-1027, *Euro French*

Inside is a haven for smokers, while outdoors a garden caters to those who don't want to "inhale." The open-air kitchen lures you in with fragrant cuisine; otherwise, you might walk right by this unique and discreet destination!

Blue Ribbon Sushi, 119 Sullivan St. (bet. Prince & Spring Sts.), (212) 343-0404, *Trendy*

Sushi girls will love this teeny tiny tucked-away place that's giving hall-of-famer Nobu a run for its money in miniature Zen style. No reservations accepted, so put your name down on the long, obnoxious list and skip to Casa La Femme (see Twilight) around the corner for a quick cocktail or groovy Moroccan tea under tented tables that are very "sheik." Meanwhile, back at the raw fish ranch, the sushi is worth the wait!

Bread and Butter, 229 Elizabeth St. (bet. Prince & Houston Sts.), (212) 925-7600, *Lunch To Go*

"I like bread and butter, he likes toast and jam . . ." Remember the *9½ Weeks* sound track? Never mind . . . Delish-nutrish sandwiches made with eclectic ingredients will make you an instant fan . . . Service is not zippy, so bypass if you're rushed!

Cafe Gitane, 242 Mott St. (@ Prince St.), (212) 334-9552, *Euro Lunch*

Downtown hipsters come here to do all the things we love to do—smoke, drink lattes, read, chat, and eat (not necessarily in that order). Somehow the food is secondary but always fresh and interesting, like the couscous salad with white grape currants. Great for a leisurely Saturday lunch, which everyone knows doesn't begin until 2 P.M.

Ceci-Cela Patisserie, 55 Spring St. (bet. Lafayette & Mulberry Sts.), (212) 274-9179, *Worthy Pastries*

This "demitasse" bakery/café is as cheerful as it is busy. Special orders from uptown save socialites from preparty anxiety.

Chinatown Ice Cream Factory, 65 Bayard St. (bet. Mott & Elizabeth Sts.), (212) 608-4170, *Exotic Ice Cream*

Asian dairy exotica. Ask for a sample and let the adventure begin. . . .

Eileen's Cheesecake, 17 Cleveland Place (bet. Kenmare & Center Sts.), (212) 966-5585, *New York Specialty*

Nineteen varieties available at your fingertips—don't say we didn't warn you: *they deliver* . . . so keep the number handy for traumatic events both real and imagined . . . Stop the madness! Wait! Pass the fork! *Psst . . . also available at Balducci's* (see GV).

Felix, 340 W. Broadway (@ Grand St.), (212) 431-0021, *Hood Favorite*

Food is irrelevant. Models, hipsters, wanna-bes, and Euro Trash alike rejoice at the cornucopia of trendsetters frequenting this bistro. Prepare to be distracted by oncoming Harleys . . . Our See Jane Go award for the cheap and chic Sunday brunch spot in the neighborhood.

Jing Fong, 20 Elizabeth St. (bet. Canal & Bayard Sts.), (212) 964-5256, *Swanky Dim Sum*

Glistening chandeliers and red crushed-velvet walls with pink table-cloths decorate this den of dim sum! Step off the second-floor escalator and be transported to a somewhat chaotic scene. Avoid weekends unless you

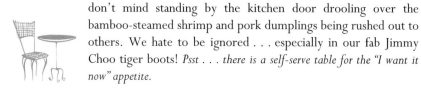

don't mind standing by the kitchen door drooling over the bamboo-steamed shrimp and pork dumplings being rushed out to others. We hate to be ignored . . . especially in our fab Jimmy Choo tiger boots! *Psst . . . there is a self-serve table for the "I want it now" appetite.*

Joe's Shanghi, 9 Pell St. (bet. Bowery & Mott Sts.), (212) 233-8888, *Authentic Chinese*

Get in line and wait (and wait some more) for the best Chinese dumplings Chinatown has to offer and that's a heavy order! Don't go for the décor . . . what décor? The original location is in Queens, (718) 539-3838, with a new MTW location that is perfect for lunch delivery. The shredded pork noodle soup is perfect on a cold day!

Jones Diner, 371 Lafayette St. (@ Jones St.), (212) 673-3577, *Cheap And Fast*

Enter this classic "diner car" with Old-World prices for cheap and greasy grub—$2.45 for grilled cheese and $3.15 for a burger. Now if you could just figure out how to swing those Siegersson & Morrison (see Treasures, SoHo) sandals you have been coveting.

Kitchen Club, 30 Prince St. (bet. Mott & Prince Sts.), (212) 274-0025, *Hip Japanese*

We stumbled upon this little Euro-Japanese fusion funky sake joint. Marja Samson and her adorable dog hold court while the kitchen whomps up her avant-garde and inventive take on Asian fare. Very groovy if we do say so ourselves! Extensive sake selection almost outshines the food.

Le Gamin Café, 50 MacDougal St. (bet. Houston & Prince Sts.), (212) 254-4678, *Coffee Bar*

Crepes, café au lait and B.Y.O.B. make this a Soho mainstay. Open with attitude until midnight . . . sulk and sip!

Lombardi's, 32 Spring Street (bet. Mott & Mulberry Sts.), (212) 941-7994, *Traditional Pizza*

No deep-dish Pizza Hut action here—although they do sport red-checkered tablecloths and a slanted floor for authenticity's sake. Only the freshest ingredients go into these delectable disks, making every bite the best Manhattan has to offer—just ask *anyone*. We, along with everyone we know, suggest the "Clam Pie," a heavenly no tomato/no cheese specialty with crispy oven baked crust.

Lupa, 170 Thompson St. (bet. Bleecker & Houston Sts.), (212) 982-5089, *Neighborhood Newcomer*

Cheaper than a ticket to Roma! Mario Batali and partner Joe Bastianich have outdone themselves, again. This newcomer is a casual, comfortable mini-Babbo (see Eats, GV) with none of the pretense and all of the panache. Lunch is the best time to chill out with no crowds breathing down your neck for your seat. Cured meats and wine are served all afternoon and sold to go. A true Roman trattoria complete with a wine list that impressed even our friends from Tuscany! *Molto bene.*

Me Kong, 44 Prince St. (bet. Mott & Mulberry Sts.), (212) 343-8169, *Vietnamese*

Innovative yet simple Vietnamese in disappointing portions but at satisfying prices. Probably not chic enough for the terrain, but enjoyable all the same.

Mexican Radio, 19 Cleveland St. (bet. Spring & Kenmare Sts.), (212) 343-0140, *Cheap Mexican*

Mellow by day, rockin' by night. Pick your poison! Serving tiny tempting tortillas. We just can't resist this place especially since they moved locations and expanded the bar! The 'ritas are the frozen type out of a machine, just like we make them in Texas!

New York Noodle Town, 28 Bowery (@ Bayard St.), (212) 349-0923, *Cheap Asian*

Bargain-basement prices for Gold Standard noodles and fish served in ample portions. Worth every minute spent waiting in this hectic neon and Formica Asian eatery. Noodle your way in, you'll be shell-shocked with palate pleasure. The best crispy seasoned soft-shell crabs anywhere.

Once Upon a Tart, 135 Sullivan St. (bet. Houston & Prince Sts.), (212) 387-8869, *Desserts To Go*

Gather friends for coffee and tarts fit for a fairy tale. The flaky pies and scones are not to be missed, especially the lemon tart. Friendly service and an authentically comfy atmosphere make this a perfect afternoon hang.

Palacinka, 28 Grand St. (bet. Sixth Ave. & Thompson St.), (212) 625-0362, *Late Night Nibble*

Open till 4 A.M. The specialty is scrumptious baby crepes from a Croatian recipe. Sounds exotic but you will love every last bite and won't do too much damage to your hips. Now all those cosmopolitans you drank earlier are another story!

Raoul's, 180 Prince St. (bet. Sullivan & Thompson Sts.), (212) 966-3518, *Neighborhood Favorite*

Exhausted from shopping and without an umbrella, hide out in this French bistro mainstay: smoky, vibey, loud, and delicious. Order the steak frites and a martini in the garden, or take the joy juice upstairs for a psychic reading while you wait . . . reservations are helpful, but then again, there are so many groovy types huddled at the bar. Staff? Attitude is everything, *ma chère!*

Sullivan Street Bakery, 73 Sullivan St. (bet. Spring & Broom Sts.), (212) 334-9435, *Baked Goods To Go*

Picturesque storefront and yummy Italian-style breads and pastries . . . You can't go wrong with the Pizza Bianca or some other reasonably priced nibble . . . For the Dough Girl in all of us without a lot of "dough"!

Va Tutto, 23 Cleveland St. (bet. Spring & Kenmare Sts.), (212) 941-0286, *Friendly / Outdoor*

Bella Tuscany with moonlit garden, affordable prices and incredible cuisine! Owned by former Gotham Bar & Grill goddess/manager Laurie Thomassino, the focus is on creating culinary delights very successfully—she runs this place like a machine, which only serves to enhance your dining experience. Our fave dishes: thin-crust pizzas with creminis and truffle oil and seafood risotto will have you singing "O Sole Mio" at the top of your lungs. Bring your friends or bring a date, just don't forget your appetite!

Yama, 92 W. Houston St., (bet. La Guardia Pl. & Thompson St.), (212) 674-0935, *Delish Sushi*

See details in Flatiron/Gramercy/Union Square, other location in GV.

❧ *Not to Miss:*

Ciao Bella Café, 262 Mott St. (bet. Houston & Prince Sts.), (212) 431-3591, *Ice Cream*

Nom Wah Tea Parlor, 13 Doyers St. (bet. Pell Street & Chatham Square), (212) 962-6047, *Exotic Ice Cream*

Novecento, 343 W. Broadway, (bet. Broome & Grand Sts.), (212) 925-4706, *Argentine Steaks*

Omen, 113 Thompson St. (bet. Prince & Spring Sts.), (212) 925-8923, *Japanese*

Woo Late Oak, 148 Mercer St. (@ Prince St.), (212) 925-8200, *Korean*

Zoe, 90 Prince St. (bet. Broadway & Mercer St.), (212) 966-6722, *Neighborhood Favorite*

Tribeca/Lower Manhattan/Other Boroughs ·······················

Alfama Restaurant, 551 Hudson Street (@ Perry St.), (212) 645-2500, *Portuguese Newcomer*

For a different ethnic experience, taste Portugal through the culinary genius of Carmen Santos. A former "Fado" singer, Santos is making waves with a creative twist on his homeland's cuisine. The Bacalhau a Bras (cod fish with scrambled eggs) is a must for adventurous diners!

Bouley Bakery, 120 W. Broadway (bet. Duane & Read Sts.), (212) 964-8362, *Celebrity Chef*

Elegant yet relaxed, this recently expanded Bouley offering once again makes magic. The smell of fresh bread wafts morning, noon, and night from the ovens, so waltz in for an early-morning coffee and croissant or waltz out at midnight after one of the best dinners in the city. The casually chic lunch is a great bet as well.

Bridge Café, 279 Water St. (@ Dover St.), (212) 227-3344, *Group Diner*

The destination if you are looking for someplace soothing to go with a group to feel like you've left the city. Not so easy to "zip" to, but it's worth the trek. Located underneath the Brooklyn Bridge in the South St. Seaport, this historic destination serves delish American fare in a setting that is the right blend of casual and big-city elegant. Nightly specials keep it interesting. No bar, no smoking, no getting around it regardless of how badly you need one.

Brothers BBQ, 225 Varick St. (@ Clarkson St.), (212) 727-2775, *Southern Roots*

"I've been livin' on the wrong side of Memphis" and here is a BBQ joint to prove that you can get authentic Southern delicacies "up North." We crave the pulled pork sandwiches and have been known to binge occasionally on the hush puppies. The place is festive and large enough to accommodate hungry girls in need of a fix! Southern accent not required.

Capsouto Freres, 415 Washington St. (@ Watts St.), (212) 966-4900, *Fine Dining/French*

Life is uncertain, eat dessert first—or at least order it—the soufflé of course. Dessert may be all you can afford. Seek out this high-end French dining experience for romance and elegance. Great place to kidnap your recently promoted beau for brunch . . . He'll feel so swept away from city life he might accidentally propose. Hint, hint.

Chanterelle, 2 Harrison St. (@ Hudson St.), (212) 966-6960, *Fine Dining*

What sets this high-end French eatery apart from the rest? Food that defies the gods from chef/creators the Waltucks and their professional artistically and aesthetically diverse staff. The well-trained staff itself is required to dine as a guest from time to time so as not to lose perspective on their guests' needs or the dining experience as a whole. A truly memorable evening awaits . . . and the food ain't too shabby either.

Mangia, 40 Wall St. (bet. Broad & William Sts.), (212) 245-4040, *Delivery*

Great for delivery in the Wall St. wasteland of mobile meals. They do offer an in-house buffet that is ultracrowded around usual lunch hours. Now get to work, chicky! Impressive in-office catering for luncheon meetings. House accounts make ordering from their delicious and varied menu a snap. Daily specials galore if you have the patience to listen to the lengthy and detailed recorded message. See other locations in MTW, MTE.

Peter Luger, 178 Broadway (@ Driggs Ave.), (718) 387-7400, *Traditional Steakhouse*

This New York standard is rumored to be the best in beef, but tasting is believing! The setting is casual, and the aged porterhouse steaks are hard to beat. The meat is actually still cooking when it comes to your table! Cash only unless you open an in-house charge.

Petite Abeille, 134 W. Broadway (bet. Duane & Thomas Sts.), (212) 791-5264, *Belgian Find*

This little Belgian treasure is open seven days a week for those looking for hearty fare, namely stews and mussels Flemish style.

Spartina, 355 Greenwich St. (@ Harrison St.), (212) 274-9310, *Trendy Italian*

Trendy Mediterranean hot spot with devilishly delicious pizzas care of Chef Stephen Calt. We love the outdoor tables to revel in our latest designer acquisition from Century 21 (see Treasures, Lower Manhattan).

Sylvia Weinstock's Cakes, 273 Church St. (bet. White & Franklin Sts.), (212) 925-6698, *Gourmet Wedding Cakes*

Wedding cake virtuoso Sylvia Weinstock is known for her breathtaking and elaborate custom-made cakes that will convince you to take the plunge just to taste the cake on the other end! No credit cards so bring a wheelbarrow full of cash. Open only M–F, by appointment.

The Lotus Club, 317 Church St. (bet. Lispenard & Walker Sts.), (212) 625-2544, *Eat and Read*

Reading and eating for the lit girl with a light appetite. Copious selection of mags and rags while you catch up on news and views over cappucino and light café fare—sandwiches and salads.

The River Café, 1 Water St. (@ Brooklyn Bridge), (718) 522-5200, *Room With A View*

A feel-good place with a perfect view of the sweeping Manhattan skyline, but the view comes with a price, so get out your Nikes . . . Cross the Brooklyn Bridge by foot (see Tripping, Lower Manhattan) or by car. It is well worth the trip, especially if you have "visitors" or are looking for a marriage proposal. *Molto romantico. Psst . . . views aside, the food is absolutely delicious!*

✦ *Not to Miss:*

Bubby's, 120 Hudson St. (bet. Franklin & N. Moore Sts.), (212) 219-0666, *Hangover Breakfast*

Odeon, 145 W. Broadway (@ Thomas St.), (212) 233-0507, *Neighborhood Favorite*

Nobu, 105 Hudson St. (@ Franklin St.), (212) 219-0500, *High-End Sushi*

    Next Door Nobu, 105 Hudson St. (@ Franklin St.), (212) 334-4445, *Casual Sushi*

    Tribeca Grill, 375 Greenwich St. (@ Franklin St.), (212) 941-3900, *Neighborhood Favorite*

✿ Good to Know:

In the mood for caviar? **Caviarteria** ensures that you are never too far away. Locations are popping up all over: Grand Central Station, Park Ave. @ 58th, Soho Grand Hotel, Tribeca Grand Hotel, The Ivy Club, or dial (800)-4CAVIAR! We can never get enough!

Treats

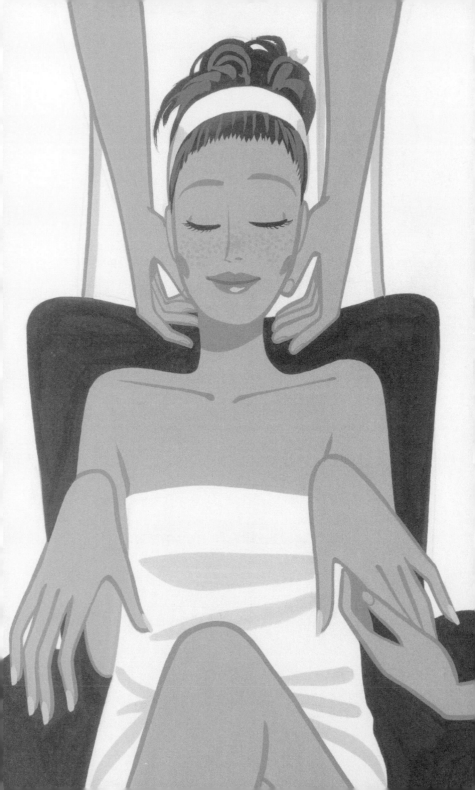

Crunch, 162 W. 83rd St. (bet. Amsterdam & Columbus Aves.), (212) 875-1902, *Hi-Tech Fitness*

Cutting-edge cardio and daily rates for traveling execs with the urge to sweat! Get with the Level 3 trainers, go for the boxing ring, cycle your heart away on the bikes with Internet access . . . First in the city to offer "Firefighter Training"—the Intense workout consists of climbing ladders, hoisting hoses, and carrying "victims." Twenty-two dollars and a picture ID will get your everywhere your body wants to go . . . Like into that little black dress in your suitcase! See other location in LES. *Psst . . . be sure to claim your frequent flyer miles from the NetPulse that lets you earn miles on United or American.*

Lavar Hair Design, 127 W. 72nd St. (bet. Broadway & Columbus Ave.), (212) 724-4492, *Hair Extensions*

Karina Castaneda is the extension guru for UWS babes of all shapes and sizes. So extend your pixie cut down to your waist before dinner! Not that you'll be able to afford dinner afterward . . . Full weave is $500 plus the cost of the hair. Call for a consultation.

Ling, 105 W. 77th St. (bet. Columbus & Amsterdam Aves.), (212) 877-2883, *Eyes & Face Care*

See details in Union Square/Gramercy/Flatiron; other location in Soho.

Liza Nails, 20 W. 64th St. (bet. CPW & Broadway), (212) 769-0300, *Quick Or House Calls*

Susan Kim rules the roost in this Asian nail emporium that is cleaner and chicer than most (hey, *Vogue* wrote it up!) . . . Regular manicure/pedicure is $30, and if you want Kim to make a house call double the ante plus cab fee. Sit amongst socialites and secretaries dipping their extremities in Palmolive! Liza personally files on the UES. Park yourself against the wall of personalized "first name only" bottles of Nailtiques—Sally, Lisbeth, Leslie, Anne . . . see other locations in UES. *Psst . . . don't forget to tip for the massage!*

Madelaine Cosmetology, 134 W. 72nd St., Second Floor (bet. Broadway & Columbus Ave.), (212) 362-0450, *Facial Plus*

We come for the two-hour facials that cost a mere $45! Classic facial with the full treatment you would get at any chichi Madison Ave. salon. They also offer manicures, pedicures, waxing, and electrolysis, with appointments as early as 8:30 A.M. for early risers!

Oz Garcia, 10 W. 74th St., Suite 1G (bet. Columbus & CPW), (212) 362-5569, *Nutritionist*

The diet guru of stellar munchers like Robert DeNiro, Winona Ryder, and Donna Karan, Garcia uses hair and blood evaluations to help him accurately determine metabolic rate and nutritional needs. One-on-one evaluations and diet plans will keep you coming back for more!

Paris Health Club, 752 West End Ave. (bet. 96th & 97th Sts.), (212) 749-3500, *Deluxe Gym*

Not just another club, this comprehensive gym feels more like a spa. In addition to the regular drill—StairMasters, EFX machines, and a lap pool—indulge in the eucalyptus steam room, cold plunge pool, or coed whirlpool (whoopie!). They also offer one-day guest passes for $18.75, good for entry to one of the 60 classes per week, including Pilates and Iyengar yoga. Now lace up those tennies . . .

Pilates Studio of New York, 2121 Broadway, Suite 201 (@ 74th St.), (212) 875-0189, *Stretch Out*

Stretch your way to slim at a reasonable $15 per class.

Reebok Sports Club/NY, 160 Columbus Ave. (bet. 67th & 68th Sts.), (212) 362-6800, *World Class Sports*

Membership has its privileges, though it doesn't come cheap! However, you will be treated to innovative fitness adventures like Rooftop Inline Skating, Rock-Climbing Walls, and Boot Camp. Also excellent swimming facilities (don't you wanna backstroke next to Vendela?) and killer spinning classes. On Functional Fridays, the gym offers several of its hottest classes simultaneously, kicking off every half hour during the peak "crunch" from 5:00 to 7:00 P.M. See other locations in UES, MTW @ Rockefeller Center.

Scott J. Salon and Spa, 257 Columbus Ave. (@ 72nd St.), (212) 769-0107, *Spa Pedicure*

Hidden beneath a beauty parlor is a haven for your toes and a waterfall to soothe the mind. Combining pedicures and reflexology, Scott will take your feet to nirvana and exfoliate up to the knees before you know it!

Two Do Salon, 210 W. 82nd St. (bet. Amsterdam Ave. & Broadway), (212) 787-1277, *Full Service*

Sacha is the up-to-the-minute up-do artist ($70). Their garden is ideal for a bridal party's prenuptial makeover. The expert staff can accommodate everyone for everything! The "spa side" of the salon offers other treatments including massage ($85/1 hour), waxing ($25/bikini), facials ($75–$90), and the usual color and cut.

⌀ Good to Know:
Great places for kids' cuts:
Cozy's Cuts for Kids, 448 Amsterdam Ave. (bet. 81st & 82nd Sts.), (212) 579-2600

Upper East Side ··

Alexandra & Alexandra's Beauty Center, 30 E. 60th St. (bet. Park & Madison Aves.), (212) 752-1071, *Exclusive Pampering*

Located next to the French Institute, this adorable, elite place is perfect when you want to spoil a friend before her wedding or be spoiled by a boyfriend trying to get out of the doghouse! You can get reasonable package deals that make this level of service seem affordable. Including such treatments as Oxigenation Therapy ($90), European waxing (the green French kind), European manicures/pedicures, and, last but not least, the recent addition of hairstylist Alfred Nardi (Jackie O's hair guru) who closed his town house to join the Center.

Asphalt Green, 555 E. 90th St. (@ York Ave.), (212) 369-8890, *Olympic Pool*

Day rates are available for the tomboy traveler at this testosterone-infused five-and-a-half-acre workout jungle. The pool is groovy, as is the almost "college campus" feel. Maybe you could join a pickup game of touch football.

Berenice Electrolysis and Beauty Center, 29 E. 61st St. (bet. Madison & Park Aves.), (212) 355-7055, *Hair Be Gone*

Well, luckily it's the twenty-first century where you're only a zap away from hairless perfection at the hands of Berenice Rothenberg, who is dedicated to bringing the most modern methods of hair removal to the city gal. Discreet, private, and professional. What more could you ask for besides your bare-o-ness! Maybe a facial, or some reflexology? Yep, they do that too.

Bloomie Nail, 1320 Madison Ave. (bet. 93rd & 94th Sts.), (212) 426-5566, *Fast Manicure*

Quick lube for the nails. Treat yourself to their back and neck massage in the special "chair" for a taste of relaxation amid the stress of midday . . . Manicure $10, pedicure $22.

Completely Bare, 764 Madison Ave. (bet. 65th & 66th Sts.), (212) 717-9300, *Hair Removal Plus*

Epilady be gone, retire your Remington! The new millennium's answer to hairballs, "staches," and other stubbly unsightlies . . . For $450, you can once and for all eradicate that bikini line with cutting-edge technology. "Relatively painless," the much-hyped Epilight system claims virtually no regrowth. You be the judge. Call ahead and ask about your free fifteen-minute "sampling" before you lay out the big bucks. *Psst . . . ask about the power peel if you are looking for a half hour micromabrasion to remove tired skin.*

David Barton Gym, 30 E. 85th St. (@ Madison Ave.), (212) 517-7577, *Look Better Naked*

We love this gym for its cleanliness and emptiness even at peak times, not to mention the elegant atmosphere and Aveda products in the locker room. We have been tempted to blow off our workout and head for the shower. Mod and sleek, not to mention beautiful, the staff is helpful and informed. Personal trainers are available to give personalized attention and introduce you to new exercise disciplines. Regular classes and two locations in the city (the other's in Chelsea) are an added boon as is the ability to buy "10-packs" if you only visit the city periodically.

Steven Dillon @ Gil Ferrer, 21 E. 74th St. (bet. Fifth & Madison Aves.), (212) 535-3543, www.GilFerrerSalon.com, *Style Maven*

We could fill this book with accolades about the fabulous haircuts by Steven Dillion. His God-given talent is that of a real artist and his long list of clients would follow him to the end of the earth. Trust him with a total hair makeover or go for just a trim. Either way, you will be blown away at the sheer perfection. You may catch him doing makeovers on *Oprah* or quietly snipping away on this quiet UES block. Best bet for best cut at any price. Cuts start at $225.

Facial Dynamics, 129 E. 80th St. (bet. Park & Lexington Aves.), (212) 794-2961, *Custom Facials*

Just learning about June Meyer alone is worth the price of this book! Meyer has had her "word of mouth only" esthetician business for 22 years, with her "no advertising/no phone book listing" policy making her a hidden treasure for those in search of flawless complexions. Incorporating eight different product lines, she customizes your facial from visit to visit depending on your skin at the moment. After an hour and a half of pure bliss (she includes feet/hand rubs along the way) you will count yourself among such Meyer devotees as Donatella! No weekends and prepare to pay from $110 to $145 depending on the "damage"! Amex and cash only.

First Nails, 1604 First Ave. (bet. 83rd & 84th Sts.), (212) 879-6500, *Quickie Nail Job*

Clean and quick, the pro manicurists are able to get you filed, polished and out the door in no time. After five years in the neighborhood, a loyal clientele depends on them for this popular ritual!

Janet Sartin Institute of Skincare, 500 Park Ave. (@ 59th St.), (212) 751-5858, *Skincare*

Get that little bottom buffed for your slinky Versace evening gown—no ripples allowed! In addition to carrying an excellent line of custom skincare products they are a full-service spa with exclusive treatments like "Body Surfing," where you slip into a power suit (No, not Armani!) that stimulates cellulite areas, or the famous Golden Spoons Treatment with Collagen Mask ($79) that incorporates the ancient Egyptian philosophy of using cold and warm stimulation. Pamper your mom with an Ultimate Day of Beauty ($248) that includes two signature treatments, manicure, pedicure, makeup application, and a light lunch! . . . *Psst . . . you must try their hair removal cream called Bare It. Call (800) 321-1779 to have your order shipped overnight.*

John Frieda, 30 E. 76th St. (bet. Fifth & Madison Aves.), (212) 879-1000, *Hollywood Hair*

John and his coterie of "whiz kids" (Orlando Pita, Christophe Robin, Danilo Rick Haylor, Kerry Warn, James Brown, Gavin Harwin to name many) have monopolized the spreads of fashion rags worldwide. See if they can work the same magic on you at his minimalist UES salon. For the Hollywood record, Sharon Dorram is responsible for the locks of Pitt, and Sally Hershberger of Meg Ryan color and cut fame works a few days a month in a private room.

Karen Wu's Therapaeutic Chinese Beauty Experience, 1044 Madison Ave., 2nd Floor (bet. 79th & 80th Sts.), (212) 737-3545 1377, Third Ave. (bet. 77th & 78th Sts.), *Chinese Spa*

A cutting-edge "spa" and alternative health center devoted to beauty from the inside out. "When our body is out of balance, or when there is a weakness in our internal system it is reflected in our skin, body tone, and mood." Come in for a traditional Chinese diagnostic examination (about 15 minutes) and you will be amazed. Next, you are told about appropriate beauty "treatments," such as acupuncture, herbal remedies, the Chinese Herbal Mask Facial, or the Vitamin C Facial, all designed to re-create balance within your body and without . . .

Kevin Mancuso @ Peter Copola, 746 Madison Ave. (bet. 64th & 65th Sts.), (212) 988-9404, *Top Haircutter*

Perhaps eclipsing John Sahag as the cutting king of NYC, Mancuso is the "mane man of Manhattan" and at $300 per cut he should be! Cindy Crawford testifies to his talents in Mancuso's book *The Mane Thing*. Girls famous and not so famous line up for a new look! *Psst . . . once a month Robyn Cosio comes from Los Angeles to Copola to wax the brows of her legions of fans. "It's like an instant face-lift," says Cosio herself. Not bad for $50 and a ton of patience.*

Kimare Ahnert, 1113 Madison Ave. (bet. 83rd & 84th Sts.), (212) 452-4252, *Cosmetic Artist*

A business for the "masses" in this luxurious town house. A true artist with cosmetics, Ahnert is a frequent referral of many top plastic surgeons in search of short-term solace for their recently reconfigured patients. Consultations begin at $75 with Kimare, teaching application is $150. Other talent artists on hand charge $55 for the consultation and $100 for the application. House calls cost a lot more but if you have the bucks, it is worth the luxury of never leaving your boudoir—Kimare is $175 Mon–Thu, $250 Fri–Sun.

Laura Geller Make-up Studios, Inc., 1044 Lexington Ave. (bet. 74th & 75th Sts.), (212) 570-5477/800-MAKEUP-4-U, *Custom Cosmetics*

Make-up whiz Laura Geller has seen her business grow from two employees to twenty-two over the past twenty years. Having honed her craft on the Great White Way on beauties like Lena and Liza, she has a low-key, hands-on approach to beauty that puts function and her client's happiness before trend! Additional services available under the same roof are waxing, haircutting, and coloring. *Psst . . . rumor has it that she is "world-renowned" for her wedding-day portrait looks and specializes in camouflaging scars, acne, and other pesky flaws.*

Liza Nails, 22 E. 66th St. (bet. Medison & Fifth Aves.)
1081 Madison Ave. (bet. 80th & 81st Sts.), (212) 517-4566, *Quick Nail Job*
See details in UWS.

Lotte Berke Method, 23 E. 67th St. (bet. Fifth & Madison Aves.), (212) 288-6613, *Body ReShaping*

If exercise were ever considered "graceful" this would be it. Celebs and socialites are addicted to this 30-year-old technique that integrates body and mind using a bit of ballet, strength training, and stretching that is sure to give newcomers the "Lotte Shake" (uncontrollable muscle twitching from sheer exertion)! Be prepared to sweat as you gently and precisely reshape your body. Don't stare at Julia Roberts if she slides in next to you at the barre . . . Classes are booked solid in this three-story town house, so make your reservations early.

Louis Licari Color Group, 797 Madison Ave. (bet. 67th & 68th Sts.), (212) 517-8084, *Hair Color*

Color god of Manhattan! No roots allowed. Seek tremendous tresses a là Susan Sarandon and Ellen Barkin. If you can't get in with Louis, ask for Kathy Gallotti, who snazzes up the locks of Katie Couric and rocker Jon Bon Jovi.

Nails By Nina, 129 E. 80th St. (bet. Madison & Park Aves.), (212) 288-8130, *Perfect Manicure*

After a 45-minute manicure from Nina you will be completely devoted. No typical soapy water (too drying), no dramatic cutting of cuticles and no harmful chemicals make this the environmental and skin-friendly experience. Good filing, hand massage, and neatly applied polish topped off with a paraffin treatment will send you to hand heaven . . . $17 manicure, $31 pedicure. Waxing available as well. By appointment only. Cash only.

Salon A.K.S., 694 Madison Ave. (bet. 62nd & 63rd Sts.), (212) 888-0707, *Cut / Color / Makeup*

Popular and bustling, this upstairs Madison Ave. salon is home to colorist Frank Friscioni and handsome French co-owner Alain Pinon, who gives an incredible cut after a heavenly scalp massage and shampoo. Word on the street is that these guys are taking over tresses everywhere! Check out resident Bobbie Brown sorceress, Maria Romano, but make your reservation in advance as she is part-time and booked months on end. And Bobbie says you just need the brushes . . . Ha!

The Spa @ Equinox, 205 E. 85th St. (bet. Second and Third Aves.), (212) 396-9611

140 E. 63rd St. (@ Lexington Ave.), (212) 750-4671, *Body & Hair Treatments*

Hot Ginger and Body Glow Rubs are the ticket! And if you have a Saturday night rendezvous with your new crush, Moty Moty (at the 63rd St. location) will custom blend hair conditioners and follow with a blow-dry for $50. M–F from 8 A.M. to 8:30 P.M., Sat. & Sun. until 7 P.M. Kabaam! You are ready for a night on the town with a glow and a gloss equal to the bright lights and big city!

The Stressless Step, 115 E. 57th St., 5th Floor, (bet. Park & Lexington Ave.), (212) 826-6222, *Tipless Too*

This is one of THE favorite affordable, no-frills places to go for bodywork. A recent move to new digs marked the addition of new services like waxing and sun damage treatments. If you are in a rush, go for the "Stress Less Express," $50 for ½ hour rubdown. Find books on maintaining your health in the front, and a nice lounge / juice bar in the back. Special facials are topped off with a relaxing steam and sauna. Prepare to pay $90 for the standard "relaxology" massage. *Psst . . . feel free to come by and use the "wet" area for a 25-dollar fee. No tipping allowed, and they mean it!*

Zendo-Shobo-Ji, 223 E. 67th St. (bet. 2nd & 3rd Aves.), (212) 861-3333, *Meditation*

Japanese meditation in a brownstone . . . A little bit like aerobics in a pagoda! Just kidding! If you are in need of some meditation tips, show up on Thursday (no reservations required) between 7 P.M. and 9 P.M. for an orientation class that is a requirement for first-timers. Could be the best $15 you have ever spent! Otherwise, once you are "mentally fit" they are open on Tuesday afternoons, most evenings and Saturday mornings.

◈ *Good to Know:*

Beauty gift for your man? For $26 you can treat him to a shave that would make "the Godfather" jealous. **Lev Zavurov @ Paul Mole,** 1031 Lexington Ave. (@ 74th St.), (212) 535-8461.

He starts with hot towels and lets his fingers do their magic by creaming, soaping, and finally razoring with the precision of a fine surgeon. A real treat for your special beau!

◈ *Not to Miss:*

Le Salon, 145 E. 72nd St. (bet. 3rd & Lexington Aves.), (212) 861-5101. Ask for Virginia.

◈ *Kids' Cuts:*

Cozy's Cuts for Kids, 1125 Madison Ave. (@ 84th St.), (212) 744-1716
Michael's Children's Haircutting Salon, 1263 Madison Ave. (bet. 90th & 91st Sts.), (212) 289-9612

Midtown West ....

Aija Lee Acupunture Center, 38 W. 32nd St. (bet. Fifth Ave. & Broadway), (212) 239-5559, *Preventive Care*

Thirty-five years of experience in acupuncture and herbal medicine. They accept most major insurance if your policy covers "preventive medicine." Prepare to pay $50 per session and book at least one week in advance as they are usually busy, busy, busy!

Anma Massage, (212) 935-2175, *Personalized Massage*
(Private residence, must call for address)

Martial Arts Hall of Famer CJ Krieger has made an art form out of the Asian "anma" massage technique, much like deep shiatsu. Also try his muscle-melting "tuina" massage and trigger-point therapies.

Art of Fitness, 39 W. 56th St., Penthouse 5 (bet. Fifth & Sixth Aves.), (212) 262-4040, *One-On-One Trainers*

Art Clyde, the owner of this skylit two-story oasis, with a private changing room and steam shower on each floor, believes in soreness. Call for your phone "consultation" and Art will help you choose a trainer based on your needs. Variety *is* the spice of life so if yoga is your thing, or kick boxing, they have you covered—$85 per session, but prices go down if you buy a group of sessions.

Club La Raquette, 119 W. 56th St. (bet. Sixth & Seventh Aves.), (212) 245-1144, *Penthouse Pool*

The best thing about this gym is the indoor swimming pool overlooking Central Park. Even though the pool is covered, they have a small but nice sundeck for the last of the remaining sun worshipers! Twenty-five dollars for the day. Bring your ID and your sunscreen! *Psst . . . they also have a full gym offering yoga and aerobics classes along with spa treatments like hypnotherapy massage.*

Dorite Baxter, 47 W. 57th St. (bet. Fifth & Sixth Aves.), (212) 371-4542, *Exclusive Spa*

A fave among the exclusive hotel concierges. Indulge yourself with the wildly popular Solar Energy Mud Treatment: a one-and-a-half-hour massage, application of mud from the Dead Sea, a facial massage, a mask, then a warm shower. The Dead Seas Salt Body Scrub cures jet lag, just be sure not to shave your legs the morning before or the salt will burn like crazy! *Psst . . . don't forget to get a special "organic wax" that manages to keep ingrown hairs away—great for the underarm or bikini areas.*

Fitness By Design, 41 W. 57th St., Fifth Floor (bet. Fifth and Sixth Aves.), (212) 759-6333, *Personal Training*

Ask for John when you call . . . No shortcuts allowed: classic training at its best! Nothing fancy here—hard work and sweat create great results! Encompassing all the modern tools (machines, free weights, kick boxing) along with good old-fashioned "staircase running" for a little added torture, uh, variety! Specializing in those that want to get serious, lose weight, and shape up!

J Sisters, 35 W. 57th St. (bet. Fifth & Sixth Aves.), (212) 750-2485, *Brazilian Wax*

Gwyneth admits she'll never be the same . . . At least her bikini line won't. Try the Brazilian, which is all the rage in Hollywood and Gomorrah. All teasing (not tweezing) aside, this nifty little den of aesthetic has the rich and beautiful flocking to be braised, buttered, and baked in a whole new way. Our pick for the best waxing this city has to offer—thirty-five minutes/$45. Virgin waxers beware . . . *Psst . . . clients are raving over the in-house specialty of eyelash extensions! Unlike faux lashes, these individual extensions adhere to the roots and last up to a month! Ask for Fatima Wadhy. Naomi Campbell swears by her.*

My Place Too, 1285 Sixth Ave. (bet. 51st & 52nd Sts.), (212) 541-8181, *Eyebrow Shaping*

Precision eyebrow shaping with a thread and no "pricking," an ancient Indian trade secret. Your brows never looked so good for so little pain! Ten dollars plus tip.

Osaka Traditional Therapy Spa, 50 W. 56th St. (bet. Fifth & Sixth Aves.), 2nd Floor, (212) 956-4322, *Romantic Massage*

If a boring business dinner has taken the best of your night, steal away for a late-night treat that will leave you as relaxed as if you had been a lady of leisure all day long! Highly rated by the local press. Go for the Shiatsu Acupressure treatment that was good enough for former President Ronald Reagan. Finish off your night with an herbal steam and an eye-opening, mind-healing Japanese hot and cold hydrotherapy bath and shower. Open from 11 A.M. to 3 A.M., seven days a week. Reservations recommended. *Psst . . . grab your "honey" and enjoy a coed rubdown at this Eastern-themed spa. You won't feel shy after you have been lathered in oil and loosened up together. One hundred dollars per person for two hours of bliss.*

Radu Physical Culture Studio, 24 W. 57th St., 2nd Floor (bet. Fifth & Sixth Aves.), (212) 581-1995, *Heavy Sweat Gym*

Cindy Crawford was at the forefront of this guru's rise to fitness stardom, and devotees follow him to the Hamptons in the summer. Radu is a firm believer that an hour is enough, and thank the Lord because he kills you each and every minute. Personalized evaluation precedes class participation. No sissies allowed!

Roxana Pintilie @ Warren Tricomi, 16 W. 57th St. (bet. Fifth & Sixth Aves.), (212) 262-8899, *Nifty Nails*

Creator of the nifty "Hardware Nail Enamel," adorably packaged in miniature paint cans, Roxana had the brilliant idea to partner with psychic Vanessa Facciola so that clients could be "read" and "filled" at the same time. Groovy Moroccan interior sports golden bowls to soak your extremities premanicure/pedicure . . . that is, if it's in the cards for you to get an appointment!

Splash Salon @ Sports Club/LA, 45 Rockefeller Plaza (bet. 50th / 51st Sts. & Fifth & Sixth Aves.), (212) 218-8600, *Last Minute*

Located in the new Sports Club L.A., this neighborhood newcomer is a nice place to pop into. Offering full-service salon treatments such as massage, color and cut, and facials. Make a bad hair day go away when you are able to "walk in" for a last-minute do!

Yi*Pak Sauna @, New Han Yang Beauty Salon, 10 W. 32nd Street, 2nd floor (bet. Fifth Ave. & Broadway), (212) 594-1025, *Korean Massage*

Okay girls, get ready for the treat of all treats in this Korean in-crowd hideaway. Walk into the tacky outer hair salon, and keep walking . . . Back, back, back into nirvana. They'll strip you, scrub you with salt and cucumbers (sometimes carrots!), massage you, pour freezing cucumber water on your head, massage you some more . . . You'll soak, steam, and get your body polished and finish with a milk-bath rinse! A little minifacial tops it off! You'll walk out a new woman and ready for cucumber tea sammies at the Plaza. No appointment necessary: $100, credit or cash.

Arrojo Cutler Salon, 115 E. 57th St. (bet. Lexington & Park Aves.), (212) 308-3838, *Aveda Concept*

Using all Aveda products you will enjoy a free head and neck treatment with every shampoo. The salon itself appeared in *Interior Design* magazine for its chic look. But the main attraction here is the Magnificent Manuella! Manuella Goncalves is your hair and makeover maven who makes house calls to boot! She is only in the salon on Saturdays. Services in the environs of $250.

Away Spa & Gym @ the W Hotel, 541 Lexington Ave. (bet. 49th & 50th Sts.), (212) 407-2970, *Day Passes*

Combine *Gattaca* with Elizabeth Arden and what do you get? Two hours of no-touch aura analysis and "pranic healing." By the way, Jane is blue. Whatever . . . For workout girls: 10,000 square feet of gym with groovy workout gear if you left yours behind. Day passes for nonmembers. Javanese Lulur Treatment ($150) is two hours of Indonesian treatment for princess brides (that's you!). The practice is traditionally performed for forty consecutive days before the nuptials. We recommend that busy women get the treatment once a month up to the big day. It includes exfoliation, full-body massage, lathering yogurt treatment and a delicious soak!

Brad Johns @ The Avon Centre, Trump Tower, 725 Fifth Ave. (bet. 56th & 57th Sts.), (212) 755-AVON, *Blond Ambition*

Look no further if you are "dying" to be blond. Specializing in caring for the blond tresses of Faith Hill to the late Carolyn Bessette Kennedy, Brad wants you to be blond too! As a rule, he likes to copy the way a child's hair looks at the beach—no ashy shades, only golden tones. Upkeep will cost you a fortune and if you can't afford it, don't go blond. He is fantastic at other shades as well. Not for the faint of pocketbook but worth every penny to those of us who have joined the cult. Three hundred dollars plus for color and highlights. *Psst . . . look for his new book called* Dyeing to Know *for more about his technique and style.*

Eliza Petrescu @ The Avon Centre, Trump Tower, 725 Fifth Ave. (bet. 56th & 57th Sts.), (212) 755-AVON, *Eyebrow Diva*

From *Vogue* to *Vanity Fair* "the Queen of the Arch" has carved the arches of everyone who is anyone! Sixty dollars for first-timers and $34 for return patrons! *Psst . . . she is so popular that she has a phone line dedicated to her clients at the spa as well as a staff trained in the Eliza way.*

Juva Skin & Laser Center, 60 E. 56th St. (bet. Madison & Park Aves.), (212) 688-5882, *Skincare*

Dr. Bruce Katz has taken the world of laser surgery to new levels with his seven-room treatment facility featuring cutting-edge (no pun intended) therapies using high-powered lasers, along with a generous array of dermatologic and spa-based treatments as well . . . Mole removal? Wrinkle maintenance? Juicy facial? Enter here.

Kenneth @ Waldorf Astoria, 301 Park Ave. (@ 50th St.), (212) 752-1800, *Socialites Hair / Nails*

The "House of Kenneth" was built by Jackie O, but the new generation of socialites agrees. Our friend Patricia, who shows off her designer purchases over lunch at La Bilboquet, gives heavy references . . . and believe us, her color looks good! Manicures and pedicures receive the brilliant benefit of being sent home with a mini bottle of polish for touch-ups . . . Finally!

Laura Norman Reflexology Center, 41 Park Ave. (bet. 36th & 37th Sts.), (212) 532-4404, *Reflexology*

The feet are the seat of soul and body according to some . . . so pamper yours with this Eastern alternative therapy and you will not only reduce stress and increase energy but perhaps catch a health problem before it hatches!

Natasha Mgaleeva @ Limpopo, 48 E. 43rd St. (bet. Madison & Vanderbilt Aves.), (212) 986-1160, *Glossy Hair*

Natasha is in the house—all the way from Moscow! She recently relocated and are we ever glad! Specializing in beautiful, sleek, straight hair that is healthy from the root and looks it. Natasha gives you a two-hour scalp treatment with intensive massage (from the Lazertique method whose products she carries). Then, prepare for the blowout of a lifetime . . . Conde Nast girls come to her by the dozen.

Oscar Blandi @ The Plaza Hotel, 768 Fifth Ave. (@ 59th St.) 2nd Floor (212) 593-7930, *Extensions Plus*

Welcome to the gorgeously renovated salon at The Plaza, perhaps better known than its landlord thanks to celeb clientele and rave reviews! Jennifer Lopez and Drew Barrymore are devoted clients. Ask for Yoshi, a seriously talented stylist. Scott Pepper, the head colorist, has been known to send you on vacation with your bottle of color. And don't forget Kyle, formerly of Brad Johns Salon, who handles the color wand with loving care. James Herndon is the resident "weave king," having started his art at 16. If "Eloise" ever grew up to be hip and famous, she would be cut and coifed here at home!

Paulo Siqueria, 4 Park Ave. (bet. 33rd & 34th Sts.), (212) 779-9270, *Eyebrow Guru*

Didn't you know "archery" was an Olympic sport? Pia Getty, Shalom Harlow and Liv Tyler swear their brows to this "gold medalist." Why won't you? Thirty dollars to $50 per session.

Power Pilates, 136 E. 57th St. (bet. Park & Lexington Aves.), (212) 371-0700, *www.powerpilates.com*, *Posture & Toning*

See details in US/Gramercy/Flatiron.

The John Sahag Workshop, 425 Madison Ave. (bet. 48th & 49th Sts.), (212) 750-7772, *Master Haircutters*

Innovative styling and undivided attention to she who sits before him! The legendary dry cut that rocked the world. Think Fiona Apple and Jewel's mod hippie hair with layers . . . Young Hollywood hipsters like Mira and Jennifer (remember the *Friends* cut?) swear by him! Three hundred dollars and up . . . $1500 on location—we never want to underestimate our readers! *Psst . . . can't get in fast enough? Try protégé David Pate for half the price and half the wait.*

The Peninsula Spa, 700 Fifth Ave. (@ 55th St.), (212) 903-3910, *Poolside Lounge/Spa*

The 1998 renovation did wonders for the rooftop pool overlooking Fifth Ave., but unfortunately they left out the spa area and it shows . . . Nonetheless, booking a "treatment and a half," gains you access to the pool for the day and full benefits, including lunch on the sundeck and use of all the facilities. Well worth the $100 plus for a day escape from the city! We suggest you ask for Betsey Leohner for a deep-tissue massage before you while away a sweltering afternoon over a good book by the pool!

Vanderbilt YMCA, 224 E. 47th St. (bet. Second & Third Aves.), (212) 756-9600, *Workout On The Run*

Featuring two pools, one strictly for laps, and 135 classes per week including spinning, yoga, tai chi, and karate. Get a personalized fitness evaluation, take advantage of locker rooms with steam and sauna. Drop-in fees for nonmembers!

Yasmine Djerradine Institut De Beaute, 30 E. 60th St. (bet. Park & Madison Aves.), (212) 588-1771, *Spa Treatment*

Offering the exclusive Semonin Jet Lag Treatment (via Anne Semonin's Paris Boutique), prepare to rejuvenate and melt under the layers of heated volcanic mud bubbling deliciously down your spine as the rest of you is massaged from one end to the other. You are then delivered into an invigorating Kohler steam shower to wash and steam your way back from oblivion! Waddle back to the table for the scintillating lime essential oil rub. Whether jet-lagged or not, this is a mind/body experience of boggling proportion! Plush robes and disposable undies . . . Ask for Liliya! *Psst . . . the house wax is a homemade "amber wax" created by Souad known to devitalize the hair, slowing its growth.*

Yi Wang, 104 E. 40th St. (bet. Park & Lexington Aves.), (212) 808-4968, *Alternative Facial*

If you need more than a cleanse from your facial, try this effective acupuncture facial. Pressure points are manipulated to tighten slack tissue! Devotees swear by it. Ninety dollars for the full treatment.

↯ Not to Miss:

The Greenhouse Spa, 127 E. 57th St. (bet. Lexington & Park Aves.), (212) 644-4449, *Neighborhood Newcomer*

↯ Good to Know:

Salon Ishi, 70 E. 55th St. (bet. Madison & Park Aves.), (212) 888-4744, *Rainy Days And Mondays*

If you are in need of an emergency trim, color job, or blowout for a special event, these folks are open on Monday for business! Schedule an incredible scalp massage or shiatsu pedicure . . . unfortunately Mondays are just for "maintenance" because "special" services are only offered Tuesday–Saturday!

Chelsea/Meat Packing

Creighton @ Vega, NYC, 36 W. 17th St., 4th Floor (bet. Fifth & Sixth Aves.), (212) 366-1792, *Color Guy*

This up-and-coming colorist will make you look as cool as you know you are. If you have had enough of the cookie-cutter hair color, let Creighton make you beautiful. Highlights run $150 and up.

HairPeace, 410 W. 14th St. (bet. Ninth & Tenth Aves.), (212) 645-8333, *Groovy Haircare*

Models and musicians flock to this loft space that sports a pool table, offers movies and electric guitars to play while you wait for your color to "take." They also have been known to throw late-night after-hours parties, so book your appointment late in the day to take part in the festivities—you might just end up at an unexpected bash!

Maximus Spa/Salon, 15 Mercer St. (bet. Grand & Canal Sts.), (212) 431-3333, *Day Spa*

Get watered at this newcomer that made a "splash" on the SoHo spa scene in the summer of 2001—literally: they specialize in a Signature Water Journey ($145) that combines several scrumptious water therapies. This elegant, unconventional salon was formerly a 6,000-square-foot newspaper plant. Facials, haircuts/color, massage (à la carte) on hand, but no waxing or nail treatments available. *Psst . . . we love the Steam Bar station for a pre-facial cleansing.*

Stone Spa, 104 W. 14th Street, 2nd Floor (bet. Sixth & Seventh Aves.), (212) 741-8881, *Unique Massage*

Stones are all the rage. (And we're not talking Jagger!) Carla Ciuffo's groundbreaking spa uses stones to "add that special healing touch" to massage. All treatments involve rubbing superheated river stones over oiled skin. Offering eleven different stone massages, such as the Beyond Nirvana Facial (70 minutes for $120) or the Nirvana Facial Express (35 minutes for $65) for those in a hurry. Set in a pretty loft space with whitewashed walls for a Zen-like effect. Open seven days a week to make sure you get "stoned" anytime you need it—11 A.M.–8:30 P.M. Shorter hours on Sunday. *Psst . . . they have the perfect gift for your friend who is too busy to make an appointment: A Hot Toe Voodoo kit that includes Apricot Seed Oil, Peppermint Lotion, Essential Oil, four "toe stones" and one "massage stone" for $39.*

The Sports Gym @ Chelsea Piers, 23rd St. and the Hudson River @ Pier 60, (212) 336-6000, *Massive Luxury Club*

How about a game of volleyball on an indoor sand beach? Or do laps in an Olympic-size pool, ice-skate year-round or run a few miles on the coldest day of the year on the indoor track. How about a ride on "Black Beauty" at Manhattan's largest equestrian center? If the variety has exhausted you, just visit the Origins Feel Good Spa! Day rates available: $40 per day or $50 on weekends.

Union Square/Gramercy/Flatiron ···

Antonio Prieto Salon, 25 W. 19th St. (bet. Fifth & Sixth Aves.), (212) 255-3741, *Celebrity Cut*

Formerly known as "fashion's best-kept secret"—now the secret is out! The handsome Spaniard has a flair for fine cuts. Think classic cuts with precise detailing—no Courtney Love looks done here. Celebrities and fashionistas flock to his hideaway, but local gals will find it welcoming too. A "loyal" stylist, Antonio still makes time for his "regulars." *Psst . . . the garden patio is open in warmer months where you can sip lemonade while your feet are rubbed in sage oil with azaleas floating in the foot basin ($35). Or try the "Out To Lunch" manicure, which will have you back to the office in 25 minutes!*

Bateman Institute, 43 W. 24th St., Suite 12B (bet. Fifth & Sixth Aves.), (212) 243-2311, *Healing Yoga*

Change your body, change your life . . . Home to one of NYC's most treasured gurus, known for demystifying ancient Eastern practices to appeal to Western sensibilities. The Bateman Technique is a way of looking at your body as architecture in relationship to the force of gravity. A spacious skylit loft is the perfect place to turn over a new leaf. Classes available in yoga or Qigong; Energentices for Life workshops and pain management too. *Psst . . . for those of you looking to become a teacher they offer yoga training and certification!*

Carapan Urban Spa & Store, 5 W. 16th St. (bet. Fifth & Sixth Aves.), (212) 633-6220, *Neighborhood Favorite*

Carapan means: "Beautiful place of tranquillity where one goes to restore one's spirit." Enter their unique world—the muted lighting, candles, incense and soft chanting lead you into an oasis of healing and beauty. Noted for aromatherapy rituals, a staff of 45 therapists performs over 400 services a week and yet you'll barely see another soul. No wonder it's a haven for celebrity clients. Adorable individual lockers with antique bags to hold your jewelry and lingerie, private bathrooms stocked with yummy products to restore—these are just a few of the treats. Sauna, pregnancy massage, Native American gifts.

Dr. Margolin's Wellness Spa, 166 Fifth Ave. (@ 22nd St.), (212) 675-9355, *Indulgence*

Open till 11 P.M. . . . and there's nowhere we'd rather spend late night than in the steaming lavender salt baths after a massage, eating organic oranges with a cool pack on our forehead! And they say being single doesn't have its advantages! Finish off with a private steam shower and there will be no living with you after such a pampering! Open seven days a week. *Psst . . . if you are suffering from chronic pain or just posture problems, ask for Sam Cagnina, the head massage therapist who works wonders. Eighty dollars for one hour.*

Jeniette, 62 E. 13th St. (bet. University Pl. & Broadway), (212) 529-1616, *Unique Brows*

According to Jeniette, faces are "not symmetrical" and neither are brows. With that in mind, she and her sister use an ancient "homeland" trick: paraffin wax and a piece of thread to create the perfect frame for the face. *Psst . . . ask for the Better Than Sex package: a body scrub, massage with aromatherapy oil, mud mask and wrap, deep hair conditioning, manicure/pedicure and lunch for $169! Maybe it is better than . . . doubtful!*

Julian Jonas @ Healing Life Center, 25 W. 21st St. (bet. Fifth & Sixth Aves.), (212) 496-8702, *Homeopathy*

After a decade of study in Japan, Jonas is certified in acupuncture as well as classic homeopathic medicine. Dividing his time between southern Vermont and his UWS digs, Jonas has a loyal following and is also well versed in nutrition counseling.

Ling, 10 E. 16th St. (bet. Fifth & Sixth Aves.), (212) 989-8833, *Eyes and Face*

Come visit the brow gurus. Tweezing and waxing, she'll sculpt a perfect pair for you and your life will change . . . Okay, just great eyebrows for $22, what more can a girl want. Ling means delicate in Chinese, and with over 20 years in the U.S., Ling's Ginseng Herbal Facial is a must for the pampered set. Take note of the most interesting skincare line for sale that rivals the best the world has to offer. See other locations in Soho and UWS. *Psst . . . notable diehards include Madonna, Wynona Ryder, Carly Simon.*

Madison Square Club, 210 Fifth Ave. (bet. 25th & 26th Sts.), (212) 683-1836, *Private Training*

Not for those who are just passing through, but those looking to make a commitment to your new workout regime (again!). Full-service pampering by a team of pros to help you achieve your personal fitness goals—even a plan to help with postpartum blues! Ninety-five dollars per session. Naturally, we love the luxurious dressing rooms complete with custom personal cherry lockers, a limestone steam shower, and plenty of glass that reflects the sunny Fifth Ave. location. Don't be surprised to catch a few models passing through. *Psst . . . they offer laundry service on premises so you don't have to haul your sweaty clothes around.*

Miwa/Alex, 24 E. 22nd St. (bet. Park Ave. & Broadway), (212) 228-4422, *Precision Cut*

It is no surprise that 20 years ago Miwa Ikegani launched her career as Vidal Sassoon's art director. Obviously "the master of the cut" rubbed off on his protégé. Her clientele includes William Morris superagent George Lane, curators from the MOMA and Cooper-Hewitt (see Tripping, UES) . . . Who says the arty can't have hip hair?

Mud Mask Personal Care Salon, 156 Fifth Ave. (bet. 20th & 21st Sts.) (212) 979-6685, *Deluxe Pedicure*

The Mud Mask Aromatherapeutic Pedicure ($33) is a must for tired city tootsies. First they use glycolic acid to exfoliate the dead skin followed by seaweed extracts to fight dehydration, then the feet are soaked in tea-tree oil and delightfully scrubbed with sea salt. The last step entails the usual strip, shape, and polish followed by a fantastic foot massage with collagen cream.

Power Pilates, 49 W. 23rd St. (bet. Fifth & Sixth Aves.), (212) 627-5852, www.powerpilates.com, *Posture & Toning*

Same thing as "power yoga," only different, here the principles of Pilates are boosted to a higher level to create faster, more furious results! "Butt" of course you will be hooked! They suggest at least three workouts a week—you'll feel it after 10 sessions and after thirty you will have a new body. If you put in the time, they "promise" results. Private, semiprivate and group mat classes available. Call for schedule. See other locations in MTE. *Psst . . . if you are a member of the UWS Equinox, 2465 Broadway (@ 92nd St.), (212) 799-1818, try their classes delivered by the same crew.*

Revolution, 104 W. 14th St. (bet. Fifth & Sixth Aves.), (212) 206-8785, *One-On-One Training*

Rocky would approve. Sweating required, no posing allowed. For $12 per class you can spin, box, and contour to your heart's content—literally! Flirty girls don't bother . . . you're better off at Reebok where the boys will notice. Run by fitness diva Terri Walsh, a former creative director at Crunch. Offering personalized and unpretentious classes in aerobics, spinning, yoga, tai chi and lots more. Classes are affordable: $12 for a single class; if you buy in bulk, $110 for 10 classes.

Sal Anthony's Scheffel Hall Movement, 190 Third Ave. (@ 17th St.), (212) 420-7242, *Dance Classes*

Located in the landmark Scheffel Hall, this nineteenth-century historic space now houses Sal Anthony's (Yes, he has a restaurant too) dance studio. Lovely details include a stained-glass ceiling in the petite hall and chandeliers on the third floor. Daily classes in Hatha Vinyasa yoga or pilates. African dance and salsa classes too. All classes are $10 each.

Tosler.Davis, 89 Fifth Ave., 10th floor (bet. 16th & 17th Sts.), (212) 229-0100, *Top Cut/Color*

Gals in the know have been chasing this talented (and adorable!) duo all over town for years! Alan and Sean have set up shop on their own, which makes them easier to find but not easier to book! Alan cuts with precision and Sean has a magic touch when it comes to color. By the way, there's no harm in having an innocent crush on your hairdressers!

Xena's Beauty Company, 158 W. 13th St. (bet. Sixth & Seventh Aves.), (212) 633-8550, *Neighborhood Favorite*

Xena is not a warrior princess but she may be able to make you feel like one! Celebrating her tenth year in business as the color aficionado for the Italian line Framesi, her salon's 1940s motif is pretty, but they promise to make you look up-to-date with their sensational cutting proposals aptly named "prete-porte." Color and cut to promote low maintenance—gotta love that! *Psst . . . open until 9 P.M. daily for those of you who can't get out of the office before* Jeopardy.

Manicure in your home or hotel? Call Barbara Mutnick, (212) 772-7486, a true pro at handling your nail needs on the spot! She is ready twenty-four/seven. Beep her on short notice or book ahead if you have the luxury. She brings the lamp, sterilized tools, creams, nail polish . . . All you need is a small towel—and an armored truck full of cash: $75 manicure/$95 pedicure.

Greenwich Village ···

Angel Feet Reflexology Center, 77 Perry St. (bet. W. 4th & Bleecker Sts.), (212) 924-3576, *Walk On Air*

Reflexology for the downtown girl in need of an overhaul. Regulars swear by it. The idea is that all of your nerve endings are in your feet, so massage away your aches and pains at the source. Don't expect an easy foot rub, as treatment is much more "pain-involved," especially if it is your first visit. Seventy dollars for the full hour, $40 for half hour sessions . . . They also make house and office calls for that midafternoon pick me up!

D. Esse, 350 Hudson St. (bet. King & Charlton Sts.), (212) 206-1655, *Miniday Spa*, www.deese.com.

Daphnee Selig is a French-trained biochemist specializing in facials, waxing and body treatments. Every treatment begins with a skin analysis followed by a choice of five facials depending on your skin's needs. The Rose Facial is all the rage among fashionistas; a one-hour treatment includes rose and lavender oils, and for the very dry . . . geranium! Fans of Eastern medicine will love the Acupuncture Facial. That time of the month? Go for the Detoxifying Body Wrap that throws in a minifacial to battle those little breakouts! Be sure to check out her personal homeopathic line of essential oils and aromatherapy skincare.

Eve, 400 Bleecker St. (bet. 11th & Perry Sts.), (212) 807-8054, *Reliable Nails*

Newly renovated and delivering yummy manicures, pedicures, waxing, facials, and electrolysis. This tiny space is often booked solid for services, so call ahead.

Integral Yoga, 227 W. 13th St. (bet. Seventh & Greenwich Aves.), (212) 929-0586, *Intimate Yoga*

A large selection of classes including lunchtime Hatha yoga and partners yoga, a wonderful meditative atmosphere. Don't miss the bookstore and juice bar/health food market next door "postlotus."

Nick's Hair Salon, 5 Horatio St. (bet. Eighth Ave. & 14th St.), (212) 929-3917, *Chic Barbershop*

This unisex barbershop has been owned and operated by Nick since 1956. Thus he knows a thing or two about cutting hair, and more than a few celebs have graced his "chair." "No-nonsense," stylish in the heart of the Village aka the Triangle! A bit tricky to find owing to its side-street entrance . . . Prices vary, in other words—negotiate! We guarantee it will be the city's best cut for the buck. Cash or check only.

Printing House Fitness and Racquet Club, 421 Hudson St. (@ Leroy St.), (212) 243-7600, *Big City Sports*

Full-service fitness with a view for a real Manhattan feel! The rooftop pool has a separate sun deck for your after-workout glow. A wide spectrum of classes and some of the best yoga offered by any city gyms! They are expanding and will have the first functional training facility in the city which includes workouts with a sports medicine twist. Membership has its privileges and will set you back $1,100.

Yana Herbal Beauty Salon, 270 Sixth Ave. (bet. Bleecker and Houston Sts.), (212) 254-6200 or (212) 254-6234, *Cozy Spa*

For relaxation in the privacy of what feels like home. Classical music combined with all natural products from California set the stage for a "getaway by day" executed by true beauty experts. Come for the facials ($65 for deep cleaning, massaging, masks) or the manicure ($12) and pedicure ($25). Grab a quick bikini wax while your toes dry!

East Village/Lower East Side

Crunch, 404 Lafayette St. (bet. 4th St. & Astor Pl.), (212) 614-0120, *Neighborhood Favorite*

See details in UWS.

ENE, 422 East 9th St. (bet. 1st St. & Ave. A), (212) 260-4040, *Funky Beauty*

Nelson Bartetel holds court in this bohemian salon. (Caution: he may be jet-lagged from his latest trip to France, where he coifed the models at the Victoria Secret fashion show!) They cover all the bases: cuts, color (mild and wild!), waxing, manicures, and pedicures. If the weather is nice, relax in the beautiful backyard accompanied by wine and cheese. *Psst . . . they close Saturdays to host mambo classes, beginners from 2—4 P.M., advanced from 4—7 P.M. Fifteen dollars per class. And Bring Baby Buster for a free cut after 3:00 P.M. on Tuesday afternoons year-round . . .*

Grace Heaven Salon, 226 E. 3rd St. (bet. Aves. B & C), (212) 253-5490, *Dry Cut*

Jane Webb is one of the few haircutters in NYC to adopt master stylist John Sahag's "dry cut" technique at one-fourth the price! Her tiny two-chair salon is so tight on space that you must book appointments as far in advance as possible. Haircuts are $65, a little more for long, thick tresses. Don't expect a shampoo at this joint!

Jin Soon Natural Hand and Foot Spa, 56 E. 4th St. (bet. Second Ave. & Bowery), (212) 473-2047, *Custom Nails*

Lucky girl, you are about to learn about the special services of Jin Soon. Formerly a manicurist to the stars, she's now settled into this lovely little place, with its unique rice paper screens and silk pillows to set the stage for your treatments. Try Spirit of the Beehive (paraffin wax, $30, $60) or Essence of Soul (sea salts, oils, and a scrub, $15, $30 respectively).

Jivamukti Yoga Center, 404 Lafayette St., 3rd Floor (bet. Astor Place & 4th St.), (212) 353-0214, *Yoga Galore*

Yoga World in grand style with 9,000 square feet of space! Notably the largest yoga studio in the U.S., they dish out some serious classes (at least 12 per day). All for the body & soul complete with fountains, incense, pastel walls, and an assortment of Zen products to free your mind and stretch your spine. Thirteen years in the biz, $15 a class. Don't bliss out too quickly or you might miss a Sting sighting.

Lisa Mitchell Salon, 90 Rivington St. (bet. Orchard & Ludlow Sts.), (212) 982-0085, *Neighborhood Favorite*

Popular Lisa Mitchell worked in Paris for a while, perfecting her craft, which entices such high-profile clients as Bridget Hall. The sleek minimalist design of the salon matches her cuts! Madison Ave. prices. *Psst . . . if you are going on a Saturday afternoon, bring your beau for a trim by her "in-house" cutter for men!*

Tenth Street Baths and Health Club, 268 E. 10th St. (bet. First & Second Aves.), (212) 674-9250, *www.rushturkishbaths.com, Unisex Sauna*

Don't expect the Clinique lady to welcome you in her little white jacket, but steam, sauna, and "melt" away your cares all the same. Open 365 days a year; for a mere $22 bucks you can lounge in the steam room, linger in the redwood sauna, come alive again in the ice-cold pool, take a Swedish shower, or get some fresh air on the sun deck. If you're adventurous, pay a bit more and they will actually whip you with an oak branch and scrub some Dead Sea salt into your skin ($35). Try not to leave in a hurry. Mostly unisex so be prepared for some gawking by wet strangers. Too much? Opt for women-only Wednesdays (9 A.M.–2 P.M.), where full nudity is permitted.

Ultra, 233 E. 4th St. (bet. Aves. A & B), (212) 677-4380, *Hip Hair*

Finding this place is like trying to find an underground nightclub . . . look for the fluorescent green door! Not surprisingly Ultra attracts a music biz clientele with its rep as the place to go for a trendy downtown cut. The salon is *Wallpaper* sleek and as busy as the front door of Halo (see Twilight). All this for $75.

Valerie, 149 Ludlow St. (bet. Stanton & Rivington Sts.), (212) 228-6833, *Celebrity Cutters*

Three stylists with loads of talent and diehard clients to match! Valerie keeps herself booked with glitteratti like Jimmy Page, Matt Dillon, and Christina Ricci . . . But, her two partners in hair crime are equally talented. Plan ahead as these three stylists keep their dance cards full!

SoHo/Nolita/Little Italy/Chinatown

Anatomically Correct, 142 Wooster St. (bet. Houston & Prince Sts.), (212) 353-8834, *Personal Trainer*

"People don't need hours in the gym," says Mike Creamer. Utilizing a combination of free weights and machines, he trains his clients in short, one-on-one sessions with one to two sets per body part—max! Most of his clients come from word of mouths like ours! Costs about $85 per session. Creamer is certified by the American College of Sports and Medicine and the National Strength and Conditioning Association.

Aveda Institute, 456 W. Broadway (bet. Prince & Houston Sts.), (212) 473-0280, *Beauty School Dropout*

Have a blast at the B.Y.O.B. Workshop: Bring Your Own Blow-dryer and a brush! For $25 receive a three-hour class that includes a hair analysis, as well as one-on-one instruction on styling, shaping and maintenance.

Brooke Siler, 33 Bleecker St. (@ Mott St.), (212) 420-9111, *Ab Pilates*

Her killer Pilates workout has buff city babes buzzing! The incentive? Class price decreases per hour as you improve—$75 to start, $25 for the more practiced. She counts Shalom Harlow, Kate Moss, and Stella Tennant among her diva devotees! No attitude, all are welcome.

Erbe, 196 Prince St. (bet. Sullivan & Sixth Ave.), (212) 966-1445, *Facial/ Massage*

Eighteen-year veterans of the SoHo scene, these folks have earned their beauty stripes! Specializing in yummy one-hour facials that focus on deep pore cleansing, steaming, masks, essential oils, and finish with toners and moisturizers using only the purest of ingredients from the in-house product line manufactured in Rome. We are particularly fond of the Mallow Cream for daytime, or the Royal Jelly for winter months!

Haven, 150 Mercer St. (bet. Prince & Houston Sts.), (212) 343-3515, *All Or Nothing*

This could be heaven for the girl looking to get a facial and a wax treatment delivered with equal amounts of care and precision. These waxing specialists offer a "less sticky" wax for "sensitive skin" containing citrus oils and vitamin E. But get ready to be Sphynx'd! According to *Cosmo* and *In Style*, Sphynx takes it all off, baby. And we thought the Brazilian was "comprehensive" . . . ouch! Another specialty is a customized facial, a skin evaluation before every facial and an appropriate treatment. They use the delicious Parisian line, Yonka, and sell it on site.

Helena Rubinstein Beauty Gallery, 135 Spring St. (bet. Wooster & Greene Sts.), (212) 343-9966, *Queen For A Day*

Colorful treats and goodies from the Helena Rubinstein collection fill the first floor, but this is not your typical makeup store as you discover what lies beneath: a 4,000 sq. ft. basement with a serene Feng Shui atmosphere. You will feel ultimately pampered by any of the treatments carefully supervised by dermatologist Karen Bureke, M.D. Scientifically formulated skin-care products based on vitamin C and Retinol are new additions to the HR line. The 60-minute manicure or pedicure is a delight. *Psst . . . ask for an application of "fake lashes." They offer the service for free if you buy the lashes! Don't panic, they are the individual kind that are applied one by one.*

John Masters Organic Haircare, 79 Sullivan St. (bet. Spring & Broome Sts.), (800) 599-2450, *Haircare*

This place is small (and we mean *small!*)—only four chairs and a few handpicked stylists available to cut your precious locks. But for those wanting all-natural hair treatments bearing the signature of the "master," it is worth the wait for a coveted appointment. Try the lavender conditioner with plant extracts.

Ling, 128 Thompson St., (bet. W. Houston & Prince Sts.), (212) 982-8833, *Eyes & Face Care*

See details in Union Square/Gramercy/Flatiron; other locations in UWS.

Make Up Forever, 409 W. Broadway (bet. Prince & Spring Sts.), (212) 941-9337, *Makeup Application*

Calling all rock stars and wanna-be drag queens! This is the place to get all your makeup needs for stage and beyond. Experiment on the wild side, or just get "done" for that fun party by a professional ($45). Or, if you want a lesson on how to create that new solo, try the lesson/application for $65. We heard that rocker Michael Stipe buys his "glitter" here. We love the Make Up Forever's face and body Liquid Makeup.

Mud Honey, 148 Sullivan St. (bet. Prince & Houston Sts.), (212) 533-1160, *Trendy Hair*

A fab place for a new "do"! Where else can you get the Nouvelle Farrah and feel like you're spending the afternoon "on the town"? The stylists' area resembles a "torture chamber" but it makes the whole coiffing experience seem quasi-intellectual, with a bit of rock and roll thrown in for good measure. Owner Michael Matula has done so well that he is opening a second hip salon and spa on Bond St. Open on Sundays and Mondays too!

Oscar Bond, 42 Wooster St. (bet. Broome & Grand Sts.), (212) 334-3777, *Manicure Plus*

It's all about feeling good at Oscar's! Specializes in waxing, haircuts and color, massage and nail care. Salon highlights: Jennifer Hall for waxing, a massage on Sundays, and all haircuts begin with a consultation and a shoulder rub to get you in the mood. Do not forget Beatrice! Her "healing hands" attract followers in droves for the regular manicure/pedicure but you should check out her individualized treatments such as a "sports" or "paraffin" . . . heaven! Costs are $20/$35 respectively and the special services are $35/$50.

Prema Nolita, 252 Elizabeth St. (bet. E. Houston & Prince Sts.), (212) 226-3972, *Wait-Listed Pedicure*

Bastien Gonzalez is the handsome Parisian who jet-sets from London (two days a week among the social and media set) to Paris (four days a week at the tragically hip hotels Costes and Bristol). On the seventh day he rests . . . except when he heads for NYC every other month to fulfill the foot fantasies of savvy stateside clientele! His secret? A special technique that is more medical (using dental instruments!) than beauty oriented. He would like to start a training program in NYC and incite a "movement" to remove every callus and crevice from all trampled soles! *Psst . . . don't miss the dynamic skincare lines like Jurlique (Australia) and Ann Semonin (Paris).*

Prince Street Reflexology Center, 177 Prince St. (bet. Greene & Wooster Sts.), (212) 353-3659, *Walk On Air*

David Cook specializes in the Ingham method of foot treatment, considered the original therapeutic reflexology. David's goal is for your feet to feel good at the end of your treatment but expect a little soreness in trouble spot areas that need "working out." The agony and the ecstasy!

Prive, 310 W. Broadway (bet. Grand & Canal Sts.), (212) 274-8888, *Neighborhood Favorite*

A cornucopia of talent makes up this trendy SoHo salon . . . Owned by Laurent Dufourg (he gave Sharon Stone her first cropped cut) and his fabulous wife Fabienne, this salon is sister to their Los Angeles home base. Scott Bond (formerly of Frederic Fekkai and John Barrett) is the Picasso of color. Christina is the "bicoastal" goddess of cut . . . if you can wait for her New York visits. Clients include Uma, David Duchovny, Elizabeth Shue, and Michael J. Fox. Haircuts start at $90, single-color process at $75, highlights $150 and up. They have the exclusive rights to Hollywood's makeup artist extraordinaire Thierry Pourtoy's fabulous cosmetics.

Rescue Aromatherapy Nail Spa, 21 Cleveland Place (bet. Spring & Kenmare Sts.), (212) 431-3805, *Neighborhood Favorite*

Hip and adorable, this is the answer to the typical no-pampering manicures you find on every block. Chic owner Ji Baek has got it down—the latest hair accessories up front, Cosabella's thong underware, hard-to-find beauty potions, and hour-long scrubbing, massaging, and "energizing" pedicures. (Complete with customized flowers painted on your toes—if that is what your mood desires!) Rescue does all that and more in style, comfort, and semiprivacy. Catch up on the latest *Wallpaper,* relaxing on velvet pillows while your feet are being aromatically massaged. Closed Sunday and Monday.

Rescue Beauty Lounge, 8 Central Market Place (bet. Broome & Grand Sts.), (212) 431-0449, *Hip Day Spa*

Brought to you by Manhattan's most chic manicurist, this satellite day spa is around the corner from the original Rescue, behind the historic Police Building. One visit and you will know why even uptowners make their way downtown to be "rescued"! Blowouts, waxing and of course manicures and pedicures, as well as expert makeup consultation and application. You'll never pick the wrong shade of red again!

SoHo Integrative Health Center, 62 Crosby St. (bet. Spring & Kenmare Sts.), (212) 431-1600, *One-Stop Tip*

Enter innovator and aesthete Dr. Laurie J. Polis's multimedicinal enclave, this is the first spa-cum–doctor's office aimed at soothing your soul *and* healing your body. Where else could you get that shot of echinachea in such stellar company as Kate Moss and Miss "Ray Of Light"? Whether you're after a pap smear, a face peel, or merely a palatable potion from the elixir bar, Polis delivers evidence that beauty comes from the inside out. Polis, a dermatologist, boasts a staff including OB-GYN, internist, ophthalmologist, homeopathic doctor, and plastic surgeon.

SoHo Sanctuary, 119 Mercer St., 3rd floor (bet. Prince & Spring Sts.), (212) 334-5550, *Women-Only Yoga*

Yoga anyone? Sneak away for a women-only hour of power at this retreat where the name speaks for itself. While yoga is the calling card, don't miss the best steam in NYC—complete with yummy white robes and slippers. Punctuality is a must for classes, tricky if you don't know where you're going or the elevator acts up—but sip on mandarin orange tea and chill out until the next class begins. *Psst . . . many of the dancers from Broadway work out here so don't even try to keep up with the "pros."*

Space, 155 Sixth Ave. (@ Spring St.), (212) 647-8588, *Hip Haircuts*
Created by four young stylists who all simultaneously defected from their swanky uptown salons for their own hip downtown digs. You may have read about Lisa Loeb's cutter, Janet Boweror, or Norman James who tends to the locks of Shirley Mason, the sexy lead singer of Garbage. Campy, cool, and fun when you need a cut and some "space"!

The Art of Beauty, 26 Grand St. (bet. Thompson St. & Sixth Ave.), (800) 238-2922, *Cosmic Makeup Artist*
Where makeup and the Zodiac meet! Owner Linda Mason is an astrological makeup artist. Tell her your birth date (sans the year, thank you), and she will assist you in picking out the most "cosmically" correct cosmetics. As an extra bonus, she also designs custom compact cases that slip easily into your purse for that "morning to nighttime" glow! Regulars include Debbie Harry, Cameron Diaz, and Jerry Hall.

The Aveda Institute, 223 Spring St. (bet. Sixth Ave. & Varick St.), (212) 807-1492, *Neighborhood Favorite*
Housed in a spacious former warehouse complete with rain-forest décor, this place is an escape from the concrete jungle . . . The Himalayan rejuvenation treatment is to die for! Try their specialty packages named after scents, like Jasmine: a 60-minute facial, full-body massage, and haircut ($230), or the Cinnamon package, or the Patchouli: a facial, body polish, and 30-minute foot reflexology ($179). *Psst . . . recent renovations made room for a school of cosmetology and estheticians.*

Lower Manhattan/Other Boroughs

Millefleurs Day Spa, 130 Franklin St. (bet. Varick St. & West Broadway), (212) 966-3656, *Exotic Day Spa*

The norm and the not so norm in spa fare collide in this exotic salon designed as an Egyptian temple! Tarot-card readings ($100 for one hour) as well as belly-dancing lessons ($20 for one hour) add spice to the traditional spa treatments like waxing ($20 for bikini) or aromatherapy facials ($85). If you are desperate for a body treat, or just need advice on your current love, Millefleurs is at your service seven days a week!

Sue Devitt, 23 Watt St. (bet. W. Broadway & Thompson St.), (212) 925-5996, *Cosmetic Guru*

Gorgeous Aussie Sue Devitt, Francisco Nars's former assistant, helped formulate the makeup line Awake Cosmetics. Inspired by the outdoors on a trip to Iceland for *Elle* magazine, she developed unique shades such as Bright Midnight, Sun Glow, and Rose Dawn that make Awake the choice of beauties like Liv Tyler, Brooke Shields, and Celine Dion. Devitt is available for consultation ($250). On a tight budget? Her first-rate assistants consult for much less, while the products stand on their own!

Tribeca Bodyworks Pilates Center, 177 Duane St. (bet. Greenwich & Hudson Sts.), (212) 625-0777, *Pure Pilates*

This is a laid-back place that welcomes all size and body styles, a remarkably clean and well-run place to "Pilates" your way to health and fitness. Pilates "virgins" are welcome, just don't forget to smile when you notice your new bod after a few of these intense classes. Twenty dollars for mat classes, $75 for private instruction.

Ula Salon, 8 Harrison St. (bet. Hudson & Greenwich Sts.), (212) 343-2376, *Manicure Deal*

Angela Charova offers the best manicure and pedicure for the money in this neighborhood. Manicure $12, pedicure $25.

✤ *Good to Know:*

John Allan's Men's Club, 95 Trinity Pl. (@ Thames St.), (212) 406-3000, *For Him*

Is your man jealous of all the pamperinig available to women in the city? If you want to give him a memorable gift, call John Allen. Since opening in 1987, this has been *the* place to pamper your man with treats to delight even the most difficult to please. This 1940s-style barbershop (albeit with all fe-male stylists) delivers the "hot towel treatment" to erase the stress of the day while sitting in a 1940s-style vintage chair. After a scalp-massaging shampoo and haircut, a manicure and hand massage, he can make his way to the bil-liard table complete with groovy Coltrane tunes and a cigar, while he waits for arguably the best shoeshine in town. Forty-nine dollars for the whole shebang!

Jipping: How much should you tip the manicurists and pedicurists? Usu-ally $3–$4 for a 10-dollar manicure and $5 for a 22-dollar pedicure.

Fitness Access Passbook, (212) 808-0765

A groovy service sponsored by The American Health and Fitness Al-liance . . . Traveling to NYC and want to workout, planning to take up Pi-lates, or just bored with your gym routine? We've got your ticket! For $65, your "Passbook" gives you access to almost every gym and fitness center the city has to offer (from two to five visits per location!) and four personal training sessions. Annual "membership" is valid from January to January and, in most cases, if you decide to join one of the facilities, your $65 fee is deducted from the total cost. Adds a whole new meaning to "club hopping," *n'est-ce pas?*

Viewpoint International, (212) 246-6000, offers private off the beaten path tours for groups of any size. Whether you're with a group of girlfriends for the weekend or a visiting "spouse," call these pros to arrange a special day on the town with the other ladies on the lam!

Trauma

Amsterdam Billiard Club, 344 Amsterdam Ave. (bet. 76th & 77th Sts.), (212) 496-8180, *Insomnia*

A charming pool hall fresh on the billiards scene, but with the flavor of yesteryear from the exposed brick walls and café fare . . . Eric Clapton and Jerry Seinfeld rack up balls along side Dick and Jane into the wee hours—4 A.M. on weekends—seven days a week, 365 days a year. A perfect way to spend Christmas afternoon? Or a sleepless night!

Apthorp Pharmacy, 2201 Broadway (@ 78th St.), (212) 877-3480, *365/24/7 Drugs*

Open 365 days a year! If you find yourself sniffling under the mistletoe or feeling like death on New Year's Eve, Apthorp's is open. Full-service pharmacy, plus all the groovy extras—the latest in cosmetics, shampoos, nail polishes.

Columbus Air Conditioning Center, 552 Columbus Ave. (bet. 86th & 87th Sts.), (212) 496-2626, *Burning Up*

Statistic: More murders are committed by women without air-conditioning than by those who have it. Rentals from $145 to $300 depending on the BTUs. Service and delivery included. Save a life and retain that fresh glow.

Drip, 489 Amsterdam Ave. (bet. 83rd & 84th Sts.), (212) 875-1032, *Dating Drama*

If you're Judy Jetson desperately in search of a husband in the 21st century, this may be the last frontier . . . Coffee-table bio books give you a peek into the psyche of a potential mate, but they don't guarantee liftoff! A mod pickup joint for the open-minded and caffeine-deprived. But we can't be responsible if you wind up with a real drip.

Extravertical Climbing Wall, 61 W. 62nd St. (@ Broadway), (212) 586-5718, *Career Emergency/Anxiety*

If the walls of your studio apartment or small hotel room are closing in on you or you're bombing in your career as a cat burglar, go climb a wall—literally! First-timers should opt for the eighty-dollar one-hour lesson that includes two free climb days. After you become a pro, you can climb the wall for a mere $9 a day. Think how much cheaper and healthier this "therapy" is than massive amounts of vodka at nearby Whiskey Park bar. *Psst . . . shoes and harness are available for rental on premises. Open 4–10 P.M. daily!*

Flik's Video To Go, 175 W. 72nd St. (bet. Columbus & Amsterdam Aves.), (212) 721-0500, *Suicidal Boredom*

Rainy night? Got the flu? Wanna stay in and cuddle? Call the 24-hour new release hotline 799-7711 and have a video delivered. NYC's largest video delivery store including some hard-to-find titles. All films must be returned the following day by midnight. Hours of delivery: seven days, 4–10 P.M. Thrifty girls, take note: three videos for the price of two midweek . . . See other location in MTE.

Frank Signorella/Astrologist & Numerologist, 210 Riverside Dr., (@ W. 93rd St.), (212) 222-4454, *Future Forecast*

Considering a job change, change of husband, or just going through a change of life? Frank Signorella is a professional astrologer and numerologist who lectures and appears on various radio and television programs. This pro offers specific services such as relationship compatibility, name selection, and marriage chart selection. Choose your topic or just come with your own issue. It will be tough to predict when he will be able to squeeze you into his hectic schedule.

Hydrosurge, 207 W. 80th St., (bet. Broadway & Amsterdam), (212) 787-3037, *Pets Only*

Is pooch "acting out" or just "stressed out"? Consider an alternative bath to sooth away his or her woes. Offering both self-service and custom grooming, Hydrosurge is the place to bring your dog for a relaxing massage bath that acts like a Jacuzzi. It is great for their skin and conditions the hair—sorry, no humans allowed in the tubs. Open Mon–Sat 10 A.M. till . . . Cost depends on the size of the dog or if you do it yourself.

More Than Parking, 540 W. 59th St. (bet. 10th & 11th Aves.), (212) 307-7886, *Cheap Parking*

Just spent your last dime on a car for summer in the Hamptons? Your college roomate wants to drive into the city and stay the week while you're here on business? No problem, just park it here—indoors for $150 a month. Freedom on four wheels!!

Stefanie Smith, 201 W. 89th St. (@ Amsterdam Ave.), (212) 873-3720, *Temporary Paralysis*

Have table, will travel! Or come to the privacy of her home studio, where 70 minutes costs $70. Stefanie is the woman to call for a massage to resolve a specific problem, such as sciatica or a knee injury. Or, just indulge at the last minute after a long day with a relaxation massage complete with essential oils and music. If you like the way you feel after she works her magic, you can join the ranks of women who have standing weekly appointments. House calls $130 for 70 minutes.

The City Church, New York, 64th St. @ CPW, (212) 832-7705, *Spiritual Crisis*

When your psychic is on vacation . . . Dr. R. Maurice Boyd, the pastor at this more-Presbyterian-than-not, nondenominational church, was formerly spiritual head honcho of the hugely popular Fifth Ave. Presbyterian. Services are every Sunday at 10 A.M. in the Cultural Ethical Society building. You will be inspired and renewed by what you hear, see, and feel at this lovely spiritual respite. The membership is diverse and friendly so don't be shy about going alone! *Psst . . . don't miss the coffee and donuts downstairs after the service.*

The Paul Labreque Salon and Spa, @ The Reebok Sports Club/NY, 160 Columbus Ave. (bet. 67th & 68th Sts.), (212) 595-0099, *Late-Night Haircare*

Full-service "Queen for a Night" setup, with haircare, nail care, skincare and massage located "in-house" at the Reebok Club. Open daily until 10 P.M. (Membership not necessary for salon/spa usage.) *Psst . . . don't miss a deep and extracting facial with Regina Viotto. Also, check out the highly coveted French cult line of skincare that celebrities swear by, Biologique Recherche.*

✦ Good to Know:

Did your roommate leave the dirty dishes for a week, again? **Roommate Finders** (250 W. 57th St.), (212) 489-6942, is the city's oldest and most reliable service.

Animal Medical Center, 510 E. 62nd St. (bet. York Ave. & FDR Dr.), (212) 838-8100, *24-Hour Vet*

Appointments by day, after-hours emergency/trauma services by night at the hands of five vets in this nine-story nonprofit teaching hospital. They handle anything from The Chipmunks to Mr. Ed, but usually Felix and Lassie. Just ask Jay McInerney and his "Babe," *Psst . . . new services include acupuncture and bereavement counseling . . . no chuckling, please.*

Artbag, 735 Madison Ave. (@ 67th St.), (212) 744-2720, *Handbag Hangover*

Drag your purse through the mud? Or maybe you wreaked havoc on your wallet. Want to redesign your mom's funky alligator bag? All can be accomplished here in one to three weeks. Specialty of the house: relining that bag you spilled Giorgio into in the mid-eighties with matching fabric . . . These guys know more about women's handbags than most women.

Check's Etc, 862 Lexington Ave. (bet. 64th & 65th Sts.), (212) 570-2959, *Memory Lapse*

Houston, we have a problem! You forgot to pay your electric bill between business trips. This place accepts payment on behalf of all of the major utility companies as well as cashes payroll checks, sells MetroCards and offers Western Union—for true traumas like a lost wallet!

Club Macanudo, 26 E. 63rd St. (bet. Madison & Park Aves.), (212) 752-8200, *Man Hunting*

Supposedly women over 30 have a better chance of being hit by lightning than finding a mate, so when a bar boasts a higher ratio of men to women who can resist? Then again we could pretend we're here for the beautiful surroundings and clouds of cigar smoke. Last call around 1:30 A.M. *Psst . . . state-of-the-art ventilation system allows one to breathe without a mask amidst 130 types of cigars lit on any given evening . . .*

Daniel Baker, M.D., 65 E. 66th St., (bet. Madison & Park Aves.), (212) 734-9695, *Drooping Jowls*

Let's face it (pardon the pun), this guy is one of the most well known surgeons in America as the guy who makes beautiful women more beautiful by way of his magical hands. He has a technique that lifts the face in a natural way that never appear stretched and pulled. Past patients call him the "ultimate artist with a scalpel." Isn't it great to grow old gracefully while looking great is your best revenge? If you have to ask the price, don't make the call.

Dial A Secretary, 208 E. 85th St. (bet. Second & Third Aves.), (212) 348-8982, *Missing Slave*

Your "right hand" has the flu but your deadline doesn't? Typing specialty shop—that's typing, not writing your thesis . . . But for those creatives who can only channel through a Pilot V6 Rollerball, they're a godsend especially when your agent wants your screenplay yesterday and it's scrawled over 50 rolls of Bounty, the quicker picker upper! Where were they when this project was due? *P.S. Transcription as well . . .*

Diamond Essence, 784 Madison Ave. (bet. 68th & 69th Sts.), (212) 472-2690, *Mining Impaired*

Far away from the realm of QVC lies the land of the true "faux" jewel. Indistinguishable from her highly overpriced sister, she calls out to savvy girls on the street. Ten minutes later you have twinkling studs worthy of Tiffany, and you've only been set back $58. Trust us—they're tasteful, remarkably "real" and great for traveling (a lost earring won't require a second mortgage to replace)! If diamonds are a girl's best friend, friendship is overrated. . . . Catalog available. Ask for Marie when shopping in the store.

Dr. Steven J. Pearlman, M.D., 785 Park Ave. (@ 74th St.), (212) 794-3434, *Midlife Crisis*

Specializing in cosmetic and reconstructive surgery of the face, neck and head, you may have seen him frequently quoted in *W, Allure,* or *Elle* magazines. Botox is the word on everyone's lips so give him a call and check out your options! Shhh . . . we won't tell if you don't!

Fashion Award Cleaners, 1462 Lexington Ave. (bet. 94th & 95th Sts.), (212) 289-5623, *Deadly Stains*

Rated by the cleaning gods as one of the top five cleaners in the world. Thirty-five-year veteran Jerry Leeds's clients ship him their soiled Chanel from as far as Paris via FedEx. If you have a spot that you think is permanent, we bet these guys can get it out. How about bright red lipstick from a delicate white straw hat? No problem—for a cool $47.50 it is good as new. Red wine on chiffon? Gone for $122.50—cough, cough. Also, try the acid-free cleaning of your wedding dress for $350.

Goodson-Parker Wellness Center, 30 E. 76th St., 4th Floor, (bet. Madison & Park Aves.), (212) 717-5273, *Stay Well*

Staying well is what it's all about at this hidden studio. Name your "cure" and they have it: acupuncture, facials, reflexology, Shiatsu massage, lymphatic drainage, Pilates, yoga . . . and colinics (we are not brave enough but models swear it is the only way to get a true flat stomach). All services are private and by appointment only. ($80 per hour, except Pilates and yoga at $75) Best of all, Goodson is a psychologist and is available at the same location! Talk about a nifty "emergency room"!

Gruen Optika, 1225 Lexington Ave. (@ 83rd St.), (212) 628-2493, *Botox Impaired Squinting*

Can't squint to see these days? With seven locations throughout the city, Gruen provides progressive and state-of-the-art optical products and services. Specializing in repairs with quick turnaround, they also boast chic opticians and personnel to help you find the perfect pair or two or three . . . Main office: ask for Susan Fein, NYC's truly chic optician.

Hyde Park Stationers, 1070 Madison Ave. (bet. 80th & 81st Sts.), (212) 861-5710, *Office Emergency*

You can find thirty-dollar hot chocolate and your very own van Gogh, but good luck finding a paper clip—except here, the UES's all-purpose stationery and office supply store. The hands-on owner is ready to help with all business need: Filofax, envelopes, faxing, writing instruments, notebooks, and customized stationery! They are also one of the few places in the 'hood that sells erudite magazines (cash only) along with frames, gift cards, whimsical books, and games. Otherwise, credit card friendly.

Jim's Shoe Repair, 50 E. 59th St. (@ Madison Ave.), (212) 355-8259, *Worn-Out Soles*

Ruining your gorgeous shoes on Manhattan sidewalks is as easy as getting caught in traffic in L.A., but luckily there's Jim's. A NYC institution, Jim has been repairing damaged soles for Bergdorf's, Gucci, and Joan & David for over 50 years. No scuff too great, no designer too difficult. This is "sole" repair heaven! They will deliver, but then you might miss all the juicy shop gossip or the visiting model with her trashed Manolos begging for mercy!

Ken Casoria@ Casa, 48 E. 73rd St. (bet. Park & Madison Aves.), (212) 717-1998, *30 Days To Fitness*

This personal trainer (and fitness author!) is best known for his Mission Control Program! Besides the cost-prohibitive fee of $2,750 for the four-week program, you must be "chosen" by the man himself. Forget interviewing this guru, he's interviewing you to test your mettle. However, the end result is supposedly life-altering if you are willing to pay the piper—er, trainer. Cardio, weights, and indoor/outdoor activities keep it fresh on a daily basis. Kiehl's products give you something to focus on for your 90 minutes of *hell*!

Lisa Linblad Travel Design, 27 E. 95th St., (bet. Madison & Fifth Aves.), (212) 876-2554, *Escape From Alcatraz*

Travel in style and "in the know." Orchestrating luxury fantasy vacations using 25 years of experience and unbelievable connections, Lisa will design a memorable trip. Prior to departure, you will receive an itinerary including restaurant and table recommendations, reading lists, must-sees, and introductions to her contacts in that area all handsomely wrapped (think Hermès meets Louis Vuitton). While everything extraordinary comes with a price tag to match ($500 initial consultation plus 10 percent of total trip cost), the information provided is truly priceless.

Madame Paulette's Custom Cleaning Services, 1255 Second Ave. (bet. 65th & 66th Sts.), (212) 838-6827, *Dry-Cleaning Phobia*

Truly beyond the call of duty cleaners . . . Devoted clients include Calvin Klein, Hermès, Geoffrey Beene, and Norma Kamali ("They're my Johnny on the spot!") Whether it's a Dior or a Levi Strauss, you'll be covered: wet cleaning, special bleaching, custom dyeing, restoration from smoke and water damage, Scotch Guarding furniture and tapestries, ionization, and upholstery overhauls . . . What else could a girl need? *Psst . . . If you're a member of the Reebok Gym, feel free to use MP's in-house services on the West Side.*

Mommy's Night Out, 147 E. 72nd St. (bet. Lexington & Third Aves.), (212) 744-6667, *Baby On Board*

Not just for expectant mothers (although this is a specialty), you can rent glorious party duds for all occasions—shoes, evening bags, jewelry, and long-distance "emergencies" are also available (ask for their catalog). The three-to-five-day rentals are affordable ($75–$185) and sparkly in sizes "petite to full-bloom."

Night & Day Locksmith, 1335 Lexington Ave. (@ 89th St.), (212) 722-1017, *Locked Out*

Never leave home without their number. But sometimes keys disappear when you've sneaked out in your nightie under your raincoat to get chocolate milk at midnight in the rain. Yoo-hoo! Mr. Locksmith! You can get an estimate, but let's face it—in that nightgown you'd pay out a king's ransom just to get back in twenty-four hours!

Norman Pastorek, M.D., 12 E. 88th St., (bet. Fifth & Madison Aves.), (212) 987-4700, *Rhinoplasty Drama*

Dying to take the plunge and get your classic Roman nose reconfigured? Norman is the doctor who understands the significance of such an important step for women, that confidence in our appearance matters. He only performs three procedures daily and makes sure that your personality drives the direction of the look. Listed in *W* magazine as one of the "Surgery Superstars" in the world.

One-Hour Martinizing, 1287 Madison Ave. (bet. 91st & 92nd Sts.), (212) 289-9874, *Immediate Removal*

Your lucky shirt just got Lucky Charms down the front and you need it for an audition this afternoon. . . . Don't despair! This is truly a one-hour-turnaround operation if you get the garment in by noon.

One Night Out, 147 E. 72nd St. (bet. Lex. & Third Aves.), (212) 744-6667, *Black Tie Emergency*

These folks specialize in renting designer gowns for Cinderella's big night out! Just make sure you have it back in good condition before the clock strikes! Great black-tie maternity attire too.

Overnight Boarding, (arrange appointment by phone), (212) 517-3847, *Hairball Hysteria*

Last-minute trip and your ex-boyfriend isn't able to take on Rover because his new girl de jour has cats? Never fear, Melissa is rated the best in happiness by those picky Upper East Side dog mommies. Her philosophy? Board pooch in a home, not a cage! Melissa also offers a daily dog-walking service. Call for prices.

Parliamo Italiano, 122 E. 42nd St. (bet. Park & Lexington Aves.), (212) 744-4793, *Illegal Aliens*

Let's speak Italian! Planning a tour of Tuscany? Transferring to Firenze? Trying desperately to communicate with your latest Roman god (although who really needs words)? Learn from the best—the staff all hold degrees from Italian universities in a gorgeous town house with Italian atmosphere. Delicious coffee and panettone for good behavior! Sign up in advance because classes get full, full, full.

Pet Taxi Emergency Service, 227 E. 56th St., (bet. Second & Third Aves.), (212) 755-1757, *Canine Crisis*

Traveling to Rio with your beloved pooch doesn't seem so impossible after all. They also offer assistance with traveling with your pet by coordinating kennels (for sale or rent), complying with airline regulations, and all other travel-related issues assuring you get your pet from here to there with safety and ease. Costs vary according to needs but prices start at $25 for a 50-block transport. *Psst . . . not a taxi in sight and you have a sick pet on your hands? They also offer a 24-hour emergency van equipped with temperature-controlled devices and drivers skilled in handling animals.*

Peppino's, 780 Lexington Ave. (@ 60th St.), (212) 832-3844, *Terminal Tripping*

Where socialites, celebs, and The Four Seasons go to get hemmed. Whether it's Zsa Zsa's feather boas or Leonardo's Dolce & Gabbana, Joseph "Peppino" Rettura and staff are up to the task. They'll deliver, and if you're in a mad dash, they'll assign two tailors to double-time it.

Philip B @ The Mark Garrison, 820 Madison Ave. (bet. 68th & 69th Sts.), (212) 570-2455, *Scalp Treatment*

Perhaps if you are Richard Branson you can afford to fly this "scalp guru" to London for a treatment (as he has done many a time thanks to Virgin); otherwise, get in line for an appointment at his tranquil offshoot at Garrison's salon . . . Prepare to not wash your locks for several days, as the conditioning maestro likes to see your scalp in its "natural" state before treating!

Tender Buttons, 143 E. 62nd St. (@ Lexington Ave.), (212) 758-7004,
Wardrobe Emergency

If you lined up all of the buttons in this place you might end up in Sri Lanka (not a bad thought)! If you are looking to update last year's jacket or simply replace a specific lost fastener, this is your place. A great feel and staff—not too pushy but full of advice if needed. Buttons of glass, buttons of tortoise, buttons of plastic, they have you all buttoned up! Prices range from 50¢ to $2,000 for a George Washington commemorative inaugural button!

Woodson Merrel, M.D., 44 E. 67th St. (bet. Park & Madison Aves.), (212) 535-1012, *Be Healed*

Western medicine meets Eastern alternative treatments . . . The combination of the two is the latest trend in health care. It worked for us!

♦ *Good to Know:*

Where to go . . . **The Plaza Athenee** (E. 64th St., bet. Madison & Park Aves.), for a quick puff and buff. The "ladies' room" is at the end of the corridor on the left. They have one for him too!

Looking for a hillside home on the French Riviera or a Tuscany castle? **Heldi Dechter @ Stribling and Assoc. Ltd.** (212) 570-2440, will find the international home of your dreams. Her other office is in Provence, so you know she has the inside scoop.

Midtown West ....

A&A Pearl Company, 10 W. 47th St. (bet. Fifth & Sixth Aves.), *Broken Baubles*

You weren't sure whether Fred had enough passion for your "inner diva" until he took your grandmother's pearls between his teeth while tangoing at the Rainbow Room. Your relationship is better than ever, but Granny is ready to cut you out of the will. A&A can repair and re-string, and possibly save your inheritance.

Angela Cosmai Salon, 16 W. 55th St. (bet. Fifth & Sixth Aves.), (212) 541-5820 or (800) 992-9585, *Wigging Out*

Excellent advice for the overtreated and "blowfried." Cosmai's other forte is corrective color. Cosmai corrected Melanie Griffith's mane after *Working Girl.* Her approach is to create believable color with highlights that "whisper rather than shout." She flies to L.A. and Florida every eight weeks. Hands-on disaster relief doesn't come cheap but can be worth it! Four hundred dollars for full color and highlights.

The Dental Day Spa, 45 W. 54th St. (bet. Fifth & Sixth Aves.), (212) 265-7724, *Say Cheese*

The usual preventative side of dentistry is mixed with the beauty angle for busy girls. State-of-the-art cosmetic dental technologies such as whitening packages, porcelain veneers, bonding, and implants are combined with the comforts of a day spa. Also aromatherapy, massage, soothing music, herbal eyelid compresses, and neck wraps. You may have read about Lana Rozenberg, DDS, in *Vogue, Elle,* and *Mademoiselle. Psst . . . book a coffee-break cleaning that will have you back at the office with a sparkling smile in no time.*

Driver's Motor Vehicle Express, 300 W. 34th St. (bet. 8th & 9th Aves.), *Expired*

If you are a fully licensed driver who needs to renew or change your expired driver's license, then get in and out of here and still have time for a nice lunch! Prepare for some lines and slow staff but the other option is worse! Open from 8 A.M.–5:30 P.M. Monday–Wednesday, 8 A.M.–7 P.M. on Thursday. Closed on Friday.

Franklin Covey, 6 W. 49th St. (bet. Fifth & Sixth Aves.), (212) 957-8827, *Discombobulation Disease*

Disorganized? While it's not a medical trauma, it could be a career derailer. Enter Steven Covey with a copy of his best-seller, *The Seven Habits of Highly Effective People,* and his covetable Franklin Covey daytime planner. Get one, now! Basics, accessories, refills, and motivational paraphernalia . . . what more could a girl need to get her act together?

James A. Farley Post Office, 421 Eighth Ave. (@ 33rd St.), (212) 967-8585, *Compulsive Correspondence*

Uncle Sam's answer to convenience—24-hour express mailing, money ordering, stamp collecting, and loitering. Whatever gets you through the night—or rain, snow, hail, blackouts.

Garden Check Cashing Service, Inc., 250 W. 49th St. (bet. Broadway & Eighth Ave.), (212) 246-0156, *Fast Money*

Cash crunch? Get it anyway you can here, where they offer Money Gram wire transfers, cash payroll checks, accept payments of local utility bills, and sell lottery tickets. Yes, they sold the one winning ticket in 1999 for $48 million! Lightning could strike twice! Open until midnight Wednesday and Thursday.

Mr. Tony's, 120 W. 37th St. (bet. Broadway & Seventh Ave.), (212) 594-0930, *Accidental Bloating*

Can't squeeze into tonight's Gucci number? Tony and his staff are well-known among Seventh Ave. fashion types. Enter the frenzy via some non-descript stairs, and you'll witness hemlines changing faster than Leon Tally at *Vogue* can blink! Alterations are kid's play and you can trust your Galliano gown to them—no prob! In a rush? They can accommodate anything. Tony will even take out the size 12 tag and replace it with a 6. He's such a doll!

Personal Communication Center, 716 Seventh Ave. (bet. 47th & 48th Sts.), (212) 459-2500, *Cell No More*

Cell phone crisis? Neil, the store manager, will get you mobile in a hurry. He carries all of the latest phone styles like Nokia, Star Tec, Erricson, accessories. The place is tiny but packed with power, so you won't be out of touch for long! *Psst . . . he overnighted a new phone to one "Jane" girl we know when hers went on the blink!*

Personal Computer Power Center, 1650 Broadway (@ 51st St.), (212) 315-0809, *Cyber War*

Crashing Windows everywhere and not a Bill in sight. Or perhaps you need shelter from all your Mac bombs. These guys will boot you up in a flash and get you on your way. Rentals? No prob. Upgrades? No prob.

Quick Trak, 268 W. 23rd St. (bet. Seventh & Eighth Aves.), (212) 463-7070, *Pigeon Strike*

Need to send that proposal by 5:30 or lose the account? Call Mark and his top-of-the-trade messengers for help. All messengers are intensely screened for reliability and in turn they are treated with respect, all adding up to better service for you and your sacred package. It's a circle of love on a bike!

Sew Fast, Sew Easy, 147 W. 57th St., 2nd Floor, (bet. Sixth & Seventh Aves.), (212) 582-5889, *www.sewfastseweasy.com, Fashion Crunch*

Home economic classes never did spark any interest for a career girl in the making! But, reality has set in and sewing never sounded so fun! Offering four levels of classes. Starting with the all-important: "RX: Fear Of Sewing Machines," ($55). Level 1 might teach you to make boxer shorts out of heart fabric for your sweetheart on Valentine's Day in one session. And for those who get "hooked," finishing up with a Level 4 series (five sessions) where you can make your own clothes with darts, linings, and learn basic fitting corrections. Also classes in knitting, crocheting.

St. Malachy's Church, 239 W. 49th St. (@ Broadway), (212) 489-1340, *Spiritual Intervention*

Also known as The Actors Chapel of New York, every desperate actor/singer/dancer comes to this Times Square spiritual, yet loose, service for Christians of all denominations and anyone else seeking a spiritual shot in the arm. Choir at 11 A.M. Sundays, other services at 5 P.M. Saturday and 9 A.M. Sunday.

The French American Reweaving Company, 119 W. 57th St. (bet. Sixth & Seventh Aves.), (212) 765-4670, *Killer Moth Attack!*

Calamity Jane's favorite spot. Burn, tear, nibble a hole in anything and you'd have to use a magnifying glass after these folks take a needle to it. Ship a garment to them, they'll repair and send it back for a small additional handling fee. So when Kitty goes for cashmere, don't despair.

The Muscular Therapy Center, 130 W. 56th St. (bet. Sixth & Seventh Aves.), (212) 957-1561, *Physical Therapy*

Meet Claudia Terlizzi and her team, Sam Katz and Elizabeth Cornell . . . Boston marathoners and the U.S. Olympic Rowing Team come to Claudia's center for every mentionable ache and pain and injury, so there is little this team hasn't dealt with. Great massage as well.

Tops Service, 845 Seventh Ave. (@ 54th St.), (212) 765-3190, *Scuffing Accident*

One-day turnaround repair for shoe fetishists! What's a girl to do when the subway grate rips the heel off her Gucci spikes? Messenger the little lovelies here and like magic they'll be brand-new! *Psst . . . for you sale shoppers, they specialize in elaborate dye jobs, so go ahead and get those chartreuse crocodile loafers for 90 percent off . . . They'll be black before nightfall!*

Virgin Records, 1540 Broadway (bet. 45 & 46th Sts.), (212) 921-1020, *Addicted To Disco*

You just left Lotus (see Twilight) and are in "dire" need of the *Abba's Greatest Hits* CD with the extended version of "Dancing Queen"? Where can you go at this hour? This megastore is open until 1 A.M. on weekdays and until 2 A.M. on Friday and Saturday!

✦ *Good to Know:*

Where to go . . . At **Worldwide Plaza** (Eighth Ave., bet. 50th & 51st Sts.), ask the guard for a key if locked (it usually is!) and the rest room is in the arcade, east of the park. Or, the **Royalton Hotel** (44th St. bet. Fifth & Sixth Aves.) on the main floor just past the reservation desk on the right.

Midtown East

All Language Service, 545 Fifth Ave. (@ 45th St.), (212) 986-1688, *United Nations Embargo*

Need a love letter translated from Flemish? Linguists are on call to translate 59 different languages with proficiency in multiple fields, such as banking, advertising or the law. Equally as prepared to deal with individuals as with government agencies, bring your shopping list for the Hispanic maid or your Brazilian lawsuit from that scooter accident, and it will be translated for you in a flash.

American Dermatology Center, 210 59th Street (bet. Seventh Ave. & Broadway), (212) 247-1700, *Accidental Self-Mutilation*

When all those saketinis wear off and you have no idea who "Pedro" is—although his name is plastered in blue ink on your behind—call Dr. Jim Baral for tattoo removal using dermalaser technology.

American Express, 420 Lexington Ave. (bet. 43rd & 44th Sts.), (212) 687-3700, *Travel Assistance*

Don't leave home without expert travel arrangements or the right foreign currency! This headquarters for the most famous credit card company provides reliable help with travel plans and the financial tools to back them up! Open M–F from 9:00 A.M.–6:00 P.M.

Avis, 217 E. 43rd St. (bet. Second & Third Aves.), (212) 593-8378, *24-Hour Car Rental*

When you need to get out of Dodge in the middle of the night . . . who ya gonna call? Avis—the plain Jane, tried-and-true, 24-hour rental-car lifesaver of Midtown East. Better to call ahead, take time to change out of your nightgown!

Center for Integrative Medicine, 333 E. 57th St. (bet. First & Second Aves.), (212) 223-5151, *Acupuncturist*

If you are in need of more than a Band-Aid, book an appointment with Dr. Bruce Oren. First visit includes a complete medical and nutritional evaluation along with your medical history. Next you will receive a diet and lifestyle evaluation and risk evaluation. The price is $200 to $275 for the tests and evaluations and future treatments are $100. Book between one to two week ahead giving you time to binge one last time on french fries with mayonnaise.

Chakra 17, Comprehensive Healing Arts Center, 401 E. 34th St. (@ Second Ave.), (212) 679-6576, *Energy Crisis*

It's time you found your universal energy. This untapped energy could be the source needed to heal all disease, be it physical, spiritual or emotional. Empower yourself by following a "healing path" at this haven for well-being. It's a pollution-free, tension-free, serene healing environment complete with a negative ion machine and EMF to block harmful radiation from electricity and cell phones. Offering colonic irrigation, massage yoga, and supervised detoxification. As they say on the answering machine, "have a healthy day"! All treatments under $70.

Counter Spy Shop, 444 Madison Ave. (bet. 49th & 50th Sts.), (212) 688-8500, *You Sly Girl*

Personal protection can be yours for the asking. In business for almost half a century, they're the leader in manufacturing this kind of equipment. Maybe you need a disguised video camera to capture straying spouses.

Maybe you'll want your own personal defense system to thwart even the boldest of muggers. Better safe than sorry.

Creative Freelancers, 99 Park Avenue #210A (no office, all services done by phone), 1-888-398-9540, *Mental Meltdown*

This nifty outfit provides and locates professional freelance talent for any and every specialized business need—illustrators, designers, graphic artists, writers, art directors, photographers, mermaids. You name it— they can provide it. And, if you're one of those hip and talented free agents, they can get you back in business asap!

Flik's Video, 1093 Second Ave. (bet. 57th & 58th Sts.), (212) 752-3456, *Suicidal Boredom*

See details in UWS.

Fredrick Bed Central, 107 E. 31st St. (bet. Lexington & Park Aves.), (212) 683-8322, *Sleeping Disorder*

Found your dream apartment and the bedroom is so small your matress doesn't fit? Founded in 1928, FBC is the only custom bed maker in NYC! Want a round bed made of a combination of wool and horsehair and absolutely no foam? Or maybe you want your ticking to be made of antique fabric you found in a Paris flea market. How about an oversize king bed? They even make mattresses to fit European bed frames. Prices range from $600 to $3,000.

Greene Luggage, 6 E. 46th St. (bet. Fifth & Madison Aves.), (212) 682-7778/(800) 831-4996, *Luggage Repair*

Luggage like new in two hours flat! They'll even pick up and haul back to your fifth-floor walk-up or that swanky hotel where you're holed up with your Latin lover! Your duffel will thank you. Since 1945.

It's Easy, 125 Park Ave. (bet. 41st & 42nd Sts.), (212) 286-8500, *Assumed Identity*

Two days before the trip you've planned to the Italian Alps for a mid-winter pick-me-up, you notice your passport has expired. Not to fear! Get these folks to do this international dirty work for you while you go about your busy life. They get all your info, schlep over to the Passport Office, stand in line and wait—and wait—while you are flitting about SoHo for a new travel wardrobe or perhaps a new travel mate?

Just Once, 290 Fifth Ave. (@ 30th St.), 5th floor, (212) 465-0960, *Cold Feet Insurance*

Choose from a huge variety of dresses to rent for use "just once." You can sport a $6,000 Carolina Herrera original for a mere $1,400. After the required two to three fittings and special dry cleaning before your big day, you will look stunning, think of all the things you could do with that extra cash! Somewhat unromantic, but very practical!

Lanciani Travel Jewelry, 510 Madison Ave. (bet. 52nd & 53rd Sts.), (212) 644-2852, *Fake Impressions*

No matter where you go, put your best foot forward—including wearing all of your jewels. Or at least, look like you are! This small chain of stores is dedicated to creating expensive-looking jewelry that is suited for travel, without fear of theft or lost luggage. The prices range from $49 for small earrings up to $1,500 for more elaborate pieces. Other locations, UES, 922 Madison Ave. (bet. 77th & 78th Sts.), (212) 717-2759, and 826 Lexington Ave. (bet. 63rd & 64th Sts.), (212) 832-2092. Also in other chichi locales such as Aspen, Palm Beach, Boca Raton, and Short Hills, New Jersey.

Madison Avenue Spine & Sports Medicine, 275 Madison Ave. (@ 40th St.), (212) 986-3888, *Spinal Entrapment*

Arrive from overseas bent over from flying coach? Try the infamous and indispensable 45-minute medical massage, only $25 for newcomers! You do need an appointment, and if you decide that once is never enough be prepared to cough up $90 for your sophomore visit.

Marcy Blum, 251 E 51st St., Suite 2N (bet. Second Ave. & Third Ave.), (212) 688-3057, *Matrimonial Mayhem*

Leave the last-minute details to Marcy! She will help with all your marriage needs. Available around the clock for those "urgent" urges to tie the knot, she will get the rings, gather all the paperwork for the license, and maybe even help warm your "cold feet"!

New York Errands, 114 Lexington Ave. (bet. 27th & 28th Sts.), (212) 481-7886, *Need a Wife?*

Here is the answer to all of your scheduling problems: This highly useful company offers four categories of service: 1) waiting (for the cable guy), 2) local delivery and pickups (pick up flowers for dinner party), 3) specialty (retrieving the Armani jacket you forgot after last night's three-martini dinner), 4) create your own (alphabetize your CD collection). The cost is $30 an hour or $15–$20 for a "city errand." They accept checks, credit cards. *Psst . . . you can call, fax or e-mail your errand orders.*

Optical Express, 122 E. 42nd St. (bet. Lexington & Park Aves.), (212) 856-0636, *Contact Sabotage*

You've scoured your bathroom sink looking for it . . . You felt it pop out in Bergdorf's shoe salon . . . Whether "it" is hard or soft, Optical Express is the fastest and cheapest game in town for contact lens replacement. Optometrists on staff are first-rate and most lenses are kept in stock.

Pakmail, 99 Park Ave. (bet. 39th & 40th Sts.), (212) 867-7823, *Secretarial Strike*

One of the most efficiently run, friendly businesses to help you go about your daily business! Services abound: mailboxes, shipping, printing (business cards, invites), messenger service, receiving packages, and best of all, an answering service, forwarding calls to wherever you are. Confidentiality is guaranteed, given their chichi Park Avenue address.

Passport Plus, 20 E. 49th St., 3rd Floor (bet. Fifth & Madison Aves.), (212) 759-5540, *Environmental Escape*

Travel Documents Inc.! Mainly a passport service, they don't mind picking up airline tickets, marriage licenses, visas etc . . . Their dream hire? You're getting married next week in Portugal, and you don't have reservations, license, passport, Chapstick, or a fiancé . . . It's amazing what money can buy!

Personal Concierge, 575 Lexington Ave. (bet. 51st & 52nd Sts.), (212) 527-7575, *Demand Dementia*

Busy New Yorkers with more money than time can hire this service to do their dirty work: restaurant reservations, theater tickets, travel arrangements, sporting events and flower delivery to name just a few . . . Quite honestly, the sky is the limit! Owner Pascal Riffaud (formerly of the St. Regis and the Ritz in Paris) says, "I'll attempt any possible—and legal—request." Period. Services by membership starting at $1,500 per year (30 requests). Platinum membership (200 favors) sets you back $8,000 annually.

Protravel International, 515 Madison Ave. (@ 53rd St.), (212) 577-4550, *Travel Agent Guru*

Booking a trip with your new baby to an exclusive hideaway that has a no-children policy? Want to take the president of Taiwan to dinner? Never fear. Clients like Elle McPherson, Rupert Murdoch's son Lachlan, and Amber Valleta are just a few of the celebs who use this amazing service. Glen Litwak and his team are able to score great deals and hard-to-get dates with top airlines and hotels and assembles tailor-made exotic destination packages. He does work with anyone who seeks his assistance and has the cash to play ball. One-on-one consultations are required ($250) for new clients and this does not include the service charge for each "mission" you give him. That ranges from $1 to infinity—depending on where, when and how you are going.

Schumer's, 59 E. 54th St. (bet. Madison & Park Aves.), (212) 355-0940, *Wine Drought*

Every fine wine has its time, but what happens when you run out of red in the middle of the roast? Call or fax these vino maestros for quick delivery until midnight. Be sure to mention if you want that Pinot Grigio chilled when you order! *Bon appetit!*

The John Barrett Salon @ Bergdorf Goodman, 754 Fifth Ave. (bet. 57th & 58th Sts.), (212) 872-2700, *Deal Breaking / Nail Breaking*

Risk your job over a silk tip? Not! One of Manhattan's tonier stylists has entered the new millennium. Now available: modem connections in the pedicure rooms. Located in the posh Bergdorf Goodman store. Enter at your own risk: a quick trim could cost you thousands as you pass the designer bags by the elevator!

Two Dogs And A Goat, 326 E. 34th St. (bet. First & Second Aves.), (212) 213-6979, *www.twodogsandagoat.com, Pet Baby-Sitters*

There is no need for your pet Shitsu to be alone while you are at the office! Animal lover/owner Charolotte Read's goal is to make sure that you have a happy and safe pet at home or away. Take advantage of her bonded and licensed services such as: pet sit, three daily visits and walks to your home ($54); play date, for a two-hour visit to play with your pet; or if you travel with your pet, try the hotel care, where your pet gets a 30-minute walk in the neighborhood or just a visit—$21.50 per hour.

Worldwide Business Centers, 575 Madison Ave., 10th Floor (bet. 56th & 57th Sts.), (212) 605-0200, *Space Shortage*

Office in a box—when the kitchen table or the hotel bar just won't do! Conference rooms can be rented on daily or weekly. Basic fee includes phone service, receptionist and private office. Secretaries are available as well. And just in case you have to go to Jakarta to seal the deal (and pick up a cool sari) they offer a travel service . . . The Mod Squad work ethic . . .

✦ Good to Know:

Need to pick up a last-minute dessert? **Desert Deliver/Wine & Roses** (360 E. 55th St., bet. First & Second Aves.), (212) 838-5411, will deliver almost anywhere! They sell goods from 39 best bake shops in the U.S. be it cheesecake or special cookies. They make you look good.

Where to go . . . **J-Lo's Tank** aka the Sony Building (550 Madison Ave.@ 55th St.). Head toward the upstairs in the back for a nice experience.

Chelsea/Meatpacking

Aaron-Hotz Locksmith, 219 W. 14th St. (bet. Seventh & Eighth Aves.), (212) 685-2779, *Locked Out*

In 75 years of lock-out emergencies, anything and everything, these boys have seen it all, including handcuffs in the wee hours of the morning. Twenty-hour hours, seven days a week.

Barbara Matera Ltd., 890 Broadway (@ 19th St.), (212) 475-5006 *Growing Pains*

It's a fact: the right "foundation" (undergarments) can shape your body better than a month's work of Lotte Berk (see Treats)! All jokes aside, Barbara custom-makes foundations, from corsets to girdles and bustles. Expect to pay big bucks, from $500 up for your secret treasure. *Psst . . . some require fittings.*

Cross It Off Your List, 404 Park Ave. (bet. 28th & 29th Sts.) 725-0122, *Help!*

Have to rely on the kindness of strangers? You bet. Pretend you have a full-time staff to manage your home and only pay an hourly fee. Running household errands, coordinating "the big move," or just overhauling and organizing closets between seasons, these folks have the ticket. Lynda Rothschilds, the owner, will cost you $95 per hour; the well-equipped staff is $75.

Evie's Personal Shopping Service @ Loehmann's, 101 Seventh Ave. (bet. 16th & 17th Sts.), (212) 352-0856, ext. 420, *Lack of Taste or Time*

Cut your shopping time in half . . . how? By not going! Ring energetic Evie, and she'll do everything for you. No request is too big, too small, or too difficult to deal with. You want it, Evie will get it or a reasonable facsimile. Gluttons for punishment can go with her and try to keep up with the whirlwind! By appointment only—Monday through Friday, two Saturdays per month.

Florent, 69 Gansevoort St. (bet. Greenwich & Washington Sts.), (212) 989-5779, *Late-night Coma*

It's always a party at four in the morning, no invitation required! Late-night eclectic and frenetic crowd makes for excellent people watching— from celebs to drag queens, don't get a sore neck from spinning it around! Open 24 hours, Friday and Saturday. Perfect for a late-night nibble in neighborhood.

L. Allmeier, 109 W. 24th St. (bet. Sixth & Seventh Aves.), (212) 243-7390, *Collar Hospital*

The cuffs and collar people. Does your husband have a favorite shirt that he insists on wearing even though it's on its last legs? Bring it in for a re-vamp! French cuffs? No problem . . . Why not add an adorable pique collar to that blue shirt of yours from last season?

Les Concierges, (appointment by phone), (212) 252-5455, *Time Crunch*

Need someone to wait for the plumber or cable guy? Pick up friends at the airport? Locate a Siberian tiger at the last minute? A monthly flat fee will bring you all of this and more. One client had his concierge orchestrate a marriage proposal—maybe yours could seal the deal!

Origins Feel Good Day Spa, Pier 60, The Sports Center @ Chelsea Pier, (212) 336-6780, *Jet Lag Relief*

Feel good you will after experiencing "The Light Tank"—light therapy for the city bedraggled or the overly jet-lagged. Who isn't perpetually life-jagged? Take advantage of this spa devoted to organically natural beauty treatments that push the envelope and defy the senses. Breathe in, breathe out. Now get a massage and vow to never pollute yourself again.

Paws Inn, 189 Ninth Ave. (@ 21st St.), (212) 645-PAWS, *Dog Gone*

Situated in a brownstone in the heart of Chelsea, this is the place for Pup to stay while the master is away. For a fee, a limousine equipped with a television (it plays *102 Dalmatians*!) will pick up your pup. The rest of his "boarding" will consist of just as much pampering, such as "nap time" after lunch complete with dim lights. Playing is encouraged on the roof deck playground. At night someone even sleeps upstairs in the bed with them so they don't get lonely without you. Costs are $40 for 15 lbs and under and $45 for over 15 lbs. *Psst . . . don't worry about dog fights breaking out, they separate the dogs by size.*

Props For Today, 121 W. 19th St. (bet. Sixth & Seventh Aves.), (212) 206-0330, *Atmospheric Ambush*

You've had six months to plan the company bash but decided you work best under pressure. It's tomorrow and you're at ground zero. By the way, it was your brilliant idea to make it a Medieval Safari—Tarzan Meets Braveheart . . . Never fear, the props are here! And the tables, and the tablecloths, and the silver, and the glassware, and the chairs, and the couches and the candlelabras.

◈ *Good to Know:*
Where to go . . . **TIDY ART** Met Life Building: (Madison Ave. @ 24th St.) Ask the guard for the Gallery and he will give you a visitor's pass and you can "potty" in peace. Passes the white glove inspection.

Union Square/Gramercy/Flatiron ············

Glow, 36 E. 23rd St., 10th Floor (bet. Park & Madison Aves.), (212) 228-1822, *Hair Overnight*

Where length is everything! Extensions are the house specialty at this cool Flatiron salon. Breezy and light loft space make this an all-around pleasant experience. Starting at $350 and up depending on the style and length. A stylist and makeup artist are on hand to help out with your other beauty needs. We love the MOP products!

Gramercy Park Animal Hospital, 37 E. 19th St. (bet. Park Ave. & Irving Pl.), (212) 477-4080, *True Trauma*

This well-known and trusted group of Manhattan vets can handle all of your pet health concerns: Dr. Jay D. Kuhlman, Dr. Tom Basso, Dr. Karen Feibusch, and Dr. Dale S. Rubin. Take your pick, and be assured that your "best friend" will be back to barking and wagging in no time at all.

L'Express, 249 Park Ave. (@ 20th St.), (212) 254-5858, *24-Hour Hangover Cure*

French infused late-night diner with breakfast all day and all night . . . Postdancing destination for omelets, cigarettes, and model watching. The food is mediocre at best, the atmosphere and your "buzz" will bind you to the slow service, but somehow you always come back time and again. What does that say about you, missy?

Nail Noble, 407 Park Ave. (bet. 27th & 28th Sts.), (212) 481-0200, *Rampant Snagging*

Keep snagging your Fogal hosiery? Need an "emergency" nail job? Here's your answer: A little file, cuticle massage, and polish, and you are good to go! Cheap, cheap, cheap.

New York Dog Spa & Hotel, 145 W. 18th St., (bet. Sixth & Seventh Aves.), (212) 243-1199, *Pampered Pet Set*

Is Fido "acting out"? Sometimes we all need a little TLC from professionals. This is a complete dog spa that specializes in the kind of day care, bathing, and grooming, boarding, and veterinary services that only a city like New York can offer. A popular procedure is call the T-touch, a gentle massage for your pooch. Rates vary according to the size. It is a dog's life! *Psst . . . be sure to allow time for you to linger at FIDO's Café and Lounge located at the spa, which allows people and their beloved canines to mix and mingle over coffee. What better way to meet that cute guy with the yellow Lab?*

Robin Epstein, 43 W. 24th St., Suite 12B (bet. Fifth & Sixth Aves.), (212) 501-3875, *Loss of Willpower*

A natural nutrition counselor and inspiration guru . . . So before you jump out of your high-rise screaming "donuts or die," let Robin talk you down off the sugar wall! One-on-one nutrition counseling teaches you to love your body by inspiring you to eat fresh wholesome food and lead a less stressed life. Soothe stress, boost energy, calm cravings, increase mental clarity, shape up your body, enhance digestion, and get a glow to go with it all. Devotees swear by the results if you are committed to the cause!

Vanishing Point, 4 W. 16th St. (bet. Fifth & Sixth Aves.), (212) 255-3474, *Attack Of Wolf Women*

This place has a two-month waiting list! And their reputation precedes them: laser hair removal that claims to permanently remove unwanted hair. Be sure to check out the VP Micro Peel, which uses fine crystals to reduce fine lines, scar tissue, stretch marks, and acne. Also Therapeutic Cellulite Massage, a noninvasive treatment similar to lipo without the surgical. Prices are reasonable. They staff three nurses and one electrolysist and have evening/night appointments for the busy woman.

Greenwich Village

Dog Wash, 177 MacDougal St., (bet. Waverly & 8th Sts.), (212) 673-3290, *Dirt Crisis*

Calling all down right dirty dogs. No we don't mean your ex-boyfriend. This is a great place to wash the grimiest of NYC pets. Two options for your four paws: do-it-yourself for $14 or let the caring and knowledgeable staff do it for you for $27.

New York One Locksmith, 350 Bleecker St. (bet. First & Second Aves.), (212) 721-3000, *Found Is the Key*

For your 24-hour lock-out needs! They will change out locks in your apartment or help you get back in when your keys are somewhere besides your purse. They promise to open your car in 10 minutes or you get 10 percent off! Don't be ashamed, it happens to the best of us "Janes" at one time or another!

Pinch Sitters, 799 Broadway, #204, (bet. 10th & 11th Sts.), (212) 260-6005, *No Kids Allowed*

Spontaneity is a dirty word to most mommies, but not anymore! This "temp" agency provides emergency childcare (approximately $12/hr.) for those who can't plan ahead. Most sitters are "creative types" between gigs, for all you creative gals between full-time work (or husbands!). Preferably call in the A.M. for the P.M. They'll try their best to find a sitter within the hour. In business since 1986 and yes, they are licensed and bonded.

Weight Watchers @ The Village Temple, 33 E. 12th St. (bet. Fifth Ave. & University Pl.), (800) 651-6000, *Cellulite Scare*

It's all about the points which WW uses to measure daily calorie intake, and the "meetings," to chat with other dieters about your latest cookie binge. WW is on the rise as one of the fastest and healthiest ways to lose unwanted pounds in a reasonable manner. This particular WW meeting has the reputation of being low-key and schmoozy. Wednesday's meetings are run by Lenore Schmidt from 10–11 A.M. and 12:15–1:15 P.M., Thursday's by Janet! Drop some weight, chat with some folks, and don't forget to count your points!

◆ *Good to Know:*
Where to go . . . **Forbes Magazine Galleries** (Fifth Ave. bet. 12th & 13th Sts.) Rest rooms in galleries feature huge wall murals from the ship *The Normandy*. Ultraclean and man-friendly too.

East Village/Lower East Side ·····································

ABC Animal Hospital, 49 Ave. B (bet. 3rd & 4th Sts.), (212) 358-0785, *Sick Pets*

Let Dr. Daniel Tufaro help you with all of your "pet" issues. After a long stint with the ASPCA his loving hands are here for your little loved one. All standard exams available ($50) as well as lab tests (fee based on tests) including ultrasounds, vaccinations ($25), and don't forget about Muffy's teeth—offering all forms of in-house dental care. Open Tuesday–Friday 8:30–6:00, Saturday 9:00 A.M.–3:00 P.M. Emergency walk-ins welcome.

Barrett Salon, 19 E. 7th St. (bet. Second & Third Aves.), (212) 477-3236, *Hair Crisis*

So, you fell prey to the age-old "cut your hair after the breakup," realized you don't have a "short hair" face. Specializing in hair extensions for downtown babes, Brazilian-born owner Adriana Trimarchi offers a myriad of choices for all your "extended" needs! In four short hours you are back to being the girl with the tresses! It will set you back $650, but let's face it, it's cheaper than a shrink!

East Village Prescription Center, 72 Ave. A (@ 5th St.), (212) 260-4878, *All You Need*

A neighborhood fixture for 55 years. Al Pacino, Robert DeNiro, and Whoopi Goldberg find their echinacea here. A full-service pharmacy, they offer an interesting assortment of homeopathy and vitamins. They also sell electronics—telephones, radios, Walkmans, irons, etc.

Felix Tailor Shop, 97 Rivington St. (bet. Ludlow & Orchard Sts.), (212) 420-9775, *Cheap Fix*

So your new suede pants from H&M stretched a whole size after one wear? Your favorite suit is deeply wrinkled from a week of being in Lost Luggage Land? Felix's specializes in custom tailoring, alterations, and pressing while you wait. Seven days a week, from 9:00 A.M. to 7:00 P.M. these folks get you in and out in a flash so you can be on your merry way looking like the perfectly well appointed diva!

Grace Church, 802 Broadway (@ 10th St.), (212) 254-2000, *Jesus Called*

When your therapist, psychic and latest gurus just don't cut it anymore, it's time to go back to the source—911 for the soul since circa 1846. Glorious and formal (yet warm) services with full organ and choir. This small church is worth joining to ensure you can get married here! Services on Sunday at 9 and 11. Not forgetting the beautiful Christmas services for those of you still in town.

Johnny Lats, 7 E. 17th St. (bet. Fifth Ave. & Broadway), (212) 366-4426, *Fat Nightmare*

Decide to turn over a new leaf at 4 A.M. after gorging yourself for "the last time"? Then belly up to the barbells at Johnny Lats, your very own 24-hour gym. Membership starts at $10 per day to $359 for a full year. Definitely for the hard-core workout gal who is looking for fitness not glamour, and a little space to move in the silence of the peaceful predawn Manhattan.

Macvision, 210 E. 6th St. (bet. Second & Third Aves.), (212) 586-8445, *Cyber Virus*

Your beloved Mac. Your beloved 50-page report for tomorrow's meeting. A bomb. Shut down. Pull the cord. Another bomb. Oh, God. Pour some pinot. Pick up phone. *Psst . . . they sell used computers if you are on a budget and have a real "Mac attack."*

Whiskers Holistic Pet Products, 235 E. 9th St. (bet. Second & Third Aves.), (212) 979-2532, *Pet Gourmand*

Kicking the holistic pet care for those in search of a more healthy way of feeding their most treasured pet. This place caters to the most discriminating palates—pet palates, that is. Organically raised catnip comes in a variety of strains for your feline's frolicking pleasure and Bow-Wow vegetarian cookies baked fresh at the bakery. How about herb-infused crackers from Abady and toys that are designed to exercise furry minds and fluffy bodies?

SoHo/Nolita/Chinatown/Little Italy

Compass Parking, 610 Broadway (@ Houston St.), (212) 598-2354, *Parking Rage*

Located on the edge of SoHo this 24-hour parking garage is a rarity. Park at Compass while you shop or eat or. . . . Parking rates are "reasonable" by city standards: between 5 A.M. and 10 A.M., two hours @ $20; $23 for a 24-hour "park-over." *Psst . . . negotiate the wash price.*

Cybercafe, 273 Lafayette St. (@ Prince St.), (212) 334-5140, *www. cybercafe.com, Cyber Love Crisis*

Forgot your G-4 at the office and need to check if "you've got mail"? Here you got access to a great cup of coffee and a sandwich while you surf the net. Minimum time is a half hour for $6.93. Ask about computer lessons if you find yourself lost in cyberland. *Psst . . . frequent visitors should inquire about the membership program that allows discounts after four hours of on-line time. Up to 30 percent off!*

Frank Andrews, 261 Mulberry St. (@ Prince St.), (212) 226-2194, *Psychic Net-Worker*

If you need a little more oomph than your therapist can offer seek the insightful and humorous advice of this 33-year veteran of all things occult. Specializing in palmistry, tarot, and psychic readings, Andrews's clientele at one time included John Lennon, Princess Grace, and Andy Warhol—don't worry, they haven't sought his advice from the grave! Visit his charming town house and all your fears of the future will dissolve in a puff of Zen In The Morning incense.

Green Castle Laundromat, 512 Broome St. (bet. Thompson St. & W. Broadway), (212) 966-2400, *Maid Hijacking*

Hey, even the hip have to spin cycle occasionally. And why would you trust that five-hundred-dollar La Perla bra to a laundry service? Do the deed in record time, in a safe and somewhat festive environment. Don't forget the Snuggle™!

Houston Auto Repair, 300 Lafayette St. (bet. Houston & Prince Sts.), (212) 226-0633, *Car Bomb*

Twenty-four-hour/full-service auto repair that can handle anything. Call the tow, fix the car, even fuel you up next door when they realize your "emergency" is an empty tank. Girls will be girls!

Li-Lac, 120 Christopher St. (bet. Hudson & Bleecker Sts.), (212) 242-7374, *Sociopathic Sugar Freaks*

PMS Suicide Intervention Plan since 1923 at this little chocolate haven for those in need or with basically any excuse to orally bliss out.

New York Earth Room, 141 Wooster St. (bet. Houston & Prince Sts.), (212) 473-8072, *Dirty Thoughts*

Have we got the dirt for you . . . literally! Piles and piles of moist brown earth fill this loft in SoHo—280,000 pounds of rich, black topsoil. A satellite of the Dia Center (see Tripping, Chelsea/MP), this peculiar sanctuary brings a strange calm to the observer through the fresh aroma of, well, dirt. The therapeutic equivalent of marathon gardening without messing up your manicure. Free admission, closed in summer.

Pearl Paint Co., 308 Canal St. (bet. Church Ave. & Broadway), (212) 431-7932, *Toxic Colors*

Whether painting your walls or the next big "thing"—you Picasso, you—this place rocks in terms of function and aesthetic. This gigantic discount store that carries everything an artist could desire. Paper, drawing utensils, and all other supplies including custom frames. As Shawn Colvin sings, "I never saw blue like that before."

Penny Babbel Couturier, 19 E. 69th St. (@ Madison Ave.), 5th Floor, (212) 879-5844, *Deadly Decay*

Elaborate reinventions of vintage clothes and fabrics. Taking your existing garment (like your grandmother's gorgeous 1940s wedding gown) and bring it into the twenty-first century. Beading, draping and embroidery? No problem. Impeccable repairs as well. Just think, you could take that Pucci scarf and create a new millennium mini!

Pierre Garroudi, 139 Thompson St. (bet. W. Houston & Prince Sts.), (212) 475-2333, *Cinderella Syndrome*

Pierre can make a dress (your dream dress from the pages of *In Style*) in 24 hours. Guaranteed. Bring a photo or choose from some of his own designs—wedding gowns, party dresses, suits, designer copies. They have fabrics in-house—wool, silk in 96 colors, cashmere—or bring your own! Price is not based on time. Most women's suits start at $1,200 whether it takes 24 hours or two days. Pierre can do most things in 24 hours, and anything with a bit more time. *Psst . . . catch Pierre's designs on the fab body of HBO's* Sex and the City *Kim Cattrall*.

Prince Street Copy Center, 159 Prince St. (bet. Thompson St. & West Broadway), (212) 982-7333, *Copies In A Pinch*

Personalized, high-quality copy service, no job too big or too small. Corporate accounts welcome. Friendly staff will help with binding, laminating, word processing, faxing, as well as copying. *Psst . . . business cards in a flash!*

Something Special, 51 MacDougal St. (bet. Houston & Prince Sts.), (212) 924-7466, *Missing Concierge*

Let Lenny take care of you (M–F 6 A.M.–6 P.M.). He's the landlord of this building, but for a mere dollar a deed, he will fax, make keys, make copies, notarize, etc. Mailboxes available for $50/month . . . Lenny is busy but reliable, and if you are really nice, he just might forward your mail wherever the wind has taken you! *Psst . . . ask to see his business cards!*

Spring Street Dental, 182 Spring St. (bet. Sullivan & Thompson Sts.), (212) 226-5039, *Calcium Deposit*

Toothache? Chip? Lost a crown in last night's soufflé? Bring your pearly whites to this family-run trauma treasure! After 40 years of dentistry, dad left the original practice to "My Three Sons." A NYC staple, these dental boys welcome emergencies. Our kind of guys!

The Village Tailor and Cleaners, 125 Sullivan St. (bet. Prince & Spring Sts.), (212) 925-9667, *Jack The Ripper*

"Ouch!" she said, as the angry piece of taxi metal tore her Jil Sander suit. "Dammit!" she said, when she realized it was the only suit she had brought on the trip. Enter Vince Rao to repair her garment at emergency pace. They pick up and deliver for a negotiable fee (free within the neighborhood), and most work is accomplished at the speed of light (five minutes for a hem).

Traveler's Choice, 111 Greene St. (bet. Prince & Spring Sts.), (212) 941-1535, *Witness Protection*

Travel agency and bookstore all rolled up into one. Travelers' journeys may sweep a "go-go girl" off her feet and into the arms of the travel agent next door who can book your safari or an upstate weekend on the spot.

Whole Foods Cooking and Private Chef, 300 Mercer Street, Suite 15M, (Waverly & 8th Sts.), (212) 460-9685, *Kitchen Phobia*

Get sweaty palms looking at the stove? Let Gloria help spice up your meals and maybe your love life too! You never know who might be next to you in her cooking classes that cater to those trying to balance a healthy diet and lifestyle with great taste. There are even recipes for hip and healthy food for kids and babies.

Where to go . . . the unisex bathrooms at **Bar 89,** (89 Mercer St. bet. Spring & Broome Sts.) (see Twilight). LCL glass automatically becomes opaque when you close the door, giving you privacy . . . hmmm . . .

Need to change your lira over to yen? Eurochange is located at 401 Broadway (bet. Spring & Broome Sts.) (212) 966-7080, 10 A.M.–7 P.M.

Tribeca/Lower Manhattan/Other Boroughs ············

Fountain Pen Hospital, 10 Warren St. (bet. Church St. & Broadway), (800) 253-PENS, *A-Pen-Dicitus*

The name speaks for itself. In 1946 Al Widerlight embarked on providing the utmost in repair service for the world's most elegant communication tools. Once you write with a great pen, you'll never go back. Win big brownie points with dad when you repair that old quill he's been using since Harvard Class of '54!

Frankie Steinz, 24 Harrison St. (bet. Hudson & Greenwich Sts.), (212) 925-1373, *Obsessive Love / Stalking / Costumes*

Staking out your ex and need a disguise? Frankie has been designing and renting madly fab costumes for the past 15 years, mainly for TV and movie companies, but welcomes individual browsers. Maybe you want to go as Marie Antoinette to your Halloween party. Or perhaps you are just looking to spice up your love life with a darling French maid's uniform! Not a retail outlet, you must book an appointment before showing up.

Meyer's Moving and Storage, 370 Concord Ave., Bronx, (212) 688-8888, *Move It*

Twenty-four-hour service in case you have to move fast. (Witness protection?) These guys are reasonable, reliable, and available at all hours— but you never know, you may have to feed them after midnight.

Midnight Express, 3838 13th St., Long Island City, (212) 921-0111, *Wee Hour Washing*

The best dry-cleaning pickup/delivery service around at incredibly competitive (even low) prices. Even though they're located in Long Island City, call before noon and they'll get it back before 10 A.M. the next day. This works especially well when the airline has lost your bag, you're wearing your interview suit, and your interview is at lunch tomorrow! Great service to and from hotels, avoiding the in-house hotel cleaning prices.

Passport Agency, 376 Hudson St. (bet. Houston & King Sts.), (212) 206-3500, *Passport Renewal*

If you have more than three days, this is the regular and economical (30-dollar) way to renew your passport. Call the Passport Agency for a by-appointment-only meeting, gather your papers, and stand in line, have cash or check ready, and within a week the little navy booklet will be in your hands.

Petmenders Animal Hospital, 158 Duane St. (bet. Hudson St. & W. Broadway), (212) 406-0970, *Pet Drama*

Animal lovers swear by the care they get here, including some pretty famous pooches and their pretty famous owners. Your loved one will be well cared for even if you or they are not celebrities.

◈ *Good to Know:*

Where to go . . . **Trinity Church,** 74 Trinity Pl. (Broadway & Wall St.), (212) 602-0800, has nice rest rooms in the back of the church in a small vestibule in the back.

◈ *Citywide:*

Brain Dead: You never know when yours will go on the fritz. Call **Dial-A-Brain at the New York Public Library,** (212) 340-0849; their researchers find obscure facts in a flash. How many bones in a newborn? What was the value of the yen in 1946? Who had the highest batting average in the 1965 World Series? You name it, they can find it, weekdays from 9 A.M. to 5 P.M.

Kitchen Emergency: **Dial-A-Dinner,** (212) 642-1222, can help if you've lied about being Julia Child or if you and your man are too worn-out to hit the town. Conjure up a five-pound lobster from the Palm or a romantic dinner at home from Patria (see US/Gramercy/Flatiron, Eats). Delivering lunch and dinner within the hour from many of the city's top restaurants with the requisite pomp and circumstance.

Over your head: When your kid's homework is too much, call on **Dial-A-Teacher,** (212) 777-3380, a service of city schoolteachers. Open 4—7 P.M.

Drugs at midnight: **Duane Reade** has a pharmacist on duty 24 hours a day at:
485 Lexington Ave. (@ 47th St.), (212) 682-5338
224 W. 57th St. (@ Broadway), (212) 541-9708
1279 Third Ave. (@ 74th St.), (212) 744-2668
2465 Broadway (@ 92nd St.), (212) 799-3172

Hands-on-help: **Susanna Green,** (917) 333-8731, was trained at both the Swedish and Ohashi Institutes. No frills included, just an old-fashioned Shiatsu/Swedish rubdown to cure the crick in your neck from lugging new Gucci luggage in and out of taxis. Madonna swears by Susanna's healing hands. House calls, $150 an hour.

Agoraphobic Delight: Call 888-HEAL-999 for massages, facials, and reflexology, brought to your doorstep when you're feeling too frail or fried to venture out. **Healing Hands** send well-trained and trustworthy "hands" to you. 10 A.M.—10 P.M., $130 an hour.

Screaming Child: Move over, Barney, help is on the way from *Julie the Starfish and Other Lullabies.* Order this delightful CD from actress Hope Harris, (212) 330-9260, *www.hopeharris.com,* and your little monsters will be entranced in no time.

Relapse: Cocaine is illegal, but calories are not. Visit **Krispy Kreme Doughnuts:**
1497 Third Ave. (bet. 84th & 85th Sts.), (212) 879-9111
265 W. 23rd St. (bet. Seventh & Eighth Aves.), (212) 620-0111
280 W. 125th St. (@ Frederick Douglass Blvd.), (212) 531-0111
141 W. 72nd St. (bet. Amsterdam & Columbus Aves.), (212) 724-1100
Two Penn Plaza/Amtrak Station (@ 34th St. & Seventh Ave.), (212) 947-7175
Port Authority Bus Terminal (@ 42nd St. & Eighth Ave.), (212) 290-8644

Ticket Drama: If you must go to a ticket counter to purchase or change your airline reservations, forget going all the way to an airport. Try a **Satellite Airline Ticket Office,** all of which have counter space for most of the major airlines:

UWS, 1843 Broadway, (@ 60th St., Columbus Circle)

MTE, 110 E. 59th St. (bet. Fifth & Madison Aves.), (212) 486-9290

MTE, 125 Park Ave. (@ Grand Central Station), (212) 986-0888

MTW, 555 Seventh Ave. (@ 40th St.)

Toxic Locks: Now that you're in the big city, isn't it time to deal with that fright wig you're sporting? **Shirley Tores,** by appointment at the John Freida Salon, 797 Madison Ave. (bet. 67th & 68th Sts.), (212) 879-1000, $55 per blowdry, will turn that "don't" back into a do in time for the opera or the office, whichever comes first. And she can handle those last-minute freak-outs.

Psychic Surgery: The older sister to Guardian Angels founder Curtis Sliwa, **Aleta St. James,** (212) 246-2420, has created her own brand of psychic surgery. After working with AIDS patients for years, she's switched gears to focus on those in entertainment and fashion. (She even wears Vamp on her toes to make us feel at home . . .) It might take her a month to fit you in, but after entering her healing sanctuary you'll never be the same. . . . Energy work, touch therapy, breathing, and a little Freud to the tune of $200 for the first visit. (You *do* have to be open-minded.)

Organizational Armageddon: Does your office remind you of Hiroshima? Does chaos follow in your wake? You need Julie at **Taskmasters,** (718) 855-8275, to whip you into shape. She'll organize everything from your paperwork to your wedding and put you back in control of your own life.

Apartment-hunting desperation: First one to find Sunday's **New York Times** wins! Try 6:30 P.M. on Saturday at Super Ego Corporation, 140 First Ave. (@ 61st St.), K&H Deli, 448 Hudson St. (bet. Molton & Barrow Sts.), and the newstand at 314 Sixth Ave. (bet W. 3rd St. & Minetta St.) Good luck!

 Roommate allergy: Trapped in a one-year lease in an adorable studio with a roommate you hate? Call **The Wall,** (718) 793-3151, for your own pressurized partition, and *voilà* . . . your own room, complete with French doors. This patented system makes the most of small spaces that already cost too much, with no permanent damage so your security deposit remains secure. And yes, Pink Floyd provided this entrepreneur with inspiration. Walls start at $799.

Couch Amputation: Panic-stricken when your new sofa won't fit through the door? **Z Brothers Trucking,** (914) 769-2178, has been "momentarily minimizing" couches in the five boroughs for the past twenty-five years. Basic disassembly and reassembly in less than an hour for $165. (Your fancy-schmancy custom-made Shabby Chic may cost you $225 because of the dowel fasteners . . .)

High-fashion bargain: Try trainee nights at these swanky babe salons for high-styling tresses for less than half the price:

Bumble and Bumble, 146 E. 56th St. (bet. Third & Lexington Aves.), (212) 521-6500

Antonio Prieto Salon, 25 W. 19th St., 1st floor (bet. Fifth & Sixth Aves.), (212) 255-3741

John Frieda, 30 E. 76th St., 2nd floor (bet. Fifth & Madison Aves.), (212) 879-1000

Frederic Fekkai Beaute de Provence, 15 E. 57th St. (bet. Fifth & Madison Aves.), (212) 753-9500

John Berrett at Bergdorf Goodman, 754 Fifth Ave. (at 57th St.), (212) 753-7300

Louis Licari, 693 Fifth Ave., 15th Floor (bet. Fifth & Madison Aves.), (212) 327-0639

Peter Coppola Salon, 746 Madison Ave. (bet. 65th & 66th Sts.), (212) 988-9404

Oscar Blandi, 768 Fifth Ave. (bet. 58th & 59th Sts.), (212) 593-7930

Saks Fifth Ave. Beauty Salon, 611 Fifth Ave. (at 51st St.), (212) 940-4000

⸙ *True Traumas:*
City Services (Visit *http://www.ci.nyc.ny.us* for all city agencies and general information, etc.):
MTA NYC Transit, for lost and found, (718) 625-6200
NYC Marriage License Bureau, (212) 669-2400
NYC Bureau of Traffic Operations, (212) 971-0770

NYC Taxi and Limousine Commission, for lost and found, (212) 692-8294

✦ *Other Helpful Contacts:*

Alcoholics Anonymous: Call for meetings by neighborhood, (212) 647-1680

Association of the Bar of the City of New York, (212) 626-7373

Better Business Bureau: Get "reliability ratings" or file a complaint (bill the $3.80 fee to your credit card), *www.newyork.bbb.org,* (212) 533-6200

Metro Assistance Corp: A nonprofit crime victims hot line, (212) 417-5160

NY Convention and Visitors Bureau: A private NYC tourism resource, *www.nycvisit.com,* (212) 397-8222

Travelers Aid Service: Help for out-of-towners, (212) 944-0013

Treasures

Allan & Suzi, 416 Amsterdam Ave. (@ 80th St.), (212) 724-7445,
Vintage Chic

The charming owners got started in the eighties by cleaning closets.
Buried deep in their fashionable friends' homes were the makings of a brilliant boutique! Find that outrageous red Valentino or some trendy consigned leopard boots . . . in this crowded space. Killer selection of Maud
Frizon shoes ranging from $30 to $70 depending on style and condition.
Prices are negotiable, so feel free to haggle for your booty.

Assets London, 464 Columbus Ave. (@ 82nd St.), (212) 874-8253,
Forward Looks

This trendy boutique has a great collection of cute shoes, handbags,
funky gifts, and select pairs of beautiful panties, but their specialty is fashion
forward international designs . . . Great selection of Dolce & Gabbana
among others, and their constant stock updating makes this a weekly shopping stop for all serious fashionistas! Endorsed by the owner of Café Lalo as
the destination for that killer outfit! *Psst . . . call 30 minutes ahead and let the
staff pull the type of items you are looking for to save time on your way to Avery
Fisher* (see Tripping, UWS).

Balducci's, 155A W. 66th St. (bet. Broadway & Amsterdam Ave.),
(212) 653-8320, *Gourmet Food Shop*

See details in GV.

Bati, 2323 Broadway (bet. 84th & 85th Sts.), (212) 724-7214, *Shoes*

Most current styles, European shoe lines, "a little piece of SoHo in the
Upper West Side." Now you'll be able to impress all of your girlfriends
with your taste and style from a secret little place!

Bonne Nuit, 30 Lincoln Plaza (Broadway bet. 62nd & 63rd Sts.), (212)
489-9730, *Baby Clothes/Lingerie*

For nonmommies, we have never gone this beserk over babies before—
baby clothing, that is! Our eyes feasted on miniature fashions and fluffies,
tiny shoes and tutus, handmade sweaters, stuffed animals on wheels, pillows that match the snugglies that match the towels that match the rattles . . . (We didn't miss the adorable nightwear for moms and the top-end

lingerie to put him in the mood to procreate). Five hundred dollars later we walked out ready to breed!

Cardeology, 314 Columbus Ave. (bet. 74th & 75th Sts.), (212) 579-9310, 452 Amsterdam Ave. (bet. 81st & 82nd Sts.), (212) 873-2491, *Special Occasion Cards*

Don't have a "heart attack" looking for the perfect way to say the perfect thing to the perfect guy, the cards at Cardeology will handle that for you! Whether you're in the market for romance, humor, forgiveness, or forgetfulness, you'll leave not a sentiment unexpressed in this incredible card emporium.

Euro Optika, 333 W. 57 St. (bet. 8th & 9th Aves.), (212) 262-5757, 288 Columbus Ave. (bet 73rd & 74th Sts.), (212) 501-7070, *Optical Oasis*

"Four eyes" are hipper than two with the selection of sexy specs in this glam-optic joint! Fashionable eyewear for every occasion. Love their sunglasses! Our pick: the indestructible golden 2.5 ounce Swedish aviators without hinges. Perfect for the traveling woman who changes planes, trains, boats, bags, and boyfriends at lightning speed.

Gracious Home, 1992 Broadway (@ 68th St.), (212) 231-7800, *www.gracioushome.com, Home Furnishings*

If you cannot find what you need for your home here, then it does not exist—and you can quote us! Paint, brooms, lampshades, candles, nails, trash cans, stepladders, sinks, curtains, washer/dryers, note cards, potpourri, extension cords, cleaning products, stenciling kits, linens, closet organizers, cedar hangers, drawer pulls, shelving, pots and pans, plus big items like outdoor grills and butcher block islands by catalog . . . Great service, delivery, and assembly for a small fee! See other location in UES.

Greenflea, Columbus Ave. (bet. 77th St. & Columbus Ave.), *Indoor/ Outdoor Flea Market*

A Sunday urban flea market on acid. For the full-on flea market junkie chick, there's a sister operation on the UES (419 E. 66th St.) on Saturdays! Stop by Spazzia for brunch (see Eats, UWS) while in the neighborhood.

I.S. Flea Market, Columbus Avenue bet. 76th & 77th Sts., *No Fleas Allowed*

You never know what treasure you might unearth at this very popular open-air flea market. Come for the bargain antique headboard you have been looking for, or find a bauble from yesteryear to get that up-to-the-minute look today! Open on Sunday only from 10 A.M. to 6 P.M.

Lincoln Stationers, 1889 Broadway (@ 63rd St.), (212) 459-3500, *Office Supplies*

Notepaper and gadgets for girls on the run—stationery, Filofax refills, Day Timers by Kate Spade, bags by Scully, Tumi, and Kipling. Printing, engraving, notarizing, and, of course, the overpriced U.S. postage stamp. Now if they only sold 25 hours in a day!

Murder Ink, 2486 Broadway (bet. 92nd & 93rd Sts.), (212) 352-8905, *Mystery Books*

If you are already a suspect "suspect," then you have solved the case! Since 1972, this store has been stocked with mystery fiction from A to Z, neatly alphabetized by author name. Special selection of true crime and out-of-print books in the alcove. Go, Sherlock!

Only Hearts, 386 Columbus Ave. (@ 79th St.), (212) 724-5608, *Trendy Undergarments*

A tiny store for tiny things. Trendy and tasteful lingerie for the capricious of heart and hearty of wallet. Famous for cutting-edge clothes to wear inside the boudoir or out if you dare, my little J-Lo look-alike! Their other store is in Santa Monica, CA.

Penny Whistle Toys, 448 Columbus Ave., (@ 81st St.), (212) 873-9090, *Kids Gifts*

Famous for Penny Whistle Books written by the founder of these adorable toy stores. Perfect for finding a gift for the kid with everything. See other location in UES.

Really Great Things, 284 Columbus Ave. (bet. 72nd & 73rd Sts.), (212) 787-5354, *Fab Fashions*

This newly remodeled store's sleek, clean architecture mimics that of its fabulous modern fashions at fabulously high prices. Ouch! Although the prices may keep you away, the sales staff certainly won't—incredibly friendly for this type of high-end merchandise. So if pocketbook permits, you can rely on their expertise.

Ritz Fur, 107 W. 57th St. (bet. Sixth & Seventh Aves.), (212) 265-4559, *Secondhand*

When discussing "gently used furs," the Ritz is the first place to come to mind with 50 years in the business of selling new and preowned furs at affordable prices. P.S. "Gently" by definition means: in 1991, when the thrill was gone, the ever-thrifty Ivana brought her full-length lynx to Ritz, instead of hacking away with her manicuring shears.

Surroundings, 224 W. 79th St. (bet. Broadway & Amsterdam Ave.), (212) 580-8982, *Flowers*

The place to order your buds while in NYC or when sending from home to your Manhattanite buddies. Top floral designers customize orders to suit the mood of the moment; the price ranges anywhere from $55 to $500. Never gaudy, always fresh, flowers go a long way in making your mark on the mover and shaker of the day. Closed on Sunday.

West Side Wine, 481 Columbus Ave. (@ 83rd St.), (212) 874-2900, *Wine On The Go*

Purchase great wines and learn a bit of geography at this groovy shop, where the wines are organized by country. The staff is incredibly helpful and the Friday wine tastings (5–8 P.M.) are a great way to connect with other aficionados! In the smart shopper category: 15 percent off same cases and 10 percent off mixed cases . . . and they deliver.

⸙ *Not to Miss:*
Face Stockholm, 224 Columbus Ave. (@ 70th St.), (212) 769-1420, *Makeup*

Upper East Side ···

Anne Fontaine, 791 Madison Ave. (@ 67th St.), (212) 639-9651), *White Shirts*
See details in SoHo/Nolita/Chinatown/Little Italy.

A. J. Gentile Grocery, 1041 Madison Ave. (bet. 79th & 80th Sts.), (212) 879-2717, *Gourmet Foodies*

Every thing at this small European food emporium is the freshest of fresh! The take-out selection includes a wide variety of sandwiches lovingly crafted every morning, including specialties like grilled chicken salad (with light mayo) on whole wheat with fresh watercress ($6.95), a nice selection of homemade soups ($5.95), as well as fresh wraps and other prepared food. The selection of fruit in the front is out of this world. Succulent grapes, fresh cut pineapple, boxes of Clementines. European flare with big city prices!

Anya Hindmarch, 29 E. 60th St. (bet. Madison & Park Aves.), (212) 750-3974, *www.anyahindmarch.com, Perfect Handbags*

Pretty bags and wallets for those who want to stand out from the predictable Prada, Gucci and Fendi crowd. Anya houses her ultrafeminine, of-the-moment designs in her perfectly situated shop. Locations in London (including a boutique at Harrods) as well as Hong Kong. Seasonal sales are a boon for those who are lucky enough to be on the list or in the area. *Psst . . . check out the special order "envelope" wallets complete with your address and stamp on the outside!*

Best Cellars, 1291 Lexington Ave. (bet. 86th & 87th Sts.), (212) 426-4200, *Deals On Wine*

Great wine for next to nothing. Best Cellars offers the best in wine at $10 a bottle and under . . . Started by a group of aficionados with over 20 years of experience in the wine biz, they created an affordable wine store for the sensitive palate and even more sensitive budget. Feel free to stop in for a taste before you buy. Knowledgeable sales staff can match a wine to a mood or a food. M–F 10 A.M.–9 P.M.

Blakes, 88 Lexington Ave. (bet. 71st & 72nd Sts.), (212) 717-8898, *Bedroom Service*

A unique type of "room service," Blakes does not do tea and toast. They actually do rooms! This handsomely appointed store is a front for their true talent—redoing your boudoir to make it a more beautiful, comfortable, and livable space. The 200-dollar design fee is then applied to purchases made in the store. Tasteful and subdued, for the most discriminating.

Big City Kite Company, 1210 Lexington Ave. (@ 82nd St.), (212) 472-2623, *www.bigcitykite.com, Play Date*

"Let's go fly a kite!" Okay, Mary Poppins—here's your chance. Selling nothing but kites since 1963, they really know how to string a girl along!

Psst . . . Plan an afternoon in Central Park: Enter on Fifth Ave. @ 81st St., grab a gourmet picnic from E.A.T (See Eats), including delicious salmon sandwiches and bottled limonade from France . . . Closed on Sundays.

Bra Smythe, 905 Madison Ave. (bet. 72nd & 73rd Sts), (212) 352-0856, *Perfect Bra*

Stocking over 3,000 bras and featuring the best selection of bathing suits year-round (just in case you get whisked off to St. Barts in November). We love the staff of trained fitters and full-time seamstresses on hand to make sure you get the perfect fit while you wait. Don't miss the excellent selection of panties and sleepwear too. European and American lines. Check in periodically for the round stands in the middle of the floor that are often considerably marked down.

Christian Labourdin, Madison Ave. (bet. 76th & 77th Sts.), (212) 249-2083, *Museum-Worthy Shoes*

Is it a shoe store or an annex to the Whitney Museum next door? Since it's situated in the old Museum shop, it's no wonder we were confused! But, finally the much-anticipated arrival of this French shoe devil is a reality. You could slip into mules made from Charvet while gazing at the exotica in custom-made curio cabinets throughout the store. We find it impossible to choose just one. Not for the faint of pocketbook!

Chuckies, 1073 Third Ave. (bet. 63th & 64th Sts.), (212) 593-9898, *Trendy Shoes*

This small boutique features shoe finds that are ultra fashion forward. Think downtown style and prices and with decidedly uptown girl looks. The cool selection of Dolce & Gabbana, Versace, YSL, and many more you won't find anywhere else. See other location in SoHo.

Cosa Bella, 7 E. 81st St. (@ Fifth Ave.), (212) 283-7564, *One-Of-A-Kind Fashions*

Beautiful clothes made in this small house of style are designed by Shannon McLean, who has a loyal following of girls in search of classic-cut dresses, coats and suits with an Italian flair (think Audrey Hepburn). Seasonal collections can be previewed and purchased. By appointment only, 10–6 M–F, unless you're in the Hamptons, where they have a South Hampton retail outfit (516-283-7564). *Psst . . . drift over to the Metropolitan Museum after your shopping spree and enjoy a coffee in the downstairs lobby bar.*

David Yurman, 729 Madison Ave. (@ 64th St.), (212) 752-4255, *Fashionable Jewelry*

Now that the Bushes occupy the White House, all things Texan are en vogue these days. Yurman is all the rage in the Big Apple, but he's nothing new to the most fashionable women in Texas, who have been ahead of the times for years. From starlets to matrons, there is something special awaiting you at this jewelry emporium. Maybe you saw Jennifer Aniston sporting the newest pieces on the cover of a recent magazine? Prices range from $575 for a modest ring to $15,000 for more flashy pieces.

DKNY, 655 Madison Ave. (@ 60th St.), (212) 223-DKNY, *Neighborhood Favorite*

The newish DKNY store brims with high-energy chic and modern spirit—17,000 square feet of "buzz" and great American fashion. For the style-conscious but also the culturally curious: artisan curios and one-of-a-kind antique exhibits fill the ground floor and are for sale. Apple computers and CD-listening stations are on hand. Clothing is "zoned" by lifestyle to help with those last-minute purchases (you need to find a cocktail dress in five minutes)! Donna has outdone herself. *Psst . . . while you hover over the unique CD-listening station, let the private shopping department do your wardrobe legwork!*

E.A.T. Gifts, 1062 Madison Ave. (bet. 80th & 81st Sts.), (212) 861-2544, *Children's Gifts*

Fantasy land for little ones (and not so little). If you are looking for a special gift for your child, niece, best friend's child, or just a little something for your coworker's birthday, you can find it here. How about an adorable miniature tea set for Suzy and a batch of magic tricks for Johnny, and a set of plastic poolware glasses for your sister? We love the recent collection of Eloise (of the Plaza Hotel fame) items. Don't be surprised if the gift wrapping is almost as fun as what's inside. *Psst . . . if you are really in the kiddie spirit, stop into E.A.T. (see Eats, UES), by the same owner, for a PB&J and Stewart's Root Beer to go.*

Edith Weber & Associates, 944 Madison Ave. (bet. 77th & 78th Sts.), (212) 570-9668, *Antique Jewelry*

The most glorious antique jewelry in Manhattan is waiting behind the little door, but don't even bother if price is an issue. Brutal, but true: This is why the salespeople won't speak to you at Dolce & Gabbana (down the block). If you need help, other than a maid to carry your shopping bags, you shouldn't darken the door. But we digress. If you need a tiara from the 1800s or perhaps a heart-shaped diamond set in platinum from the thirties, Edith can fulfill your every fantasy. Just remember, fantasy will cost you.

Emilio Pucci, 24 E. 64th St. (bet. Fifth & Madison Aves.), (212) 752-4777, *Power Prints*

He's baaaack! After dipping out of the limelight for a decade or so, Pucci is hot hot hot all over again. nothing new to worldly fashionistas who clued in the first time circa 1970. Emilio, an Italian aristocrat-cum-designer, created many vivid geometric prints gracing the closets of fashionable women for years. Scarves and dresses are a must for every "It" girl of the nouveau Mod Squad! Closed on Sundays.

Encore Designer Consignment 1132 Madison Ave. (@ 84th St.), 2nd floor, (212) 879-2850, *Next To New*

Would you dare buy a Versace dress from last year's collection for $175? We betcha! A real secret find with pieces from all of the Madison Ave. social sets, this store was started in 1954 with a policy of not accepting clothes over two years old; however, some exceptions are made for great design. Chanel suits for $500, Armani sweaters for $100, and Escada zebra boots for $175.

Equipment, 872 Madison Ave. (@ 71st St.), (212) 249-2083, *Chic Fashions*

Not just shirts anymore. Enter off of Madison Ave. into the ultimate sportswear collection with neverending French allure. The tone of the line is set by fashionable Manhattanite Siobhan Callahan, who always pushes the envelope with her combination of fashion-forward clothes and a dose of vintage whimsy. She makes it look easy, and the staff will make you look utterly chic, mod, and tasteful as well!

Fresh, 820 Madison Ave. (bet. 80th & 81st Sts.), (800) 977-7736, *Bath And More*

Milk never quite smelled like this before. This sleek urban fragrance and bath product jungle will leave your senses reeling and your pocketbook screaming. It's very "in," according to international press coverage in *People* and *Wallpaper* magazines. Need we say more? Might as well prepare yourself to take the botanic bath. *Psst . . . if you have blown your budget on "lotions" and still need something new to wear for your business trip,*

drift around the neighborhood. It is filled with high-end designer consignment and thrift shops.

Gracious Home, 1220 Third Ave. (bet. 70th & 71st Sts.), (212) 517-6300, *www.gracioushome.com, Home Furnishings*,
    See entry in UWS.

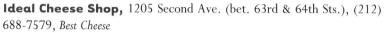

Ideal Cheese Shop, 1205 Second Ave. (bet. 63rd & 64th Sts.), (212) 688-7579, *Best Cheese*
    "It tastes better with cheese," says the ad, and certainly they were tasting from this selection. With 45 years under their belt, these folks know their "mold." If a cheese exists on earth, they have it . . . But don't offend the Cheese Gods by asking for "low-fat" anything. We make an annual pilgrimage each fall for their "to die for" truffle cheese!

Il Bisonte, 22 E. 65th St. (bet. Fifth & Madison Aves.), (212) 717-4771, *Timeless Leather*
    Longtime favorite of the "I want a sturdy Italian bag that will get better with time" crowd. Based out of Florence, Italy, this teeny-tiny outpost has a nice selection of bags, belts, totes, wallets, journals, and luggage. Sturdy and stylish graduation gift for your niece who is traveling Europe for the summer.

Il Papiro, 1021 Lexington Ave. (bet. 72nd & 73rd Sts.), (212) 288-9330, *Writing Papers*
    This extremely fine Italian stationery store carries hand-marbleized writing paper from Florence. Other gift items too tempting to ignore: leather-bound photo albums and small table frames. Engraving would be overkill, so don't even ask. If you are planning a trip to Italy, you lucky girl, visit their five locations in Florence and Venice.

Jaded, 1048 Madison Ave. (@ 80th St.), (212) 288-6631, *Custom Semi-precious*
    Custom-made, one-of-a-kind jewelry for the belle of the ball in search of unique adornment. (And what woman doesn't want to be adored and adorned?) Two full-time designers are ready to help create and modify the perfect addition to that little black dress. Exclusive U.S. representation of Roman designer Diego. The prices are reasonable and you are sure to find a unique piece. *Psst . . . Michael's Resale Shop, (1041 Madison Ave. bet. 79th & 80th Sts., 212-737-7273) across the street has that designer little black dress on*

consignment from the closets of many UES ladies-who-lunch. Get the dress for next to nothing, blow the rest at Jaded!

Joseph, 796 Madison Ave. (bet. 67th & 68th Sts.), (212) 327-1773, *Best Pants*

Should be called the Pants Pantry. Pants, pants and more pants from this London-based designer. The fit is excellent *if* you can fit in them at all—better skip dessert . . . for a year. Second location downtown in SoHo (115 Greene Street) has men's styles as well. Stop by after you have gone to Lotte Berk (see Treats) to show off that stretched and streamlined torso.

Julius Lowy Frame & Restoring Co., 223 E. 80th St. (bet. First & Second Aves.), (212) 861-8585, *You're Framed*

The *crème de la* in antique frames and reproductions. If money is no concern, name your request, they can make your wish come true. The staff is well versed in all styles of art and qualified to help you choose the perfect mat and frame to suit your painting. They also offer the conservation of oil paintings and restoration of furniture and antique frames. Known in art circles as *the* definitive place.

Kate's Paperie, 1282 Third Ave. (bet. 73rd & 74th Sts.), (212) 396-3670, *Paper Goods Plus*

See details in GV, other location in SoHo.

Kitchen Arts & Letters, 1435 Lexington Ave. (bet. 93rd & 94th Sts.), (212) 876-5550, *Alternative Books*

Calling all bookworm foodies. The mecca for cooks who read, write and stalk Martha Stewart over the Internet, this bookstore and gallery devoted exclusively to food and wine—where else could you pick up a gastronomic memoir and eggplant-shaped note cards in one pit stop? The gallery part of the store features antique food labels, restaurant postcards, crate labels, early food packaging, and other tasty memorabilia.

Laterrine, 1024 Lexington Ave. (@ 73rd St.), (212) 988-3366, *Pottery*

If you don't have time to visit Lisbon to restock your china cabinet, visit Laterrine for the latest in gorgeous Portuguese and French pottery and earthenware. The shop is cluttered with gorgeous things (our kind of place!). Mugs, platter, bowls, and complete dinner services by special order. No one will know you got it Stateside!

Lingerie On Lex, 831 Lexington Ave. (bet. 63rd & 64th Sts.), (212) 755-3312, *Neighborhood Favorite*

Smashing collection of Euro lingerie—like La Perla, Cosabella (those fabo thongs), Les Charmel. Difficult bra sizes are a specialty. We found the cutest Day-Glo bikinis and St. Tropez sarongs hiding out in the back! Oh, and a little Italian lace nightie, four sexy bras, a bustier, 14 thongs, some slippers, lingerie soap, and a new boyfriend! *Psst . . . Brooke, Mariah, and Cameron have been bra-spotted . . .*

Liz Lange, 958 Madison Ave. (bet. 75th & 76th Sts.), (212)879-2191, *Mom-To-Be-Fashions.*

Expecting mom-to-be like Elle McPherson, Elizabeth Shue, and Paulina flock here for glam gear to cover tummies at all stages. Lange, a former *Vogue* editor, has a collection of clean and modern styles without all of the "cutesyness" associated with maternity clothes. Pretend in these cool "notso obvious" duds that you're still a virgin . . . just don't take it too far and smoke.

Lobel's Prime Meats, 1096 Madison Ave. (bet 82nd & 83rd Sts.), (212) 737-1371, (800) 556-2357 for dry-ice orders, *Top Butcher*

The Pope orders from here. Need we say more? Earth Angels order holiday turkeys or exotic meats (stuffed pheasant to die for!) from these fifth-generation butchers. Prepare to feel your mouth water! If you are preparing to play Julia Child for your new beau or family, this should be the first stop on your ingredient list.

Marina Rinaldi, 800 Madison Ave. (bet 67th & 68th Sts.), (212) 734-4333, *Plus-Sized Design*

Delicious designs for the "curvaceously blessed" or those who prefer pizza and petit fours to Pilates and Perrier. Italian manufactured with sumptuous fabrics and flattering cuts, and tailoring is available on site for those last-minute nips. All for the Rinaldi label with collections that include dresses, suits, blouses, sweaters, and outerwear. Sizes 10–22. Open till 7 P.M. on Thursday nights and closed on Sunday.

Martine's Chocolate at Bloomingdale's, 1000 Third Ave. (@ 59th St.), (212) 355-5900, *Chocolates*

All roads for NYC gals still lead to Bloomingdale's. And for good reason—the chocolate on the sixth floor. Made on premises, Martine's transcends chocolate as we know it. Indulge in their self-described "dessert." As it glides across your tongue, envision the butter form Charent. Experience raspberries from the Alps. Embrace the Bostonian chocolate. But don't wait too long—shelf life is about as long as that bad boy you picked up last night!

Penny Whistle Toys @ 1283 Madison Ave. (@ 91st St.), (212) 369-3868, *Kids Gifts*

See entry in UWS.

Rita Ford Music Boxes,19 E. 65th St. (bet. Fifth and Madison Aves.), (212) 535-6717, *Unique Gifts*

If my mom had known Rita, I might not have a jerky version of *Coppelia* as the sound track to many of my adult nightmares. Music box fantasy land, complete with accessories. (Why would you need a music box accessory? If you have to ask . . .) Best of all, you can *customize* your box—you want Bocelli, you want *Carmen,* you want Iron Maiden? Well you can't have Iron Maiden, it's a music box, not a CD player. Great for gifts for the person with everything.

Roberta's Lingerie, 1252 Madison Ave. (@ 90th St.), (212) 860-8366, *Luxury Lingerie*

The ultimate in European lingerie. You won't actually blink at the 400-dollar black lace teddy, you will fall under its spell! Exceptional personalized service will get you in and out before you can say "thong." Wear a hard-to-find panty that you love? Most likely they'll have it or know how to get it. Indulge!

Sherry-Lehmann, 679 Madison Ave. (@ 61st St.), (212) 838-7500, *Old-World Wines*

This Old World wine shop has been family-run since Prohibition ended and offers international service to a global clientele. Limited space requires the use of paper and pen to jot down your selections which then are retrieved from "below" and sent on their way inside glorious Toulouse Lautrec–designed paper bags. (If you don't drink, go for the sacks!) Never hesitate to ask for help and if you don't see a particular vintage, consult the "big book" on the counter as not all are visible to the shopping eye! *Psst . . . gracious selection of kosher wines.*

Slane & Slane, 30 E. 74th St. (bet. Madison & Park Aves.), (212) 452-0850, *Custom Jewelry*

Sisters Landon and Heath are the designers of this hotbed of juicy jewels. Set in the parlor of a century-old brownstone, the kilim-covered chairs in front of the fireplace are so comfy you may want to move in! It's the perfect environment to linger over South Sea pearls and clusters of gems set in Baroque-style 18-karat gold. You may notice them on the likes of Gwyneth and Winona! *Psst . . . our glamorous friend Hope's door-knocker silver and blue topaz ring looks great with just about everything—and sometimes nothing!*

Trouvalle Française, 552 E. 87th St., 3rd floor, (@ York Ave.), (212) 737-6015, *Exclusive Linens*

By appointment only—that's the first thing you need to know before you get too excited. Muriel Clark's shop is located in a classic New York town house that feels more like a home. Count on delicious 100 percent linen sheets and tablecloths that are covered with beautiful handwork. Don't be surprised if you cross paths with a stylist from *Martha Stewart Living. Psst . . . she has some lovely clothing too.*

Urus Books, 981 Madison Ave. (bet. 75th & 76th Sts.), (212) 772-8787, *www.urus.com, Antique Books*

"The story behind every great book seems to be that it's been stolen or lost at war." Hidden above the Carlisle Hotel, this is nirvana for the rare-book lover. Specialty: art books. Find literary jaw droppers like a nineteenth-century sailing manual or perhaps an eighteenth-century best-seller by Louis XVI's groundskeeper—"Let them eat cake!"

White On White, 888 Lexington Ave. (@ 66th St.), (212) 288-9218, *White House*

This place may have a few home furnishings that are not white, but not very many. Housing some of the city's prettiest things, painted furniture, custom linens, ceramics, antique china cabinets, and much more for you to drool over. We dare you to leave without something pretty for your home or apartment. Gift registry available. *Psst . . . be sure to venture downstairs for a double whammy of beautiful objects of desire!*

Zitomer, 969 Madison Ave. (bet. 75th & 76th Sts.), (212) 737-5560, *Mini Department*

Stocked with every single beauty, bath and health product ever made, but don't count on too friendly service. Downstairs you will find hair accessories, cosmetics, vitamins, hairbrushes, faux jewels, handbags, hats, candles, and anything else your heart and mind desire. Venture upstairs for great undergarments from designers like Only Hearts, Moschino, and more. Don't miss the great travel accessories too. If you can weed through the goodie jungle, you might make it to the back where your Prozac prescription awaits. *Psst . . . in-house charge account and delivery available.*

⚘ *Not to Miss:*

Chloe, 850 Madison Ave. (@ 70th St.), (212) 717-8220, *Designer Comback*

Clyde's Chemist, 934 Madison Ave. (bet. 73rd & 74th Sts.), (212) 988-8508, *Drugstore, Not*

Crate and Barrel, 350 Madison Ave. (@ 60th St.), (212) 308-0004, *Setting Up Home*

Diesel, 770 Lexington Ave. (@ 60th St.), (212) 308-0055, Trendy Italian Clothes

Janine Dray, 1021 Madison Ave. (bet. 76th & 77th Sts.), (212) 771-8239, *wwwjaninedray.com, Custom Designs*

Linda Dresner, 484 Park Ave. (@ 58th St.), (212) 308-3177, *No Hassle Designer Frocks*

Nicole Farhi, 10 E. 69th St. (bet. Fifth & Madison Aves.), (212) 223-8811, *Neighborhood Newcomer*

Vera Wang, 991 Madison Ave. (@ 77th St.), (212) 628-3400, *Wedding Destination*

Midtown West ···

Alberene Cashmere, 435 Fifth Ave., (bet. 38th & 39th Sts.), (212) 689-0151, *Cashmere Find*

Affordable cashmere sounds like an oxymoron but it's true. No girl's wardrobe is complete without a few smart pieces. How about a black crew neck (about $199) or a heather gray cape? It all comes from Scotland in an abundance of colors and styles. Great gifts such as scarves and socks for your hard-to-please mother-in-law!

Carnegie Spirits, 849 Seventh Ave. (bet. 54th & 55th Sts.), (212) 977-3039, *Wine & Spirits*

A refuge amid the chaos of Times Square. Once you step in and hear the classical music you will be relaxed and able to choose from their selection of chilled wine, including half-splits of champagne and kosher wines.

Daily Blossom, 787 Seventh Ave. (bet. 51st & 52nd Sts.), (212) 554-4600, *Fine Flowers*

If you want to wow someone with your good taste, then you have found your "blooming" match in the talented Simone. Every arrangement is unique and made from only the finest fresh flowers that money can buy. They deliver anywhere in the city for a 10-dollar fee. *Psst . . . if you are stopping by the actual store and not ordering by phone, they're to the left of the main door of The Equitable Center.*

Fellissimo, 10 W. 56th St. (bet. Fifth & Sixth Aves.), (212) 247-5656, *Gift Emporium*

Searching for "it"? You'll probably find that unexpected treasure for friend, spouse or self at this elegant four-story town house, home to an exclusive specialty store. Browse among the best of the best in home accessories, eclectic clothing, and gifts as you feel transported to an exotic locale by your luxurious surroundings—complete with spiral staircase leading to the most intimate of tearooms. In fact many come solely for tea and resident psychic, but who can pass up that delish pashmina calling your name!

Gotham Book Mart, 41 W. 47th St. (bet. Fifth & Sixth Aves.), (212) 719-4448, *Literary Haunt*

Started over 80 years ago by a woman named Frances, the store set out to prove that the literary will inherit the earth, or at least outlive the average TV junkie. Frances died at the ripe age of 101 and left this huge selection of new and used books as her legacy. Latch on to a liberal bookwormy clerk for guidance and perhaps dinner at 8:00.

Grande Harvest Wines, Grande Central Terminal (Graybar Passage/Lexington Ave. side), (212) 682-5855, *Wine On The Go*

Fine wine, anyone? This antique-laden wine store is the perfect place to pick up something fast. But no wino could afford their price point. They are "very selective with a highly defined focus." Plan to find many of your favorites from California, France and Italy along with some newcomers worthy of an evolved palate but not cost-prohibitive for the budget-conscious!

Jazz Record Center, 236 W. 26th St., 8th floor, (bet. Seventh & Eighth Aves.), (212) 675-4480, *Vintage Vinyl*

All the "cats" hang here, so you jazzy gals be on the lookout. Find 50,000 titles, mostly LPs, as well as 350 videos and books at this ultimate shrine to this genre. Rarities such as the first commercially produced LP from Charlie Parker ($10,000) abound.

Mason's Tennis Mart, 911 Seventh Ave. (@ 57th St.), (212) 757-5374, *Love Tennis*

Whether you're U.S. open material or just like the look of white shorts on your tan legs, Mark Mason and crew have the goods. The enthusiastic staff of tennis junkies can help match your style and strength to the perfect Prince, Head, or Yonex. And if Miss Fancy Pants wants an exotic racket, they can special order.

Michelle Roth, 24 W. 55th St. (bet. Fifth & Sixth Aves.), (212) 245-3390, *Wedding Gowns*

Australian owners Michelle and Henry, a brother/sister team, greet you at the door of this lovely studio for a perfect prenup experience. Home to some of the most "royal" wedding gowns: lines such as Elizabeth Emanuel (creator of Princess Diana's taffeta train), although these days she is designing Galliano-like sleek glamour in lieu of the puffy sleeves that Di brought into chic. *Psst . . . don't miss the sample sales that happen here every January and August.*

Museum Of Modern Art Design Store & Bookstore, 11 W. 53rd St. (bet. Fifth & Sixth Aves.), (212) 708-9700, *Special Gifts*

What gift can you buy for your friend's going-away party? What about your boss's birthday? Oh, it's your parents' twentieth anniversary tomorrow. Artsy girls make this a destination even if there is no time to linger over the Miros across the street. With a huge renovation in late '99 (we thought they were great before) this marvelous museum store is chock-full of well-designed and useful products for gifts of all seasons. Don't miss the Finnish garden tools by Fiskar that are a must for the pruning princesses in your life! Discounts are offered to MoMA members.

Ray Beauty Supply, 721 Eighth Ave. (bet. 45th & 46th Sts.), (212) 757-0175, *Beauty Supplies*

Ray carries 150 different shampoos and conditioners, professional curling irons and flat irons (baby Saffires), shaving products, hair sprays, and most definitely the best selection of handheld hair dryers. Closed on Sunday. Call ahead if you are looking for something specific that may need to be special ordered. Closed on Sunday.

Remains, 19 W. 24th St., 2nd Floor (bet. Fifth & Sixth Aves.), (212) 675-8051, *Unique Lighting*

This little boutique lighting gallery is a resource for many of the top interior designers. If you're looking for something ordinary, don't look here. If you need something special or spectacular, come on in!

Rizzoli, 454 W. 57th St. (bet. Fifth & Sixth Aves.), (212) 759-2424, *Elegant Bookstore*

Italian booksellers doing what they do best—selling style in a stylish setting. Interiors of both NYC stores are worth documentation in their own right. Among the most extensive, comprehensive collection in the city, some whimsical and fun little books as well as perfect gifts for your office mate. Known to feature top writers in reading series throughout the year as well as high-profile signings. See other location, SoHo.

Sam Ash, 160 W. 48th St. (bet. Sixth and Seventh Aves.), (212) 719-2299, *Musical Instruments*

The most extensive discount music store in the world—instruments, DJ equipment, computer hardware and software. Basically, if it makes a sound, it can be found here and shipped worldwide. Staff is friendly and blessedly well informed. We spent hours over the harmonica section alone. However, never underestimate the beauty of your man's air guitar. . . .

Tagger, 66 W. 47th St. (@ Sixth Ave.), (212) 730-2225, *Discount Jewelry*

Little "gem" of a jewelry kiosk in the heart of the diamond district. Owners Dorite and Sholomo will help you find your heart's desire—diamonds, pearls, gold, and more. And if they don't have what you want, they will get it or make it for you. Repairs done with expert care, replacement copies are no problem when that stud goes down the drain. Prices are excellent for the quality of workmanship. Closed on Sundays. *Psst . . . if this is your first visit to this district, don't get sidetracked—head straight for these trusted folks.*

The McGraw Hill Bookstore, 1221 Sixth Ave. (@ 49th St.), (212) 512-4100, *Intellectual Pursuits*

If you like brainy types, venture down the stairs in front of the huge McGraw-Hill building. Reference books for the high-minded individual: philosophy, economics, cyberspace, religion, psychology. Sorry, even Dante is considered lowbrow for these folks! A little fiction and a selective group of travel books are on hand for the intellectual in search of "deeper meaning." *Psst . . . they happily special order items not in stock! Not as quick as Amazon but a bit more personal.*

Toga Bike Shop, 110 West End Ave. (@ 54th St.), (212) 799-9625, *Bicycles*

Honestly we don't even own a bike, but this place is groovy. Incredible 70 percent discounts on top-end European lines for the serious cyclist. They specialize in boxing your bike for the air—air travel, that is—and who doesn't want to bike on her own cycle in Bora Bora? Now if we just had a ticket . . .

♦ *Not to Miss:*

Crane & Co, *Fine Writing Paper,* 59 W. 49th St. (@ Rockefeller Center), (212)582-6829

Harry Winston, 718 Fifth Ave. (bet. 54th & 55th Sts.), (212) 245-2000, *Diamonds Abound*

McCreedy & Schreiber, 37 W. 46th St., (bet. Fifth & Sixth Aves.) (212) 719-1552, *Cowgirls*

The New York Look, 570 Seventh Ave. (@ 41st St.), (212) 382-2720, *Little Black Dress*

Variazioni, 37 W. 57th St. (bet. Fifth & Sixth Aves.), (212) 980-4900, *Trendy Looks, look for 7 other locations throughout the city.*

Midtown East

Amish Food Market, 240 E. 45th St. (bet. Second & Third Aves.), (212) 370-1761, *Food Shop*

Cheese, cheese, and more cheese—180 varieties to be exact. Olive oils, vinegars, breads are just some of the delicacies at this full-service food shop. Step back in time to this truly Amish enlave. Adorable and well-stocked. No flirting with the boy behind the counter, it may be against his religion!

Bridge Kitchenware, 214 E. 52nd St. (bet. Second & Third Aves.), (212) 688-4220, *Cooking Utensils*

Looking for a heart-shaped grill for your sweetie on Valentine's? If anyone has it, these people do. Wander the aisles with New York's best chefs and most serious amateurs. So before you put the little pot in the big pot one more time, treat yourself to a real double-boiler at Bridge. The finest of European cookware, utensils and accessories under one roof.

Cosmetic Show, 919 Third Ave. (@ 56th St.), (212) 750-8418, *Discount Cosmetics*

This little find is hard to find, with no signs or product-stocked windows to show you the way. Look for a black-glass office building but don't go there—turn left, go in the double doors, and look for a small sign that says "Cosmetics, Fragrances." Inside you will find many prestigious lines at shockingly low prices. Erno Lazlo, Lancôme, Elizabeth Arden. They don't have everything, but it is worth a sweep if you are up for the hunt and feeling lucky! And if your new Lazlo Hydra Therapy soap you bought for a mere $2.50 is not enough of a bonanza . . . that price includes the tax!

Dallek, 269 Madison Ave. (@ 40th St.), (212) 684-4848, *Office Furniture*

"We make offices work," is the motto of this exclusive office furniture center. Sleek and modern, offering pieces for the smallest cubes to the largest conference rooms. Seasonal sales offer great bargains.

Jimmy Choo, 645 Fifth Ave. (@ 51st.), (212) 593-0800, *Designer Shoes*

Who but this Brit to arrive Stateside and give Manolo Blahnik a run for his money in the world of outrageously sexy footwear. Sapphire-crystaled sandals on spikes with ankle-wrapping straps for miles. Jennifer Lopez and Mariah Carey fight it out in the aisle for the latest in Choos! Guess what? They're relatively pricey $$$$. *Psst . . . brides-to-be: don't miss the selection of exquisite bridal shoes so expensive you can't afford to get "cold feet"!*

Kavanagh's Designer Resale Shop, 146 E. 69th St. (bet. Lexington & Third Aves.), (212) 702-0152, *Designer Secondhand*

Preowned clothes for those who want a Chanel suit for a fraction of retail, about $900. Mary Kavanagh was once director of personal shopping at Bergdorf Goodman (see MTE). High end and high style are the ticket here. You will find labels like Tod's, Prada, Hermès, and Gucci to tickle your fancy and delight your husband at your frugality!

Leonidas, 45 Madison Ave. (bet. 51st & 52nd Sts.), (212) 980-2608, (800) 900-2462 (to order), *Belgian Chocolate*

These heavenly Belgian chocolates are sold by a helpful staff for gifts or personal selections (oink!). We recommend milk chocolate hazelnut beauties or chocolate-covered orange peel . . . not that we've had any recently (okay, yesterday, but only a bite!) Great gift idea—bring to a friend's dinner party, buy as a houseguest present, or have them shipped cross-country for your best friend's birthday.

Librairie de France/Libreria Hispanica, 610 Fifth Ave. (in the Rockefeller Center Promenade), (212) 581-8810, *The Dictionary Store*

At a loss for words? Not anymore. Over 8,000 dictionaries covering 100 languages will make you the most articulate girl on this continent and all others! Teach yourself a new language on tape, or if you're brushing up, buy that new novel off the top of the Parisian literary charts. It's here and waiting, multilingual lit girl! Now that's a mouthful!

Pink Slip, 107 E. 42nd St. (MC-81/Lexington Passage), (212) 949-9037, *Undergarments*

This is one pink slip you won't dread! Started as a flea market kiosk two years ago, this full-fledged lingerie boutique carries mostly American brands (heavy on the CK). Great selection of bras, panties, and sexy sleepwear. Check out their new Grand Central Terminal location, created for those who forget to pack their panties for a weekend trip to the country.

Takashimaya, 693 Fifth Ave. (bet. 54th & 55th Sts.), (800) 753-2038, *Elegant Emporium*

He's Tokyo, you're Paris—this is where you meet. One of the more unique stores on Fifth Ave., Takashimaya is five floors of the best of both worlds, blending Japanese and Western sensibilities in a way that values function over aesthetic—just look at that gorgeous toilet cover! Heavenly shopping: from linens to loungewear, women's accessories to men's travel gifts. Don't miss the incredible personalized skincare lines at the back of the first floor, or ignore the florist and terrace shop that overwhelms the senses with sights and smells.

T. Anthony, 445 Park Ave. (@ 56th St.), (212) 750-9797 or (212) 750-7042, *Sophisticated Leather*

Expensive totes fit for when you have finally "made it" and want to make a big investment in legendary luggage. Since 1946, T. Anthony's sophisticated luggage has been carried by the social crème de la crème and several royals (the Duke and Duchess of Windsor). Now you too can tote in style with their elegant and timeless travel pieces. Closed on Sundays. *Psst . . . bright colors for easy spotting on the conveyer belt at Heathrow!*

The Complete Traveler, 199 Madison Ave. (@ 35th St.), (212) 685-9007, *Travel Books*

Packing for your latest adventure, don't forget to pop in this premiere travel bookstore where the most obscure destination becomes as navigable as next door. Bora Bora, anyone? Dusseldorf or Detroit, they've got you covered. Both new and used titles for sale.

The Terence Conran Shop, 409 E. 59th St. (@ First Ave.), (212) 755-9079, *Designer Home*

Strangely located below the Queensboro Bridge, Sir Terence opened his Manhattan shop in 2000 with a bang! Touted as the "champion of chic," this London-based designer has brought his populist-minded philosophy Stateside: make good taste available to Everyman. Well, at least to every monied man! This is some of the most civilized home-furnishing loot to be assembled under one roof. If you have an eye for good design, you will not leave here empty-handed. His Zeitgeist collection is a swirl of colorful, cheap plastic products that are fun and functional. Pièce de résistance? The Conran-designed furniture: huge velvet-upholstered sofas and slabs of acid-etched zinc ageless cocktail tables.

✦ *Not to Miss:*
Bergdorf Goodman, 754 Fifth Ave. (bet. 57th & 58th Sts.), (212) 753-7300, *Fashion Institution*
Fendi, 720 Fifth Ave. (@ 56th St.), (212) 767-0100, *Designer Duds*
Tiffany & Co, 727 Fifth Ave. (@ 57th St.), (212) 755-8000, *Proper Gifts*

Tourneau, 500 Madison Ave. (bet. 52nd & 53rd Sts.), (212) 758-3265, *Timepieces*

Chelsea/Meatpacking

Abracadabra, 19 W. 21st St. (bet. Fifth & Sixth Aves.), (212) 627-5194, *Make Magic*

Ever want to make your boss or your boyfriend disappear but feel the Mob is too messy? Poof! Visit this magic superstore! We must warn you that it's such a blast you can easily be sidetracked from your task at hand. Bubbles on the street entice you in to view the floor-to-ceiling stacks of gags, tricks, and gadgets to entertain and amaze. Magic shows at 3 P.M. on Sunday are perfect for the kid in all of us!

Andrea Rosen, 525 W. 24th St. (bet. Tenth & Eleventh Aves.), (212) 627-6000, *Modern Art HQ*

Contemporary art with an edge and attitude. Newly relocated to this daring little art block, this gallery and dealer will not disappoint the collector in search of something just a bit outside the box.

B & B Gallery, 601 W. 26th St., 14th Fl. (bet. Eleventh & Twelfth Aves.), (212) 243-0840, *Custom House Furnishings*

Run by two sisters, Nuala and Ann, whose résumés read like the Who's Who of cool. These fab gals do double duty as operators of their successful photographer's studio and ultrachic gallery/boutique owners. Its ever-changing inventory is a rare mix of objects from around the world: one-of-a-kind jewelry, baskets from Bali, African mud clothes, and much more. Check it out. You never know what they have "in store" for you! Open for business only on Tuesday, Wednesday, and Thursday.

Comme Des Garcons, 520 W. 22nd St. (bet. Tenth & Eleventh Aves.), (212) 219-0660, *Fashion Forward*

It took some nerve to leave their old digs in SoHo to Prada, but it was well worth the leap! The facade of the new store mimics its fashions—Japanese, avant-garde, futuristic. Proceed through the cast-aluminum tunnel door and begin the Comme Des Garcons experience. Men's fashions as well but much of the look is genderless. *Psst . . . while in the neigh-*

borhood: art galleries galore! Including the Paula Cooper Gallery (see Tripping, Chelsea / MP), another SoHo defector.

Find Outlet, 243 W. 17th St. (bet. Eighth and Ninth Aves.), (212) 243-3177, *www.findout@findoutlet.com, Discount Designer*

For the discriminating bargain shopper, Find is quite a find. No digging, groveling, group dressing, and 50–80 percent off such cutting-edge designers as Helmut Lang, Tocca, and Vivienne Westwood. Carrying all the "of-the-moment" looks, it is a haunt of fashion stylists and magazine editors. Designers love being able to unload "leftovers" without tarnishing their image at the hands of generic bargain basements. Closed on Monday. No Amex. One last tip: the staff is actually knowledgeable and helpful. See other location in Nolita.

Foliage Paradise, 120 W. 28th St., (bet. Broadway & Seventh Ave.), (212) 989-3089, *Orchids & More*

Located in the "flower district," this place is a plethora of plants for all of your green thumbs! The staff is incredibly helpful; ask one of the in-house design specialists (Carlos is king!) about helping "landscape" your new apartment or swanky new corner office. Their huge variety of orchids make great gifts. Delivery available in the city for $10—worth it if you are ordering more than one.

Jeffrey New York, 449 W. 14th St., (bet. Ninth & Tenth Aves.), (212) 206-1272, *Funky Designer Clothes*

"Barney's Goes Meatpacking" . . . This flagship store, launched by the New South's answer to a fashion Svengali, is every woman's answer to "creating a look." Jeffrey will take the affluent stylish gal by the hand and personally change her world, or at least her wardrobe. High-end and tres chic, this establishment is rumored to bring its very keen-eyes shopper into direct competition with ex-neighbor Barney. You go, Jeffrey!

Out Of Our Closet Consignment, 136 W. 18th St. (bet. Sixth & Seventh Aves.), (212) 633-6965, *Secondhand*

A swanky, much-written-about, top-end consignment store frequented and endowed by models and Europeans. Many of the items for sale are direct from the designer showrooms so you can always find something special. If you eyed last season's Dolce & Gabbana coat, this would be the place to hunt. Hermès bags, Gucci suits, Chloé sunglasses . . . Do we have you running from your closet to theirs yet? *Psst . . . head across the street to the sister store that has even more "chic" fashions like Chanel gowns or a Prada suit for one-fourth of what the cost was last season on Fifth Ave.*

Portico Outlet, 233 Tenth Ave. (@ 24th St.), (212) 807-8807, *Deal For You*

Fab furniture fiesta! Located a tad out of your way but well worth the detour—this outlet carries high-end designer items that have been discontinued or discounted at the main store (see SoHo). That does not mean that you won't find exactly what you're looking for, you just have to look harder! Offering great furniture, linens and bath accessories for at least 20–50 percent off retail. *Psst . . . found the perfect headboard for your new apartment? Make an offer they can't refuse! (They will negotiate.)*

Powers Court Tennis Outlet, 132 ¹/₂ W. 24th St. (bet. Sixth & Seventh Aves.), (212) 691-3388, *Discount Tennis Gear*

Tennis merchandise at a big savings that could be the best you will find in the city. Brand names for shockingly low prices. Clothing, racquets, footwear, and more. Closed on Sunday.

Wolfgang Thom @ Decor Floral, 227 W. 29th St. (bet. Seventh & Eighth Aves.) (212) 279-9066, *Designer Florist*

Painter turned floral designer Wolfgang turns the simple into the romantic with his beautiful minimalist arrangements. He is also known for bold sweeping statements using wondrous mixtures of blossoms, branches, and seasonal berries or leaves. Drop his number in monsieur's coat pocket (with your address at the bottom!).

Flatiron/Gramercy/Union Square

Anthropologie, 85 Fifth Ave. (@ 16th St.), (212) 627-5885 or (800) 309-2500, *www.anthropologie.com, Emporium*

Dear See Jane Go, How can I avoid spending a fortune to get my new apartment and old wardrobe up to speed before I am discovered and made famous by a stranger on the subway? A little bit of everything fun and functional (Remember Urban Outfitters? Same people, chicer material)—cool candlesticks, soap, necklaces, drawstring pants. Catalog available. See other location in SoHo.

Beckinstein, 2 W. 20th St. (bet. Fifth & Sixth Aves.), (212) 366-5142, *Redecorating*

Calling all Suzy Homemakers! If the urge to nest is in your blood or if you just need the fabric for some new pillows to give your old couch new life, they have you "covered"! An unassuming storefront, but they do offer some of the best fabrics and services for your home. Whether you are looking for custom window shades, bedspreads, slipcovers, or just the fabric to do it yourself. Open seven days a week and until 8:00 P.M. on Thursday for those who require night shopping.

Belle Fleur, 11 E. 22nd St. (@ Broadway), (212) 254-8703, *Custom Flowers*

Not just your ordinary flower shop, this is a "floral studio," a girly-girl's dream. Owner Meredith Waga Perez gets her peonies, lilacs, roses and hydrangeas flown in from Europe. Known for her personal touch using unusual vases, tailoring the arrangment to your target, and the best bonus—hand-calligraphied cards. The envelopes bear her signature sticker, a tiny pressed flower. Isn't it great to stop and smell the roses?

City Opera Thrift Shop, 222 E. 23rd St. (bet. Second & Third Aves.), (212) 684-5344, *Thrift Bonanza*

The highest-quality vintage fashions, especially for the "thrifty girl" in you. YSL and Ungaro often under $75. What more could a girl wish for? If it is good enough for the editors of *Vogue,* who frequent the shop, then it will most likely hold up to your standards too. Happy hunting for the sake of Carmine!

Kenneth Cole, 95 Fifth Ave. (@ 17th St.), (212) 675-2550, *Bridemaids Shoes*

If you don't know about Kenneth Cole from their cutting-edge advertisements then you must be living under a rock! The real find are the *peau de soie* bridal shoes, seen on the trendiest of city girl bridesmaids. Great shoes, up-to-the-minute styles in basic colors for a price that won't drain your monthly budget.

La Petite Coquote, 51 University Pl. (bet. Ninth & Tenth Sts.), (212) 473-2478, *Exclusive Lingerie*

Attitude aside, this is one of the best places downtown to shop for your girly-girl undergarments. The store is packed with some of the best-known lines like La Perla and Cosabella as well as some lesser-known but no less exceptional lines. *Psst . . . great place to send your man if he is looking for your Valentine's Day present. Just hope he doesn't get too side-tracked when he sees Christi Turlington poring over the bras!*

Otto Tootsi Plohound, 137 Fifth Ave. (bet. 20th & 21st Sts.), (212) 460-8650, *Trendy Shoes*

Slaves to fashion? Great-looking shoes on the edge edge edge. Most shoes come from England, France or Italy. And no, Tootsi Plohound does not stand for "uncomfortable shoes made in Europe" although beauty is pain and pain is beauty. Also well-done copies of the latest Prada and Gucci at great prices—comparatively speaking, of course. Other location, MTE.

Ten Thousand Things, 137 W. 19th St. (bet. Sixth & Seventh Aves.), (212) 352-1333, *Be-Jeweled*

Bypass Barney's and Bergdorf Goodman to find these goodies directly at the one true source. (Though they do have different creations at all locations.) A tranquil brick-pathed studio—mucho gallery vibe. This gem is co-owned and designed by David Rees and Ron Anderson. They will guide you through the collection of precious stones set on oxidized chains. You might have noticed their jewels sexily draping the necks of Julia Roberts or Susan Sarandon.

Greenwich Village

Balducci's, 424 Sixth Ave. (@ 9th St.), (212) 673-2600, *Fine Food Shop*

Quintessential gourmet grocery but prepare to mortgage the farm. Linger and browse the exotic delicacies mixed with high-end staples. The prepared foods are equally as enticing and delicious. Excellent choice for "gift baskets" and holiday shipping worldwide. See other location in UWS. *Psst . . . grab a bite on the run at the delish café across the street.*

Bond 07, 7 Bond St. (bet. Broadway & Lafayette St.), (212) 677-8487, *Neighborhood Favorite*

Selima Salaun, an optician, is the mastermind behind this beloved shop. A delightful boutique filled with a little bit of everything—antiques, cosmetics, children's clothes, assessories, shoes and more! Highlighting young, up-and-coming designers like Amy Chan. Small collections of sexy eveningwear and her exclusive line of sunglasses are enough to keep us coming back.

C.O. Bigelow Chemists, 414 Sixth Ave. (bet. Eighth & Ninth Sts.), (212) 533-2700, *Beauty Emporium*

Known as the downtown place to pick up hard-to-find beauty imports. This is a chic apothecary with a history to back it up—it's 160 years old. (Mark Twain used to fill his prescriptions here.) Check out their innovative signature makeup line, Alchemy. The buzz words are homeopathy, alpha-hydroxy, tea tree, and organic. Check out their new catalog, or shop here and ship all over the world. Call 1(800) 793-5433. *Psst . . . you may spot Uma Thurman sniffing aromatherapy or buying razors for her Hawke.*

Flight 001, 96 Greenwich Ave. (@ Jane St.), (212) 691-0001, *www.flight001, Travel Gear*

Dedicated to all things you need to travel—and what you never knew you did! Named after the first flight around the world, Pan Am's Flight 001, you will have a ball just looking and dreaming of your next holiday. From the bizarre to the necessary . . . bags, guides, and many globe-trotting goodies.

Kate's Paperie, 8 W. 13th St. (bet. Fifth and Sixth Aves.), (212) 633-0570. *Paper Goods Plus*

New York treasure—it's the only place where the wrapping paper will cost you more than the gift! Fancy and sassy, besides fulfilling your every paper fantasy, they offer nifty "gal gifts" like Day-Timers, photo and specialty albums, gorgeous paper by the pound, and pens. See other locations in UES, SoHo.

Kenny Valenti Showroom, 247 W. 13th St. (bet. Broadway & Seventh Ave.), (212) 967-7147, *King of Timelessness*

With more than 100,000 designer items in his "by-appointment-only" showroom, Ken is ready to meet your needs when it comes to chic designer ware from seasons past: maybe it was the seventies maybe it was last year! Call ahead and ask for favorites like Stephen Sprouse, Geoffrey Beene, and Zandra Rhodes. You can bet you will find a fabulous top to go with the elegant Dries Van Noten skirt you found on sale last week at Loehmann's (see Chelsea, Treasures)!

Once Upon A Time, 36 E. 11th St. (@ University Pl.), (212) 472-6424, *Antique Jewelry*

When it comes to jewels, good things always come in small packages. So enter this teeny tiny (7'x11') store where consistent high quality, high product turnover, high-quality customers reign. Owners Kitty Savage and John Williams cater to the educated consumer who knows what she wants and how much she should pay, so great deals abound. Rumor has it they specialize in engagement rings. Maybe you should leave this page open at your boyfriend's house?

Rockit Scientist, 43 Carmine St. (bet. Bleecker St. & Seventh Ave.), (212) 242-0066, *Alternative Recordings*

Find offbeat music for the offbeat music snob at this left-of-center retail outfit for the open-minded. A one-man operation, owner John Kioussis tries to cover every base in Western World Hip music since 1955—whatever that means. We do know he specializes in sixties rock and soul, and has a respectable selection of reggae and jazz.

Savon, 35 Christopher St. (bet. Sixth & Seventh Aves.), (212) 463-SOAP, *Bathing Beauties*

A bath product bonanza in a closet (literally! This place is teeny!). After a delish brunch at Les Deux Gamines, trot across the street to this fragrant oasis for the bath and body. We don't know how they did it, but every new chic item for hair, skin and body (including bubble sports) is tucked within these inviting walls! Create a minispa at home for the first snowy winter's night. Prepare to exfoliate!

Strand Bookstore, 828 Broadway (@ 12th St.), (212) 473-1452, *Neighborhood Find*

Delightful chaos for the lit girl. Perhaps the most extensive (though discombobulated) collection of secondhand books in the world. No air-conditioning in the summer almost makes perusing the piles an erotic adventure to rival *Cat on a Hot Tin Roof*. You can always locate hard-to-find books on psychology like *On Love and Lust* by Theodor Reik. The basement is equally vast although our arms are always too full to venture that far.

Transfer International, 594 Broadway (@ Houston St.), (212) 941-5472, *King Of Consignment*

Allessandro is "the man" when it comes to high-end, high-fashion consignment items by designers such as Prada, Helmut Lang, Hermès, and Gucci. Don't let the nondescript exterior fool you. Head to the floor to raid overstuffed racks including luggage from time to time. No official dressing rooms but feel free to strip on the spot. No one is looking at anything but that white Prada mink-collared coat! *Psst . . . if you are "looking to unload," he will pay you cash on the spot. Some great men's stuff as well.*

Warehouse Wine & Spirits, 735 Broadway (bet. 8th & Waverly Sts.), (212) 982-7770, *Discount Spirits*

Planning a party for 500 and want to maintain your standards in fine wine? Never fear, the Warehouse is here with incredible discounts. Find some great buys on high-end wines and spirits that will make you the toast of the town. Grab a cart, you will need it.

East Village/Lower East Side ···

Altman Luggage Company, 135 Orchard St. (@ Delancey St.), (212) 254-7275, *Low Cost Luggage*

Deep discounts make the trek to Altman's well worth it! If price is a concern, the friendly staff will help outfit your travel needs within your budget. Stock is enormous although somewhat traditional, but for 30–50 percent off we don't mind being a bit plain-Jane in the suitcase department.

Cherry, 185 Orchard St. (bet. Houston & Stanton Sts.), (212) 358-7131, *Fine Vintage*

High-end hippie wear, seventies rock-'n'-roll gear and all the crazy accessories to complete your retro look. Nice selection of vintage La Rose shoes (some even gently used), like those of Joan Crawford and Marilyn Monroe that recently sold at Christie's auction house. Some odd one-of-a-kind furniture pieces show up on the floor. Cool stuff for the girl who's serious about her fun clothes.

Corinna & Foley, 108 Stanton St. (bet. Essex & Ludlow Sts.), (212) 529-2338, *City Duds*

These two highly talented Manhattan girls have made a haven for half vintage and half new clothes to create the look you want. Women of all sizes and styles will find truly great high-quality clothes. Anna Corinna is the creative vintage buyer and Dana Foley is the buyer of all new fashions. Together they make a magical team that is just what you need to feel new again, as least for Saturday night. Open 1:00–8:00 P.M.

DDC Lab, 180 Orchard St. (@ Houston St.), (212) 375-1647, *Cool Jeans Too*

We love our excursions to this little Orchard St. shop and bet you won't walk out empty-handed! We love the stark white interior and espresso bar that allows for sipping while we ponder the pros and cons of the leather slippers against the sporty loafers we have been eyeing for weeks.

Economy Foam Center, 173 E. Houston St. (@ Allen St.), (212) 473-4462, *Discount Stuffings*

Down pillows at a downright affordable price! We found just the right European square bed pillows we have been searching for high and low. If you are allergic to down, they carry pillows made from varying degrees of down and other elements such as Dacron. Now you have enough pennies left over to buy those Pratesi sheets you have been eyeing on Madison Ave.

Jutta Neumann 317 E. 9th St (bet. First & Second Aves.), (212) 982-7048, *Sole Searching*

Taking orders for custom shoes daily. If you can't face 8th St., head up to Jutta's place and handpick your style (30 to choose from), your shade (over 50) and your texture—from the sublime suede to the outrageous (and outrageously expensive) python! Be pedicured and ready to trace your foot for a fitting. It takes about three weeks to make your concoction and plan to pay around $180–245 depending on your choices. The custom handbags are to die for!

Kim's Video And Music, 6 St. Marks Pl. (8th St., bet. Second & Third Aves.), (212) 505-0311, *Offbeat Video*

Where can you get the hardest-to-find independent obscure foreign films? Here. Check out *M* by German director Fritz Lang. Then swing to the back where an incredible selection of alternative music awaits—world/ techno/Latin, etc. Pick your poison for eyes and ears.

Mark Montano, 434 E. 9th St. (@ First Ave.), (212) 505-0325, *Fun Clothes*

This tiny powder-puff pink place is packed with Mark's sexy and playful designs. Come out with a sexy lace-trimmed corset or a Mongolian fur bag sure to catch "someone's" attention when you swish your way through the velvet ropes of Lotus (see Twilight, Chesea). The best in financially feasible and fashionable fun! Don't pass up the 25-dollar tiara to complete your look!

Other Music 15 E. 4th St. (bet. Broadway & Lafayette St.), (212) 477-8150, *Neighborhood Favorite*

Fugitive clerks from our fave alt-music spot, Kim's Video on Bleecker, have ventured further into alternative music store land. Already expanded to a staff of twenty from its humble origins of three, Other Music has launched itself for those interested in the musical "outer fringes," great concert tix, and the ever-dividing sections of niche music. Devoted to anything "nontraditional," this success story leaves the mainstream to their friends at Tower Records across the street!

Resurrection, 123 E. 7th St. (bet. First Ave. & Ave. A), (212) 228-0063, *Vintage Chic*

Set in an old mortuary, this place houses exellent vintage. It's Pucci. It's Dior. It's Chanel. OK, it may be a bit tattered but it's worth the price of admission—pun intended. Frequented by Hollywood stylists and models alike, you'll definitely walk out with something to die for. Even fashion biggies like Narcisco Rodriquez and Anna Sui shop here themselves. Rock and roll T-shirts and leather to fit the most rebellious of moods. *Psst . . . look for a Resurrection annex on the mezzanine level at Henri Bendel on Fifth Ave. @ 56th St. (MTE) or check out the second location in Nolita.*

St. Marks Bookshop, 31 Third Ave. (bet. 8th & 9th Sts.), (212) 260-7853, *Intellectual Bookies*

Alternative bookshop, alternative shoppers. East Village vibe. Heavy on design and design lit. Specializing in small-press publications. Open till midnight every night. Moonlighting? You'll find plenty of research room and material here. Note: One of the city's largest Women's Studies sections. *Psst . . . finish your night of research with a chilled sake at the cool sake bar hidden above the barbeque noodle shop named Angel's Share (see Twilight).*

Tokio, 764 E. 7th St. (bet. Second & First Aves.), (212) 353-8443, *Designer Resale*

This is a dark and sexy little consignment shop for better finds than your fashionable big sister's closet! You will be so chic in you new Prada skirt that cost a fraction of what you would have paid on Madison Ave. Open seven days a week.

TG-170, 170 Ludlow St. (bet. Houston & Stanton Sts.), (212) 995-8660, *Trendoid Alert*

Get the "Lower East Side Look" from the gal who created it. Terri Gillis, a pioneer in the young cool downtown fashion scene, still embraces the new and daring. Prepare your hips for a tight squeeze into some of the more avant-garde pieces—that is, unless you're fifteen and don't have any yet! All jokes aside, get great cutting-edge fashion at *really* great prices.

Zao, 175 Orchard St. (bet. Houston & Stanton Sts.), (212) 505-0500, *Emporium*

Think of Colette in Paris mixed with a downtown gallery space and forward fashions . . . violà! The world according to Zao! Owned by Tarihi but housing more than their own wares: Barbara Bui python jackets and Yoshiki Hishinuma shirts to name two and check out the trandy Burberry. Check out the hot home accessories: Japanese-inspired plates, coffee-table books, and other cool items for the girl on the go! We are happy with our recent purchase of *The Art of Barbie* and the latest recording by Brazilian Gil Gilberto. Don't miss the outdoor garden space in the back of the store for a downtown minibreak before you hit the racks. Extra style factor: their shopping bags are enough of an inspiration to "buy"!

SoHo/Nolita/Chinatown/Little Italy

Amy Can, 247 Mulberry St. (bet Prince & Spring Sts.), (212) 966-3417, *Custom Handbags*

Fashionable Manhattanites flock here for these unique handbags by Amy Chan. You may have seen her specialty look, the detailed mosaic tile bag ($150–$400), around town or in *In Style* magazine—they'll definitely update last season's little black dress for one last night on the town! The beach bags are reasonably priced for custom looks. Historical trivia: the shop itself is located on the site of John Gotti's old social club.

Anne Fontaine, 93 Greene St. (bet. Prince & Spring Sts.), (212) 343-3154, *White Shirts*

Okay, gals, let's sing along . . . "Where oh where is my perfect white shirt . . . Oh where oh where can she be?" Here. Made in France. Cotton from Switzerland. Lycra from Des Moines (just kidding!). Poplin, pique, stretch, twist, iron, no-iron, organdy, tie at the waist, tuck in, leave out. White shirts are popping up all over and we love that such a fashion staple remains popular. See other location in UES. *Psst . . . with each purchase, discover a rose sachet tucked into your shirt.*

Anthropologie, 375 W. Broadway, (bet. Spring & Broome Sts.), (212) 343-7070, *www.anthropologie.com, Emporium*

See details in Flatiron/Gramercy/US.

The Apartment, 101 Crosby St. (bet. Prince & Spring Sts.), (212) 781-5754, *Home Furnishings Experiment*

Imagine being invited to a fabulous couple's loft and allowed to take anything home with you . . . from the Matisse to the Captain Crunch. Seriously, this one-of-a kind retail "environment" is owned by a forward-thinking design couple. You can buy anything inside this 3,000 square-foot mock-abode, including food in the kitchen and art on the walls. How about some French toothpaste in the bathroom and a Philippe Starck toothbrush to match? On weekends, actors have been known to "inhabit" the apartment and lounge around in pjs ordering pizza and vegging out in front of the TV, just to make sure you feel at home in their apartment.

A.P.C, 131 Mercer St. (bet. Prince & Spring Sts.), (212) 966-9685, *Casual Unisex*

Parisian basics one step above the Gap and Banana Republic (our Stateside faves). Ideal for upscale basics that won't be out of style after one season. They also have a killer mail-order business, so if you'd rather shop between 1:00 and 4:00 in the morning (you night owl), this is phone fantasy fulfillment! *Psst . . . check out the groovy gifts for him or her in the back of the lofty plank-floored shop.*

Area . . . id, 262 Elizabeth St. (bet. Houston & Prince Sts.), (212) 219-9903, *Mod Furnishings*

This Nolita newcomer is every bit as stylish as its name suggests. In fact, the "style police" in the media have been all over this place. Modernism is the word. Some new Italian furniture and some very carefully chosen older items will make you feel like a Bond girl on the search for interiors. Prices are acceptable for such highly coveted and stylish fare.

Artmide, 46 Greene St. (bet. Broome & Grande Sts.), (212) 925-1588, *Light My Room*

Technologically advanced lighting via Italy. This group of designer craftsman provide the latest and greatest in lighting options—from funky torchiers to slightly conservative desk lamps.

Barbara Bui, 115 Wooster St. (@ Prince St.), (212) 625-1938, *Must Have Fashions*

"I'll take one of each, please . . ." Known for her sumptuous fabrics and classic coats and skirts *à la Françias*—the action now revolves around the "must-have" T-shirt and pants line.

Bark Frameworks, 85 Grand St. (@ Greene St.), (212) 431-9080, *You're Framed*

Jeb Bark takes framing seriously, catering to a clientele of serious collectors, serious artists (Jasper Johns), and serious museums (The Met). The handmade frames are cranked out at a snail's pace (two a week) for a queen's ransom, but it's art we're framing here, not your candid photo of you and Jude Law outside the door at the *Late Show with David Letterman*.

Blue Bag, 266 Elizabeth St. (bet. Houston & Prince Sts.), (212) 966-8655, *Best Handbags.*

Every bag you can imagine. Couple Pascal and Marnie Legrand have staked out new territory on Elizabeth St. from their flagship store in St. Bart's to tout their exotic handbag wares to celebrities and girls like us. Specializing in hard-to-find designer brands: Harve Chapelier, Rosamunda, and Marie Bouvero. Some footwear à la the islands—sandals, slides, etc.

Camper, 125 Prince St. (@ Wooster St.), (212) 358-1841, *Comfy Shoes*

Beauty is pain, but style can be quite comfy at this home for utilitarian lace-up shoes from $140 a pair. Pronounced "cahm-Pear" by those in the know, these trendy babies will take you anywhere but Mt. Everest in style and comfort. There are a multitude of styles from which to choose: we go for the amazingly vibey assortment of suede and canvas signature looks. Great gifts for any man—Dad or Dude.

Catherine, 468 Broome St. (@ Greene St.), (212) 925-6765, *Girly-Girl Clothes*

Flying solo after her stint in the Diane Von Furstenberg camp, Catherine Maladrino has managed to seduce the likes of style babes Elizabeth Hurley and Kristin Scott Thomas into her funky Audrey Hepburn–esque designs. Parisian style meets SoHo with baby blue leather capri pants, bias-cut chiffon dresses, and sporty cowgirl-inspired straw hats à la the ever-cool Lucinda Williams.

Ceramica, 59 Thompson St. (bet. Spring & Broome Sts.), (212) 941-1307, *Coveted Gifts*.

Gorgeous complete collections of ceramic design based on a 400-year-old Renaissance pattern. Something for everyone on your "list" (simple candlesticks for $10 to elegant serving platters for your artsy friend's wedding @ $250). Martha Stewart sightings—you be the judge.

Chuckies, 399 Broadway (bet. Spring & Broome Sts.), (212) 343-1717, *Trendy Shoes*

See details in UES.

Elizabeth & Vine, 253 Elizabeth St. (bet. Prince & Houston Sts.), (212) 941-7943, *Fine Wine*

Tiny little wine seller in this hot little 'hood . . . Girly moment: Saturday wine tastings 5 P.M. to 8 P.M., wine reps on hand along with delish crackers, cheese and fruit—taste and nibble to your tummy's content, then grab a Spanish wine for your friend's paella feast. Delivery from 2 P.M. until 9 P.M.

Erica Tanov, 204 Elizabeth St. (@ Prince St.), (212) 334-8020, *Feminine Finds*

Step into this retail oasis for a Zen-like shopping experience that will leave you rested and energized. Tanov's own line includes pretty, feminine fashions that often incorporate antique components like handmade antique Indian lace cuffs. Other items to look for: high-end bed linens, baby clothes, lotions, and candles. Other location in San Francisco.

Find Outlet, @ 229 Mott St. (bet Prince & Spring Sts.), (212) 226-5167, *Discount Designer*

See details in Chelsea/Meatpacking.

5S, 98 Prince St. (bet. Mercer & Greene Sts.), (212) 925-7880, *Beauty Products*

Created as a division of Shiseido cosmetics, this sleek and modern-looking store is one-stop shopping for "natural" beauty seekers: products made of natural herbs and colors that encompass elements of aromatherapy for all skin types. Order by phone at (877) PHONE 5S. Diehards like Drew Barrymore swear by these products.

Fragments, 107 Greene St. (bet. Prince & Spring Sts.), (212) 334-9588, *One-Of-A-Kind Jewelry*

Boutique jewelry at its best in this informal host to 40 hot, up-and-coming as well as established designers. Indian beading, silver, semi-precious stones and rhinestones too! A little bit for every taste and budget, you and friends will have fun poring over the eclectic cases—buy something to wear tonight or for a sparkly gift!

Gates Of Morocco, 8 Prince St. (@ Elizabeth St.), (212) 925-2650, *Neighborhood Favorite*

The latest in fashionable geography. Let the Berber Babe in you go wild in this emporium housing all things Moroccan. In addition to clothes in rich jewel tones and velvets with ornate patterns, they also sell a nice variety of mosaic tile, pottery (love it!), carpets, and various other throws.

Hat Shop, 120 Thompson St. (@ Prince St.), (212) 219-1445, *Mad Cap*

A bona fide millinery shop that features its own line and countless other "outside" designers—mostly from New York, of course! Stylish "Madhattanites" can grab a summer's straw hat to protect their Botox'd forehead or a chic fedora for those cold winter days. You will find style as well as function at this downtown treasure.

Hedra Prue, 281 Mott St. (@ Houston St.), (212) 343-9205, *Cool Clothes*

Want to add some "cool" quotient to your tired executive wardrobe? Look no farther: these club-inspired looks translate to your everyday life, if not to the boardroom. Modern clothes like corduroy dresses and colored leather jackets; great accessories like nameplate necklaces and rhinestone belts at moderate prices. Save your big bucks for that haute couture suit . . .

Ina, 101 Thompson St. (bet. Prince & Spring Sts.), (212) 334-9048, *Consignment Fashions*

"Used" designer clothing will leave you feeling anything but! Fashion editors, models, and insiders go here for their impulse shopping urges and splurges. The owner has a tight connection to the fashion world, so many of the items that pack the little shop have been worn only once on a catwalk by Kate Moss! So tuck your "new" Gucci bag under your arm and strut yourself over to Bond St. (see Twilight) for some suddenly affordable sushi.

Kate's Paperie, 561 Broadway (@ Prince St.), (212) 941-9816, *Paper Goods Plus*

See details in GV, other location in UES.

Kerquelen, 44 Greene St. (bet. Broome & Grand Sts.), (212) 582-3007, 430 W. Broadway (bet. Spring & Prince Sts.), *Tasteful Shoes*

This newcomer to the SoHo area is an absolute find if you are a shoe freak: stilettos, strappy sandals, pumps galore! The buyer obviously has great taste, and the selection is considerable. Cool music and industrial chic surrounding add ambiance to your shoe binge!

Language, 238 Mulberry St. (@ Prince St.), (212) 431-5566, *International Boutique*

"It's a small world after all"—and these folks have put the best of it under one roof! You'll find a deliciously exotic mix of goodies forecasting up-and-coming trends in fashion and décor: West African masks next to a huge stash of cutting-edge Latin-American designer duds along with the best from the likes of John Bartlett and Chloé.

Liquid Sky, 241 Lafayette St. (bet. Prince & Spring Sts.), (212) 279-0005, *Funky Fashions*

Not to be confused with the cult movie, this is the place to find the latest in funky/techno/hip-hop finds. Cutting-edge, you'll either "get it" or you won't . . . Like their new takes on Pan Am flight bags.

Malia Mills, 199 Mulberry St. (bet. Spring & Kenmare Sts.), (212) 625-2311, *Ultimate Swimwear*

The newly created Swimsuit Suicide Hot Line recommends this painless adventure in prevacation/presummer bikini-and-maillot shopping. Millions of styles and colors allow you to mix and match to your heart's content, or at least until the sight of your tush in the mirror doesn't cause you to hyperventilate . . . Open seven days a week 12–7.

Marc Jacobs, 163 Mercer St. (bet. Houston & Prince Sts.), (212) 343-1490, *Hot Designer*

The "it" boy of the decade . . . Aptly crowned Mr. Cool Guy by us "Jane" girls. He designs awesome cutting-edge clothes in a nonthreatening way—you've just gotta have it—now—when you see it. If you have to ask the price, it's out of your budget. But somehow you will find a way to finagle that fabulous little camel jacket.

Moss, 146 Greene St. (@ Houston St.), (212) 226-2190, *Futuristic Home*

Anything from Moss is not your usual anything. With its cutting-edge style and innovative designs Moss remains one of our favorite spots for furniture, housewares, great gifts someone who appreciates design with an intellectual slant. Closed on Mondays.

Nancy Koltes at Home, 313 Spring St. (bet Mott & Mulberry Sts.) (212) 219-2271, *Luscious Linens*

This linen "closet" carries the most beautiful Italian lines this side of Tuscany. Gorgeous sheets, Scandia Down and a yummy selection of "imported" bath products. Affordable yet not discounted by any stretch of the imagination, so don't miss her "Cool Down Sale" in August. *Psst . . . the stainless-steel sleigh bed that displays all of the goodies can be special ordered if you want to take her bedroom home with you!*

Pearl River Mart, 277 Canal St. (@ Broadway), (212) 431-4770, *Neighborhood Favorite*

Everything Chinois. Load up your basket, you Hatsumomo wannabe! Chopsticks, lanterns, dresses, slippers, pjs, and other Chinese doodads will put you well on your way to conjuring the Far East. It's a finding frenzy for next to nothing. Get out your Christmas list, even if it is August, for all your friends and coworkers! *Psst . . . it's a great place to spend your lunch hour if you are one of the lucky girls serving jury duty!*

Pumpkin Maternity, 225 Lafayette Street (@ Spring St.,), (917) 237-0567, *Moms-To-Be*

Not to be confused with Cinderella's carriage this groovy shop is a lifesaver to all those who refuse to give up being chic just because of a bun in the oven! Former rocker Pumpkin Wentzel has every trimester covered in style. Kelly Preston and Melanie Griffith both have sported Pumpkin's cool duds, and now you can too. Faux-leather pants (stretch of course) and a merino-wool coat are just the ticket to feel beautiful while carrying your precious cargo! By appointment only.

Rizzoli Bookstore, 454 W. Broadway (bet. Prince & Houston Sts.), (212) 674-1616, *Elegant Bookstore*

See details in MTW.

Ruby, 70 Spring St. (@ Broome St.), (212) 941-4145, *Antique Stuff*

Spacious and inviting: UltraSuede ottomans, perhaps an Eames sofa from the fifties, a pink girlie bicycle from Amsterdam circa 1975. A mix of modern and art deco—what pieces they do have are special. Just browse amidst the beauty. Perhaps you'll find a bicycle built for two. *Psst . . . don't miss the vintage clothing at the rear of the store.*

Shi, 230 Elizabeth St. (bet. Houston & Prince Sts.), (212) 334-4330, *Sleek Housewares*

Minimalist Japanese French Zen with flair—basic inspiration to unclutter your life and your living room without giving up style. Colorful porcelain dinnerware and creative French lighting round out the designs. Loosely based on sculptor Gnaghuchi's paper lamps. Great for gifts for the Feng Shui–inspired friend.

Shu Uemmura, 121 Greene St. (bet. Prince & Spring Sts.), (212) 979-5500, *Skincare*

Don't let the sophistication frighten you away. This is the ultimate cosmetic and skincare playground. Its 20-foot counter holds everything you need—sinks, towels, brushes—to play "face"! No hovering salespeople convincing you to buy that color you know won't work—you pick, apply, change, reapply. Fun and cost-effective "try before you buy" method. Mail order via catalog @ (888) 540-8181.

Spring Street Gardens, 186 Spring St. (bet. Sullivan & Thompson Sts.), (212) 966-2015, *Fresh Flowers*

Just say no to baby's breath! A must for anyone who despises having to "weed" those overdone flower arrangements. Grab a simple bouquet on your way to a dinner party or just treat yourself to some Rubrum lilies. Expect the height of freshness, but don't expect to find a stem left behind in the afternoon, they sell out daily to enforce their "no wilting" policy! Don't miss the lovely little garden on the premises. Delivery available on Manhattan Island only. Closed in August.

Stream, 69 Mercer St. (bet. Spring & Broome Sts.), (212) 226-2328, *Avant clothes*

Fast-forward fashion big-time! This new sparkly boutique was decorated solely to debut the lines of these cutting-edge cutters—Dirk Bikkembergs, Kostas Murkurdis, and Myth plus many more from the international scene. Makes our mouths water. Bargain hunters beware, our Bikkemberg boots from the early nineties retailed at $700, so take a deep breath as you turn the tag!

Thompson Chemists, 137 Thompson St. (bet. Houston & Prince Sts.), (212) 598-9790, *Glamour Girl*

A seriously Euro-style pharmacy with high-end hair products (Phyto Plage, Rene Futerer) along with homeopathy, nifty accessories, vitamins and Tweezerman! They'll deliver same day anywhere in the city, including your hotel. In SoHo? Delivery within the hour. Models frequent, so the products are very *au courant*. Ask about their Menopausal Compound (tick tock, tick tock). Insurance accepted on scrips and they ship anywhere.

Ting's Gift Shop, 18 Doyer St. (bet. Pell & Bowery Sts.), (212) 962-1081, *Ultimate Girl Gift*

Owned by a mother/daughter duo (we love that), this little Chinatown treasure is a great place to buy those great authentic Chinese slippers that designers are ripping off for millions these days! They have a great selection at reasonable prices . . . and they get your busy butt in and out in a jiffy! *Psst . . . great gifts for your best friend's birthday!*

Tracy Feith, 209 Mulberry St. (bet. Spring & Broome Sts.), (212) 334-3097, *Feminine Finds*

Fellow Texan Tracy Feith is no urban cowboy. He has been stirring up the fashion world for the past two years with his explosive schizophrenic combination of color and fabric. Cherry-pick your favorite piece from this collection (one is enough they are so outrageous!) and let it add a little spunk to your Saturday night . . . if not your life!

What Comes Around Goes Around, 351 W. Broadway (bet. Broome & Grand Sts.), (212) 343-9303, *Very Vintage*

Superstylish vintage clothes from all periods. Cool suede jackets, pretty vintage dresses and stuff for "him" as well as antiques and collectibles. We have never walked out of here empty-handed. Helpful and knowledgeable sales staff. Put your name on the list as The Cupping Room (see Eats) next door and enjoy hunting.

Yohji Yamamoto, 103 Grand St. (@ Mercer St.), (212) 966-9066, *Designer Clothes*

Every item is a work of art, and the store itself is a gallery of white. Pushing the envelope for the true fashion maven, Yamamoto manages to create wearable, functional fashion, much of which is reversible—meaning twice as much wear. Carolyn Bessette Kennedy was a devotee. After one look, you will be too, if you can afford it.

Zero, 225 Mott St. (bet. Prince & Spring Sts.), (212) 925-3849, *Fashion Forward*

Designer Maria Cornejo's gallery-style shop offers every girl an opportunity to look "up-to-the-minute" but not beyond it. Innovative twists on classic looks make this a "must" on your shopping list. *Psst . . . take a gander at her hubby's (Mark Borthuica) fashion photo books also on sale here—it's all-in-the-family fashion!*

✦ Not to Miss:

Costume Nationale, 108 Wooster St. (bet. Spring & Prince Sts.), (212) 431-1530, *Italian Fashions*

Jill Stuart, 100 Greene St. (bet. Prince & Spring Sts.), (212) 343-2300, *Pretty Dresses*

Portico Bed & Bath, 139 Spring St. (@ Wooster St.), (212) 941-7722, *More Than Towels*

Scoop NYC, 532 Broadway (bet. Prince & Spring Sts.), (212) 925-2886, *Hot Looks*

Sigerson Morrison, 28 Prince St. (bet. Mott & Elizabeth Sts.), (212) 219-3893, *Pretty Shoes*

Smith & Hawken, 394 W. Broadway, (bet. Spring & Broome Sts.), (212) 925-0687, *www.smithandhawken.com, Garden Goods*

Tribeca/Lower Manhattan/Other Boroughs

Bark, 369 Atlantic Ave. @ Boerum Hill, Brooklyn, (718) 625-8997

We spend more than half our lives on our backs . . . sleeping, you naughty girl! So why not do it on the crème de la crème, the yummy of all yummy linens from Egypt, India, and beyond. Owner Linda Downey presents a jaw-dropping array of gorgeous bedding and bath products. Frolic in your new silk kimono, luxuriate in your overflowing bubble bath, roll yourself seductively onto that duvet wearing nothing but a smile and some hot Hard Candy lipstick.

Calligraphy Studios, 100 Reade St. (bet. Church St. & W. Broadway), (212) 964-6007, *Writing Paper*

What girl doesn't want to leave her mark on society? What better way than with your own individually designed monogram? For the people at Calligraphy Studios, personalized stationery is a way of life. For $2,000 they'll create your own stationery "wardrobe" (Quincy Jones has one, why don't you?), including, letterhead, envelopes, note cards, and calling cards. Or if it's just gorgeous hand-calligraphied wedding invites you're after, they're up to that task as well.

Frankie Steinz's Costumes, 24 Harrison St. (bet. Hudson & Greenwich Sts.), (212) 925-1373, *Costume Diva*

A former accountant gone costume designer extraordinaire, Frankie's designs are madly inventive and fab. So if you're looking to wow everyone at that theme party, get the jump on Halloween or just satisfy his "fetish" (you vixen!) this is the place to reinvent yourself. By appointment only, with a corporate monopoly of "The Biz," she will let individuals browse to their fantasy's content. Prices swing from $50 to $175 accordingly.

Kleinfeld and Son, 8202 Fifth Ave. (@ 82nd St.), Brooklyn, (718) 765-8500, (888) 383-2777, *www.kleinfeldbridal.com, Wedding Dress Emporium*

When else do you have the opportunity to waste thousands of dollars on something that will turn yellow in the attic over the next thirty years? The wedding dress of your dreams, from high-end couture to homemade type frocks. Some say it is worth the trek from Texas to have every option available under one roof—an average of 1,000 gowns are housed at all times. Names you know include Scassi, Dior, and Herrera. Closed on Sunday and Monday; Saturday is by appointment only.

New York City Custom Leather, 156 Ludlow St. (bet. Rivington & Stanton Sts.), (212) 375-9593, *Custom Pants*

Many believe Agatha Blios makes the best custom leather pants in the country. Her signature is a sixties-inspired lace-up and flare leg. But she will cut any pattern to your liking. She claims that the secret to her success is that she uses the best cowhide that is "soft but not wimpy." They range from $700 to $1,000; expect to wait about one month from the initial fitting to delivery. But appointment only. *Psst . . . rock stars like Sheryl Crow and the president of the Hells Angels have filled their leather needs here.*

ReGeneration, 38 Renrick St. (bet Spring & Canal Sts.), (212) 741-2102, *Mid-Century Mod*

On a groovy sofa search? Take the time to seek out this hard-to-find "find" on a little street in Tribeca—they are the "King of Communal Seating" (as in couch, not love-in)! Incredibly priced vintage and new sofas in the "Mid-Century Modern" aesthetic with contemporary flair. Highly touted by the press, their pieces are highly sought after. Look for the work of these design icons: Risom, Jacobsen, Knoll, Eames . . . Yum!

The Girdle Factory, 218 Bedford Ave. (@ N. 5th St.), Williamsburg, Brooklyn, (718) 486-9599, *Vintage Finds*

Don't let the name alarm you, this place is more "vintage" than "vise" . . . if you want a supervintage handbag that has not been picked over by every wanna-be in Manhattan, make the trek! You'll be deciding between the brown crocodile Kelly or the dark green leather clutch before you can remember to suck in your tummy! Some other fashions on hand such as leather jackets in the 150-dollar price range.

Totem, 71 Franklin St. (bet. Broadway & Church St.), (212) 925-5506, *www.totemdesign.com, High Design Home*

"The Objects That Evoke Meaning"—ready to upgrade from that snazzy Scandinavian (aka IKEA) bookshelf your law school study group helped you assemble years ago? Totem is your ticket into the world of young contemporary designers ready to decorate your home in the latest mod designs. From the whimsical and inflatable to Darth Vader's couch, you'll find fun, funky and functional.

✦ *Good to Know:*

South Street Seaport: For those who can't live without the mall even in the big city . . . we pity you, but we've got you "covered" with all the regulars—Gap, Banana Republic, J. Crew, etc. Here's that Manhattan twist: the pier offers the best view of the Brooklyn Bridge. And to be honest, we had a blast pretending to be in suburbia! Take the 4, 5, 6 train to Brooklyn Bridge or don't stay after dark—it's tough to find a taxi, so plan ahead.

Remember, there is no sales tax in New York State on clothing purchases under $110. While that cuts out the Fendi purse, you can still save on a pair of Cosabella panties or two.

✦ *Citywide:*

Insider Info: **Fashion Update Tours,** (718) 377-8873, adds a whole new meaning to cleaning the closet. You'll need to after their tour of the garment district's sample sales. Monday through Friday, 10 A.M.–12 P.M., take your best shot and weed through top designers' latest at 50 percent off retail. The 75-dollar charge per girl may seem steep, but not compared to what you'll save . . . Bring cash and attitude. *Psst . . . subscribe to their quarterly magazine that allows you to navigate solo for a mere $70 a year.*

Bargain hunter: **Findasale** is a service listing all of NYC's premier sales on any given date. Log on to *www.findasale.com* or call (212) 271-6373.

Favorite Fragrance: With 270 stores across the nations, **Perfumania** is *the* place to find your favorite scent at ridiculously low prices. Don't be afraid to ask for obscure brands, and don't worry about getting a knockoff—it's the real thing. They can discount because of the sales volume.

If you're into bargains, the **S & B Report** is the monthly bible for showroom sales and consolidated designer markdown events, such as Henri Bendel, Giorgio Armani, Catherine etc. Call (877) 579-0222 to find out how to get on the list or log on to *www.snbreport.com* for up-to-the-minute scoop.

✧ *And Don't Miss*

Auto, 805 Washington St. (bet. Gansevoort & Horatio Sts.), (212) 229-2292, *Groovy Gifts*

Situated in a gallery-like setting, this little shop houses fab one-of-a-kind items for you, not to mention your house, friends, dog, sister, or anyone else. Handmade jewelery, unique leather goods, vintage scarf-covered pillows by Vera (remember her from the 1970s?), kitsch travel journals, and more. The buyers have taste and they are ready to share it. *Psst . . . Move Lab, 803 Washington St., (212) 741-5520, next door, is also filled with unique gifts. Check out the artwork (it's for sale) while you cruise the mod space. An adorable garden in the back allows you to go back and forth between the two stores!*

Neena Richter, by appointment only, (212) 570-6552, *Vintage Bags*

Do you know a savvy Jane girl who does not incorporate a vintage "something" into her wardrobe? If you want the best of the best old handbags this side of Paris, then Neena, a chic city girl herself, is your connection. She scours the world for top-of-the-line goodies. Name your passion: Gucci, Pucci, Dior, in addition to lesser known, yet highly desirable designer bags. Make last year's simple black suit look "in" with an antique pocketbook. Prices vary.

Twilight

Calle Ocho, 446 Columbus Ave. (bet. 81st & 82nd Sts.),
(212) 873-5025, *Sexy Hot Spot*

Backlit glass, funky caged fans and faux-Cuban murals provide the perfect backdrop for all of your pan-Latino fantasies, culinary and otherwise . . . And God knows on the UWS a little fantasy goes a long way. If you still have room after drowning your girl troubles in luscious Caipirinhas, prepare your palate for a spicy tango. Use the mirrors, you've never looked better. *Psst . . . inquire about the Salsa Sunday Brunch featuring live music to spice up your weekend.*

Evelyn Lounge, 380 Columbus Ave. (@ 78th St.), (212) 724-2363,
Open Late

For the uptown girl looking for a downtown experience. The four rooms suit all of your lounging needs: the main floor (opens at 5:50 P.M. daily) is lovely with a great fireplace surrounded by a combination of exposed brick and sizzling red walls. Linger for a drink before you head downstairs for some tapas and port. The comfy and ecclectic assortment of couches sets the stage for great conversation or romance! *Psst . . . don't be surprised if your date dashes for the groovy cigar room the minute you excuse yourself to powder your nose. Live music on Wednesday and Thursday, and a DJ spins cool tunes on Friday and Saturday. Open till 4 A.M.*

Merchants, 521 Columbus Ave., (bet. 85th & 86th Sts.), (212) 721-3689, *www.merchantsny.com, After Work*

Perfect after-work hot spot that has remained ultrapopular since its inception. The bar is an open-style centerpiece that allows all eyes to be on you or your eyes to be on everyone! Not so much a meat market as a cornucopia of opportunity to meet Mr. Right or just Mr. Right Now. Waltz past the heavy draperies into the cozy "inner sanctum" lounge for a little tête à tête or drag him out to the sidewalk café and flirt up a storm *en plein aire!* See other locations in UES and Chelsea.

Northwest, 392 Columbus Ave. (@ 79th St.), (212) 799-4530, *Quiet Cocktail*

How could a group of fabulous Manhattan guys create the perfect late-night hang for Manhattan girls? Will wonders never cease but Northwest fits the bill for quiet relaxed cocktails solo or with friends any night of the week. The stellar lounge is situated above their cozy downstairs bar and small restaurant that serves inventive and reliable fare at career-girl prices, and even offers outdoor seating when weather permits! Definitely not for women only, this is a great place to bring your stressed-out and famished beau for a low-key evening that you both will enjoy.

Potion Lounge, 370 Columbus Ave. (bet. 77th & 78th Sts.), (212) 721-4386, *www.potionlongue.com, Mod Patrol*

Austin Powers and the Nouveau Bond would definitely drink here. Order up a tubular concoction of colorful top shelf liquors and cordials mixed with exotic *jus de fruit* whose layers dance chimerically on the optically lit stainless-steel bar. When you're finally dizzy from staring at the bubbling water window, pour your personal potion over ice for some oral enjoyment and wander through flickering candles to the velvet banquettes. It's otherworldly, it's magical, it's seduction in a glass. Open Tues.–Sat., 6:30 P.M.

St. Nicks Pub, 773 St. Nick's Ave. (@ 149th St.), (212) 283-9728, *Live Music*

The Apollo for future jazz greats. Monday night jam sessions are the breeding ground for tomorrow's stars. All are here and paying their dues before heading downtown to the famous Blue Note. You owe it to yourself to take a big bite out of the Big Apple and check out Adam Vasquez—the current darling and jazz great in the making. Once again, go with others and make transportation plans—taxis are sporadic uptown after hours.

♦ *Not to Miss:*

Fugiyama Mama, 467 Columbus Ave. (bet. 82nd & 83rd Sts.), (212) 769-1144, *Sip 'N' Sushi*

Shark Bar, 307 Amsterdam Ave. (bet. 74th & 75th Sts.), (212) 874-8500, *Soulful Scene*

Ruby Foo's, 2182 Broadway (@ 77th St.), (212) 724-6700, *Bar Scene*

Bar, 247 E. 81st St. (bet. Second & Third Aves.), (212) 396-9928, *Neighborhood Newcomer*

Don't miss this adorably hip and hidden "bar" across the street from Etats-Unis (see UES, Eats). We went for a quick glass of vino and stayed all night! A chic modern atmosphere with incredible wines by the glass and premade gourmet nibbles. They do have tables, but it is much more fun to chat with the friendly trendy staff at the bar while you wait for "him." Who knows, you may wind up wandering across 81st for dinner! Wine and exotic beer (so don't ask for Bud Light).

Bellman's Bar @ The Carlyle Hotel, 95 E. 76th St. (bet. Madison & Park Aves.), (212) 744-1600, *Old New York*

Classic and timeless, so put on that little black dress with your pearls. The crowd is somewhat "older" but age *is* a relative concept and who doesn't like older men? The bartenders are straight out of a Doris Day and Rock Hudson movie complete with white jackets and little black bow ties. Do not miss the homemade potato chips that go so well with a Bombay martini! A cover charge applies some nights after 9 P.M. when they have live entertainment. *Psst . . . the legendary Bobby Short has been performing here seasonally for 35 years, so don't forget to ask for a schedule.*

Brandy's Piano Bar, 235 E. 84th St. (bet. 2nd & 3rd Sts.), (212) 744-4949, *Live Music*

In the mood for camp and cross-dressing? This little nightspot has that gritty piano bar thing happening, complete with chanteuse acting as cocktail waitress. Morning, make merry with drag queens who sing along. And actually catch Broadway ingenues honing their pipes and paying their rent. Great place to drift into after a scrumptious dinner at Elaine's on Second Ave. bet. 88th & 89th Sts.

Comic Strip Live, 1565 Second Ave. (bet. 81st & 82nd Sts.), (212) 861-9386, *www.comicstriplive.com*, *Laugh Out Loud*

Launching pad for Fashion Barbie Shoshanna's ex-beau. (That's Jerry Seinfeld, FYI.) Small and very popular (they don't have lines this long in Moscow), be sure to plan ahead. There are many familiar names, but the key is in the undiscovered! Drink to meet the minimum, laugh until you almost . . . never mind! Call for show times.

Dorrian's Red Hand, 1616 Second Ave. (@ 84th St.), (212) 772-6660, *Classic Bar*

Do stop by this family run restaurant/bar for some good food and fun. The best time to enjoy this perennial favorite is during the week, when you can enjoy a burger, a beer, and a ballgame in front of the crackling fire. The crowd is always colorful, a mixed bag of local barflies, television stars like John Enos from *Melrose Place,* baseball stars (NY Yankees like David Wells, who celebrated his perfect game here, and Met's pitchers like Al Leiter), and big-name politicians like John McCain. Look for the adorable Jimmy Dorrian, usually on hand to add that extra sparkle. Open till 4 A.M., even on a Sunday in January.

DT/UT, 1626 Second Ave. (bet. 84th & 85th Sts.), (212) 327-1327, *Laid-Back Leisure*

Downtown/Uptown. The rare lofty casual space located on the tony UES. If you are a black-turtleneck-wearing beat poet singer/songwriter running from Madison Ave. justice, you can seek political asylum here. Great space for a laid-back evening—occasional performances by the aforementioned artsy-fartsies. Generous selection of desserts and coffees. Ample beer and wine bar for the boozy broads. FYI, unless it's a close relative, don't get stuck sitting center stage on amateur night. Could be painful!

Iris and B. Gerald Cantor on the Roof of The Met, 1000 Fifth Ave., (@ 82nd St.), (212) 535-7710, *Rooftop View*

Just spend one afternoon at the Met's roof garden bar and you will know where they coined the phrase "I Love New York." Every day is a public cocktail party here against the breathtaking backdrop of Central Park. Plenty of cold beer and slushy margaritas are served from noon till shortly before the museum's closing. Seats in the shade are nabbed early, so bring a wide-brimmed hat and some SPF 30 for sunny afternoons. Open seasonally, weather permitting. Perfect spot to solve your life's issues while people-watching and flirting.

Le Charlot, 19 E. 69th St., (bet. Madison & Park Aves.), (212) 794-1628, *Sexy Hot Spot*

A dark and charming bistro with an aloof staff. The french fries are a great companion to the mussels while you sip away on fabulous wine and try desperately to hear what the person next to you is saying! No table dancing allowed even though we have witnessed it on occasion after the lights dim late into the night. Alert: cute boys 24/7 with and without green card.

Mark's, @ The Mark Hotel, 25 E. 77th St. (bet. Fifth & Madison Aves.), (212) 879-1865, *Hors D'Oeuvres*

The bar at the Mark Hotel has really great bar food. It's too dead to be considered a true twilight destination, but the clubby feel at the five o'clock hour is second to none for conversation, cocktails and heavy hors d'oeuvres. Who needs dinner when you can have such delicious cocktail fare. *Psst . . . order a picnic backpack prepared by the "executive chef" of the hotel. This gourmet insulated pack is filled with light summer dishes such as chilled asparagus with a truffle vinaigrette or marinated smoked salmon with a red onion caper dressing and topped off with an assortment of petits fours. Make sure you don't go dutch!*

Merchants, 1125 First Ave. (@ 62nd St.), (212) 832-1551, *www.merchantsny.com, After Work*

See details in UWS, other location in Chelsea

Park View at The Boathouse, Central Park Lake (East Park Dr. @ 72nd St.), (212) 517-2233, *Seasonal Only*

This deliciously romantic hideaway makes you feel far away from the city grind. Craving nature? Then take your lover or your friends for a tranquil retreat, but in NYC nature doesn't come cheap! The bar can be a fun spot to wait for your table. The Venetian-style gondola boats cruising the lake are the perfect backdrop to your lovely night out (May–Sept)!

Subway Inn, 163 E. 63rd St. (bet. Lexington & Third Aves.), (212) 223-8929, *Ultimate Dive*

Technically could be considered UES but no one there will claim them . . . It's a real dive dive dive. Clink glasses with the rich and famous or perhaps the homeless—this is truly a social melting pot. Big bar, booths, and tacky chachki add to this atmospheric dump with a great jukebox and cocktails at rock bottom prices. It is OK to just let your hair down every once in a while.

The Cocktail Room, 334 E. 73rd St. (bet. First and Second Aves.), (212) 988-6100, *Mod Squad*

Another Shaggadelic episode brought to you by the owners of the infamous club Shine, 30 *enormous* original cocktail creations greet you at the bar. Great place to meet on the UES for drinks after work to be assured that you will actually hear what each other has to say, though it does get packed and loud as the night unfolds so be prepared to pick up the pace a bit. Happy hour: 5–8 P.M. daily. Gigantic cocktails available till 1 A.M. Wednesday–Saturday. The live DJ puts an extraspecial "spin" on things.

Midtown West ....

Algonquin Lobby @ The Algonquin Hotel 59 W. 44th St. (bet. Fifth & Sixth Aves.), (212) 840-6800, *Elegant Lobby Bar*

Literary legends William Faulkner and James Thurber once hung their hats here and probably consumed a few beverages as well while they made their mark. The historic oak-paneled lobby is still a great place to convene for civilized postwork libation and conversation. Settle into one of the spacious groupings of overstuffed velvet sofas and high-backed leather chairs, but leave your Winstons in your Fendi bag: no smoking in the lobby, ladies! The adjoining Blue Bar features live piano music, carbaret-style shows, and an elegant menu.

Bryant Park Grill, 25 W. 40th St. (bet. Fifth & Sixth Aves.), (212) 840-6500, *Rooftop View*

Come here in the summer and hang out on the rooftop bar that overlooks picturesque Bryant Park. Something of a singleton scene, so if you can't beat 'em, join 'em! The light menu is just perfect for an enchanted evening! *Psst . . . Monday nights in the summer, the city shows classsic films on a big outdoor screen in the park. Grab your blanket and enjoy* To Kill a Mockingbird *with a few thousand other city dwellers.*

China Club, 268 W. 47th St. (bet. Broadway & Eighth Ave.), (212) 398-3800, *Neighborhood Standard*

One of the city's most classic destinations for nightlife. The drinks are a million dollars each but worth it for the loads of fun you can have if you hit it on a good night, and that means mostly Mondays. The space is huge and the music is good. Not your newest but definitely a grand dame of clubs!

Churrascaria Plataforma @ Belvedere Hotel, 316 W.
49th St. (bet. Eighth & Ninth Aves.), (212) 245-0505, *Brazilian With A Group*

Delicious Brazilian caipirnha-infused destination with succulent meats of all variety. Don't plan on sticking to your diet tonight. Just pretend you are dancing in the streets of Buenos Aires with a flower in your hair and a smile on your face! Party central for groups and festive occasions.

Float, 240 W. 52nd St. (bet. Eighth & Broadway), (212) 581-0055, *Cool Dance Club*

Pioneering in this no-man's-land of nightlife, this pseudoindustrial haunt caters to a somewhat international crowd with fresh flowers, great boissons, loud music, and marginally clad go-go dancers to keep it festive and feisty. The downside to this trendy scene is the "line and list" situation out front, but you can gain entry with a bit of patience and the right pair of shoes. Open Wed–Sat.

Flute, 205 W. 54th St. (bet. Broadway & Seventh Ave.), (212) 265-4169, *Romantic Date*

Bubbly sin den. Only champagne will pull you out of the doldrums on a winter weeknight, so sneak down the staircase to tickle your nose with Taittinger. This basement (cozy as opposed to depressing or reminiscent of your childhood) was once a speakeasy during Prohibition. Now, they serve some 100 champagnes and prohibit very little. The crowd is stylish and ready to toast, but not tango, the night away!

Grotto @ The Michelangelo Hotel, 777 Seventh Ave., (bet. 49th & 50th Sts.), (212) 333-3311, *Hotel Bar*

Step out of the hustle and bustle of Seventh Ave. and go downstairs to a spacious cocktail haven. Connected to, but not affected by, the stuffy Michelangelo Hotel, you will always be able to find a seat (leather smoking chairs!) and a delicious cocktail served by some of the nicest waitstaff in the city! Cigar smoking allowed, but there is enough space to escape it. *Psst . . . limited bar food available.*

Library Bar @ The Paramount Hotel, 235 W. 46th St., (bet. Broadway & Eighth Ave.), (212) 764-5500, *Be Seen*

We were bored, we were trendy, we were in the music business and needed an overpriced cocktail immediately among like minds and bodies. We wound up ascending the George Jetson grand escalier to the second-floor bar conceptualized by Philippe Starck. We found lots of young and glamorous professionals dangling their legs and gold cards at the streamlined bar. Out of the corner of both eyes we watched black-and-white art films on high-definition TVs . . . on the way out we blew a kiss to the "beyond hot" bellman who undoubtedly models for Calvin on the side. Another night for voyeurs on the chic side of Gotham.

Morrell Wine Bar and Café, One Rockefeller Plaza (@ 49th St.), (212) 262-7700, *Wine Bar*

Same people who brought us the renowned namesake wine store (see UES, Treasures) have opened a wine bar offering 100-plus wines by the glass. If you are in the mood to read a very long wine menu and taste some of the best wines the world has to offer, then this is your place! Some selections are $60 a pop, but as we always say, "life is too short to drink cheap wine!" We even spotted some folks from *The Wine Spectator* hanging out here. What better endorsement? *Psst . . . for a "mere" $50 you bargain hunters can try the Monday night tasting menu which pairs three courses from the dinner menu with five three-ounce "tastes" of wine to match!*

Nirvana, 30 Central Park South (bet. Fifth & Sixth Aves.), (212) 486-5700, *Sunset View*

Located on the fifteenth floor overlooking Central Park this dreamy setting could be the nirvana of romantic date locales. This is equal opportunity date central! Wrap yourself into your sari and enter this big city haven. With the city lights as a backdrop, the mood is set for a spicy rendezvous for two! We don't even mind the occasional tourist . . . Tolerance is probably the sign of the true Brahmin!

Swing, 349 w. 46th St. (bet. Seventh & Eighth Aves.), (212) 262-9554, *Alternative Dancing*

Blast to the past and join the Trendy Twenties (and a few thirtysome-things) in their attempt to reinvent swing dancing for the new millinneum. It's fun! It's festive! It's borderline ridiculous, but grab a few friends and a few cocktails and join the "swing" of things as if it was Hollywood 1947. Thursday nights bring George Gee and His Make-Believe Ballroom Orchestra. Try lessons any night at 7 P.M. Good clean fun to be had by all, just don't step on anyone's toes!

Vodka Bar @ Royalton Hotel, 4 W. 44th St. (bet. Fifth &
Sixth Aves.), (212) 869-4400, *Hotel Hideaway*

Hideaway with someone (or preferably already be "some-one") in this circular bar located in this trendy lobby. Beautiful people dwell and sip chilled vodka here . . . lots and lots of vodka. The floor-to-ceiling leather walls add a nice backdrop to the localized debauch-ery. Very close quarters guarantee that you will "get close" after a few drinks—so pick your poison and your partner with care! Great place to see sparkly people doing sparkly things.

Whiskey Park, 100 Central Park South (@ Sixth Ave.), (212) 541-8385, *Afterwork Meatmarket*

One of NY's after-work hot spots, Thursday nights bring out Midtown-ers in droves. Meaning some "suits," some music-industry types and visitors in the know. As one of the "pack" of bars owned by Randy Gerber, aka Mr. Cindy Crawford, this bar is cosmically connected to Ian Schraeger's latest fixer-upper, the legendary Essex House. PR diva Allison Bozak brought us here to give us a sneak peek of the next Gerber/Schraeger creation. Puff, puff, sip, sip . . . another martini, please!

Midtown East

Asia de Cuba @ Morgan's Hotel, 237 Madison Ave. (bet. 37th & 38th Sts.), (212) 726-7755, *Famous Owners*

As the name suggests, this fusion hot spot is still a velvet-rope destination with attitude. Bouncers with headsets provide titillating drama as you enter the exotic, sexy two-story restaurant/bar. Be the center of attention and ac-tion in the middle of the dining room or retreat to a white-curtained booth for more intimacy. Upstairs is a Euro-Zoo, so be prepared to stick your Jimmy Choo out and trip any oncoming babes attempting to steal your sofa! If you be-friend a bouncer, he just might stake one out for you, my flirty little friend!

Au Bar, 41 E. 58th St. (bet. Madison & Park Aves.), (212) 308-9455, *Late Night Only*

Picture this: Once upon a time, there was a club to rival all clubs. Then, as time wore on and the luster rubbed off a little, it reinvented itself for the Eurowealth and carefree danceoholics. If your Prince Charming wears a turban and arrives in a Rolls or perhaps orders Dom Pérignon in six languages depending on his mood, pay the 25-dollar door fee and dance the night away to the best of Euro-dance mixes in a sophisticated and sexy hot spot. The end. Open 7 days a week until 4 A.M. *Psst . . . feel free to order late-night breakfast before he whisks you into the dawn. Sun, Mon, Tues, the fee is less at $10 after midnight and free before the bewitching hour.*

Campbell Apartment, 15 Vanderbilt @ Grand Central Terminal (@ 42nd St.), (212) 953-0409, *Hidden Bar*

Since the 1998 renovation of Grand Central Station, the surprises just keep coming. This bar is housed (and well hidden) in the former office of 1920s tycoon John W. Campbell. If you have trouble finding it, ask around . . . someone will know where to point once you are in the terminal. The Florentine-inspired ceiling is so spectacular that you won't even have a chance to notice your "spectacular" bill. Dress code enforced so don't arrive in your tennies and jeans.

Divine Bar, 244 E. 5th St. (bet. Second & Third Aves.), (212) 319-9463, *Wine Bar*

See details in Lower Manhattan.

Guastavino's, 409 E. 59th St. (bet. First & York Aves.), (212) 980-2455, *Girl's Night Out*

Welcome to Terrance Conran's (see Treasures) shrine aptly nicknamed the "gastrodome" combining two of his two personal penchants: food and good design. Located under the Queensboro Bridge, this is Conran's first American restaurant complex. (He has opened nearly two dozen others around the world.) Located in a soaring turn-of-the-century building with 40-foot tiled vaulted ceilings, how could he miss? A must see! Try the house specialty drink: the Flirtini! Reservations are recommended for seating.

King Cole Bar @ The St. Regis Hotel, 2 E. 55th St., (@ Fifth Ave.), (212) 753-4500, *Elegant Cocktails*

Located in the lobby of the St. Regis Hotel, this lounge is a mecca for those looking to meet and greet in Old World style. It's a small space but somehow never feels overly crowded or cramped . . . or too smoky. A huge Maxfield Parrish painting stares down at you as you make your way through the door and settle in for an ice-cold beverage. You will see wheeler-dealer businessmen with their mistresses, the occasional actress (like Uma) holding court and your regular city dwellers post–black-tie function.

Le Colonial, 149 E. 57th St. (bet. Lexington & Third Aves.), (212) 759-0808, *Hot Spot*

Fifties Ricky Ricardo in white smoking jacket meets *The Year of Living Dangerously* in this high-end French Vietnamese boite. Swanky, genteel, and full of big-city charm (fabulous plantation shutters and white tablecloths), don't miss the FI FI FO or the upstairs bar. Some EuroTrash allowed for flavor, but mostly ample couches and snacks provide a great respite—as long as you can stay away from the wolves at the bar, unless of course you want to be caught.

The Pen Top @ The Peninsula Hotel, 700 Fifth Ave. (@ 55th St.), (212) 956-2888, *Rooftop*

Ditto the above, but tone down the high drama and throw in a hotel and a glassed-in lounge that spills out onto an Astroturf-lined terrace. Expensive cocktails (and light fare) for those that travel in expensive suits with expense accounts. Take the elevator to the 23rd floor and enjoy until 1 A.M. nightly.

Top Of The Tower, 3 Mitchell Place (@ Beekman Tower, 49th St. & First Ave.), (212) 355-7300, *Room With A View*

Romance abounds. Breathtaking views of the East River from the 26th floor take you back to the days of Doris in a cocktail sheath and Rock in a tux. Old guard waiters whisk Manhattans, martinis, and marischino cherries within the blink of an eye, leaving you and him plenty of time to spoon, and dance and of course bat your new fake eyelashes.

Water Club, 500 E. 30th St. (@ East River), (212) 683-3333, *Outdoor Cocktails*

Floating on a barge, staring at the East River, feeling the breeze in your hair, having drinks and oysters on the deck . . . what more could we want? Perhaps a taxi . . . which is nearly impossible to find at night, so come prepared with a car service. Bliss on the water but in the city. Who says you shouldn't rock the boat?

5757 @ The Four Seasons Hotel, 57 E. 57th St. (bet. Madison & Park Aves.), *Grand Space*

This is one of the most elegant spaces in all of the great island of Manhattan! I.M. Pei designed a masterpiece of a hotel and the bar on the second floor feels right at home here. It's upscale, to say the least, and serves chichi cocktails fit for a princess, so look the part before you venture here. The tables are tough to snag, but it's festive to sip Cosmos at the bar with friends. The place sizzles with excitement, but don't try it on weekends when you must prove yourself with your hotel room key for entry!

Chelsea/Meatpacking

Blue Water Grill, 31 Union Square West (@ 16th St.), (212) 675-9500, *Neighborhood Favorite*

Owned by famed NYC restaurateur Steve Hanson, this wildly popular Union Square destination is stylish (marble walls and vintage stucco ceiling) without being tragically hip. Or maybe you're just stopping by after a day at the office for a pick-me-up cocktail! We've been known to play canasta on the outside veranda with Daffy Duck playing cards, but that's another story. . . . The seafood menu is fabulous and the 100-year-old building is a NYC landmark!

Bongo, 299 Tenth Ave. (bet. 27th & 28th Sts.), (212) 947-3654, *Neighborhood Favorite*

This is such a cool lounge/restaurant that you may even be the coolest girl on the block for suggesting this place to meet for drinks and some awesome seafood at the bar. It's fun and delicious. Special drinks include Bongo Bellini or the Blue Bongo. They play great tunes too. Just go!

Cafeteria, 119 Seventh Ave. (@ 17th St.), (212) 417-1717, *Late Night*

Not! White, sleek, mod, fashion crowd, late late late, etc . . . Comfort food for the highly glossed and coifed, who slink in for mac and cheese or turkey meat loaf after a night on the town. Eavesdrop on the glitterati. No hairnets allowed—only hot D&G-clad waiters. Don't miss the space-age lounge downstairs for late-night toddies and a party-like scene.

The Cooler, 416 W. 14th St. (bet. Ninth Ave. & Washington), (212) 229-0785, *Alternative Club*

You never know what's going to happen at this avante-garde meatpacking bar . . . no pun intended! Located in an old converted meatpacking plant, the décor is the actual equipment of yesteryear. It sounds scary, but it is an underground experience for those looking to branch out . . . way out! Nightly DJs spin hard-core hip-hop or drum'n bass, or stop by on Thursday night to catch a rising rap star doing his thing for a 10-dollar cover.

Eugene, 27 West 24th St. (bet. Fifth & Sixth Aves.), (212) 462-0999, *Velvet Rope*

Who wouldn't want to be seen at this latest trendy night spot in the Flatiron District? Models, yuppies, and those who think they are flocking in by the taxi full. The space itself is huge, with couches, oversized mirrors, and velvet curtains giving it the feel of a 1940s supper club. This was, after all, the heart of all the action in New York at the turn of the last century too! Open until 4 A.M.

Glass, 287 10th Ave. (bet. 26th & 27th Sts.), (212) 904-1580, *Ultra-Mod*

We used to call this area the wild, wild west, but it is fast becoming *the* place to hang. This brand spanking new lounge/restaurant is a digitally created space inspired by the aerodynamics of a sleek car—a perfect destination for thirsty gallery hoppers. Think Plexiglas and upholstered leather set in a modular space complete with flattering lighting. Put on your best Jean Gautier skirt and prepare to sip Mojitos and snack on sea bass ceviche. Open from 5 P.M.–3 A.M.

Hell, 59 Ganesvoort St. (bet. Greenwich & Washington Sts.), (212) 727-1666, *Lounge*

We don't mind going to hell and back for the devilish scene at this joint. Even Hades knows the need for perfectly chilled martinis, red walls and a jukebox with cool tunes. Live on the edge mingling among this "mixed" crowd . . . girls, boys, and everything in between—50 percent straight, 50 percent not! This dark little dungeon can't help but make you feel up to no good. Just say the devil made you do it! Don't fight over which song to play in the jukebox that is packed with great CD's.

Hogs & Heifers, 859 Washington St. (@ 13th St.), (212) 929-0655, *Get Rowdy*

Willie Nelson on the jukebox and two women dancing on the bar—that just about sums up this late-night hot spot in the meatpacking district. Behind the bar are taxidermy draped with multicolored bras "discarded" by the rich and famous. After several beers and a game of pool you too might join Julia

Roberts in the now infamous and expected "bra toss." Will Dennis Quaid's reputation ever be the same after his romping night here? The clientele is largely gentrified, so don't be intimidated by the string of Harleys out front.

Lotus, 409 W. 14th St. (bet. Ninth & Tenth Aves.), (212) 243-4420, *Fun Emporium*

The fashionable and fabulous arrive by the limoload at this trendy and notably swanky nightclub/restaurant that is inspired by resorts in the Far East. Four levels of quasi-exotic fun. The basement houses a dance space that is moody and mysterious, complete with a bamboo dance floor that supposedly is "softer on the feet" (thank God—ours are killing us!). The main floor houses the restaurant serving "French/American" with a late menu starting at 11 P.M. The mezzanine lounge is for an eye-batting cocktail, and lastly, the top-secret VIP room upstairs is like a Balinese hut. *Psst . . . ask about renting a little space for your private affair.*

Lot 61, 550 W. 21st St. (bet. Tenth & Eleventh Aves.), (212) 243-6555, *Neighborhood Favorite*

Starts off small and intimate thanks in part to partitions, and as the night unfolds so does the ultimately cavernous sprawling den of Chelsea night crawlers. Literally, partitions pull back to unleash the full industrial magnitude of this landmark on the Chelsea club scene. A beautiful fireplace on one end gathers the gallery shopping set for postmodern cocktails and revelry. Stay for one drink or stay all night and look for P. Diddy and entourage to roll in around 1:00 A.M. Just have patience (or a bodyguard) for a taxi on a slow night in the remote neighborhood.

Merchants, 112 Seventh Ave. (bet. 16th & 17th Sts.), (212) 366-7267, *Neighborhood Favorite*

See details in UWS, other location in UES.

Rhone, 63 Ganesvoort St. (bet. Washington & Greenwich Sts.), (212) 367-8440, *Wine Bar*

Former garage space blossoms into a sexy wine bar on a mission: introducing Manhattanites to Rhône Valley wines. There are 200 choices on any given day (at least 30 by the glass). Sit at the bar for hours and taste them all! Just be careful climbing down! Prices range from $6 to $14 a glass, and bottles are reasonable as well. This dimly lit and minimalist loft is actually quiet and the crowd feels laid-back and local. The food is secondary but the fresh regional cuisine makes a nice complement to your wine. Don't expect a lot of help in choosing from the waitstaff but the reference guide *Wines of the Rhône Valley* is perched on the zinc-topped bar to compensate.

Serena @ The Chelsea Hotel, 222 W. 23rd St. (bet. Seventh & Eighth Aves.) (212) 255-4646, *Neighborhood Hot Spot*

It's all the rage . . . for now! Situated under the infamous rock and roll Chelsea Hotel—remember *Sid and Nancy*? The steps take you down into a large space that is broken into three nice-sized "dungeons" for socializing with your "dragon" in dimly lit interior—okay, it's just plain dark in here! Glamour girls abound, speckled with groups of "goths" having a ball.

Slate, 54 W. 21st St. (bet. Fifth and Sixth Aves.), (212) 989-0096, *Open Late*

So you just want to stay out a bit longer (it's 2 A.M. on a Tuesday and you're between jobs so what) with that cute boy you met at Clemetine's earlier in the evening. This Chelsea destination is open until 4 A.M. (yes! Pseudonuns ready for some irreverent post-Mass pool). *Wallpaper*-chic pool hall set in a loft space with so many pool tables availability is not a prob. And for late-night munchies, don't miss the fabulous food on hand. *Psst . . . inquire about Saturday morning lessons offered.*

Suite 16, 127 Eighth Ave. (@ 16th St.), (212) 627-1680, *Neighborhood Newcomer*

Don't be misled by the sleepy name of this joint. See and be seen at this Chelsea scene. There is a velvet rope policy at the door and saying you know the owners John Dorrian, Michael Dorrian, and Andy Fiscella won't help—so does everyone else! It's sleek and chic with its *Wallpaper* good looks. Put on those new hip-hugging pants you got at H&M today and prepare to party! Too many celebrities to mention are flocking by the limo load.

The Tonic Restaurant & Bar, 108 W. 18th St. (bet. Sixth & Seventh Aves.), (212) 929-9755, *Quiet After Work*

An ultracivilized bar on the edge of Chelsea that attracts as much attention for its excellent restaurant (chef Chris Gesualdi formerly of Montrachet) as for its happening bar scene. Don't overlook the landmark gorgeous mahogany bar (circa 1890). The simple bar menu is as tasty as the main dining area. Meet for a drink and then let the night take it from there! High-end chic American on the one hand, trendy pub atmosphere and eats in "the tavern" on the other. Each will delight the senses and the palate in its own way.

Union Square/Gramercy/Flatiron

Bar Demi, 125 ¹/₂ E. 17th St. (bet. Park & Third Aves.), *Wine Bar*
Tiny elegant 12-seat wine bar owned by chef Diane Forley of Verbena (see Eats). Tiny is the key—in fact, it is so small it only gets "half" a street address! Serving seasonal tiers (like the kind you usually see at a formal tea) of flavorful finger food to match your half bottle or glass of vino. This food is made with feeling, and you will feel fantastic, if not light as a feather, after your "demi" experience!

Cedar Tavern, 82 University Pl. (bet. 11th & 12th Sts.), (212) 741-9754, *Historic Hangout*
The real McCoy of taverns . . . booze, burgers, and NYU students abound. Serving until 3:30 A.M. We heard there was a groovy glass-enclosed roof garden, but we've never sauntered beyond the gorgeous bar formerly inhabited by William de Kooning and Jackson Pollack.

Centro-Fly, 45 W. 21st St. (bet. Fifth & Sixth Aves.), (212) 627-7770, *Dance Club*
Located in the former Tramps space, this slick and trippy place is on the lips of every downtown party girl! It's not a huge space but enough to accommodate several different "scenes" in which to make a scene! The décor is psychedelic, and there is a groovy circular bar near the back overlooking the dance floor. Was that Mary J. Blige tripping the light fantastic?

Cibar, 56 Irving Pl. (bet. 17th & 18th Sts.), (212) 460-5656, *Cigar Friendly*
With cigar bars popping up in the nineties faster than internet start-ups, this one added a feminine twist. Cozy couches and the idyllic setting of Irving Place will make you feel right in sync with this cigar bar world. The crowd is usually a good ratio of boys to girls, and the martinis are excellent! If a man in a suit is your type, then you have found your stomping ground! If you can't stand the

smoke, seek refuge in one of the small outdoor spaces in front and back.

Coffee Shop, 29 Union Square West (@ 16th St.), (212) 243-7969, *Late Night*

Just like your high school sweetheart, this fun trendy Brazilian cosmopolitan "diner" is always there when you need it. Food is great, and it's open late late late for you night-owlettes—an unpublished 5 A.M. Owned by ex-model Carolyn Benitez, wife of producer "Jellybean," this is a great place for the traveling gal to dine solo *au bar*—lots to look at and talk to. Go back beyond "the ladies" and enter another world—the World Room (an eatery within an eatery) brings a different menu and atmosphere (brick-oven pizzas and fireplaces). So whether you're there to observe and be observed or to snuggle at the fireplace, Coffee Shop does a lot more for you than caffeine.

Enoteca I Trulli, 122 E. 27th St. (bet. Park & Lexington Aves.) (212) 481-7372, *Wine Tastings*

Tuscan food of the highest order is accompanied by an unparalleled list of wines by the glass. Feel secluded and tucked away from the masses in this opera-filled hideaway bar. The spare menu is filled with choice cured meats, cheeses, olives, and 42 wines by the glass or the "flight," a three-glass set of two-ounce tastes. Compare and contrast for a truly Italian snack or move to the larger dining room for a more elegant experience.

Irving Plaza, 17 Irving Plaza (@ 15th St.), (212) 777-6800, *Live Music*

This small but inviting ballroom is known as one of the best places in the city to see great music from national touring acts. Excellent acoustics without sacrificing intimacy make this a SRO situation most nights. You will be surprised who you can catch on any given night! (They sometimes do two or three shows to accommodate all of the ticket buyers.) From Jewel to The Beastie Boys with a little Trisha Yearwood thrown in for good measure. Tickets sell out fast for hot shows but some same-day walk-up purchases are possible.

Jazz Standard, 116 E. 27th St. (bet. Park & Lexington Aves.), (212) 576-2232, *Live Music*

This is a hip place to see authentic jazz without any hassles. Situated in the basement of the sleek eatery aptly named 27 Standard. Put on that cute little number you bought at the Barneys Warehouse sale and get lost in the music while you sip some Brunello di Montalcino vino. Cover ranges from $10 to $15 per person but is money will spent.

MBC Music Studio, 25 W. 32nd St., (bet. Broadway & Fifth Ave.), (212) 967-2244, *24-Hour Karaoke*

Unleash the diva in you at this authentic Korean karaoke house. This place is ideal for those girls who are too shy to sing in public but have a real urge to belt one out. For $30 an hour, a private "living room" is provided with door, lock and key. Sing until your heart's content—we are pretty sure that they are soundproof! Whew. Grab a few beers from the cooler in the front and grab a few friends for a late night filled with lots of laughs.

Pete's Tavern, 129 E. 18th St. (@ Irving Pl.), (212) 473-7676, *Historic Saloon*

One of the oldest operating bars in the city, circa 1864. If these walls could talk you might hear O. Henry speak, literally . . . he made the place famous! Take in the original tin ceiling, tile floors and rosewood bar before you order a pint with your pals. (It would be a shame to order white wine here!) Could have a celebrity sighting or two. The cheeseburgers are gargantuan so wear your Prada stretch pants for the festivities.

Spa, 76 E. 13th St. (bet. Fourth Ave. & Broadway), (212) 388-1060, *Dance Club*

This place is hot—and we're not talking about the trendy downtown boys hanging out at the waterfall bar. Groovy interior, baby! Steven Lewis designed a club that is both simple yet lavish, cool yet cozy . . . even more cozy on the dance floor, my lovelies! We are particularly fond of the sauna-inspired bathrooms that are perfect for primping before we melt into a comfy banquette to observe the happening crowd of nubile flesh dance the night away. *Psst . . . be sure to bring your prettiest friends or a connected buddy, the velvet rope is so hard to get past that we have even been turned down on a crazy busy Saturday!*

The Belmont Lounge, 117 E. 15th St. (bet. Park Ave. & Irving Pl.), (212) 533-0009, *Low-Key Hangout*

Hang with the best of them at this "divey" Union Square hot spot offering something for everyone. Couches, coffee tables, and a game room with backgammon bring the lounge concept to new heights. Hobnob with celeb patrons who have lounged here

(Marisa Tomei, Leonardo DiCaprio) Wed.–Sat. DJs spin records but don't get too caught up in the beats because they don't have a cabaret license! Spring and fall allow you to spill into the garden for a breath of fresh air or a moonlight kiss.

✏ *Not to Miss:*

Old Town Bar, 45 E. 18th St. (bet. Broadway & Park Ave.), (212) 529-6732, *Historic Building*

Greenwich Village ··

Bar Six, 502 Sixth Ave. (@ 12th St.), (212) 406-8017, *Euro Delight*

Neighborhood haunt for the Euro-born and inclined. What a cool place—smoky and loud—it has its own brand of charm for late-night French Moroccan nosh crowd and late-night whispers in the dark. *Psst . . . beat the smoke and the crowd for a festive postwork drink.*

Bowlmor Lanes, 10 University Pl. (bet. 12th & 13th Sts.), (212) 255-8288, *Alternative Fun*

Let's go bowling! A mainstay for the NYU crowd, it's also one of the city's most popular fetish late-night activities. Monday night is "Night Strike," where you bowl to live DJ music in black light until the wee hours—definitely on a first come/first serve basis at a mere $12 a pop (shoe rental included). Any other night, you have free rein to run amuck with your glow-in-the-dark ball and your vintage league shirt, bowling away the blues with your buds!

Bottom Line, 15 W. 4th St. (@ Mercer St.), (212) 228-7880, *Live Music*

For 25 years the Bottom Line has been one of the best places to sit and listen to music. That's the key: sit and listen. Mostly showcasing singer/songwriter types from the folk, rock, country and jazz world who have major label record deals, no amateurs are allowed, but you will be delighted by the eclectic lineup during any given week. Low on charm, high on talent. Tickets can be purchased ahead of the show, or you last-minute ladies can stop by and take your chances.

C3 @ The Washington Square Hotel, 103 Waverly Pl. (bet. McDougal St. & Sixth Ave.), (212) 555-9515, *Hidden Lounge*

This is one of city's best secrets! Tucked in the back of the Washington Square Hotel (see Tripping), there is a small, romantic bar serving killer cocktails. The room is beautiful with varying shades of brown and fruitwood tones. Speaking of fruit, try one of the specialty cocktails like a blood orange martini made of fresh squeezed juice or the famous apple martini that is made by fabulous bartender Julie. Rumor has it that she personally ferments the apples used in her concoctions. Have a good time; just don't tell anyone else about this unspoiled hideaway. Open daily from 4 P.M.–midnight. *Psst . . . opt for the jazz brunch served on Sundays. Make a reservation and check out who's playing each week and other related news at www.c3jazz.com.*

Chumley's, 86 Bedford St. (bet. Barrow & Grove Sts.), (212) 675-4449, *Historic Dive*

A onetime speakeasy, an illegal pub during Prohibition, it's still not so easy to find—they just never got around to putting a sign up! Here's why: taking liberty with their street address, the common restaurant phrase to "86" something was started here during Prohibition to signal "illegal" patrons of the police's imminent arrival and scoot them out the secret entrance/exit at 86 Bedford, an unmarked door. Warm and inviting with a jukebox to keep your toes tapping for hours to come. Goth kids beware—weekends are packed with yuppies.

Hudson Bar & Books, 636 Hudson St. (bet. Jane & Horatio Sts.), (212) 229-2642, *Conversation Conducive*

This English library–style bar attracts a "refined" crowd that enjoys savoring scotch while chatting about their latest bedside book. The cozy nook in the back is perfect for relaxing or reading while you sip your Chivas in peace. *Psst . . . wear cool specs to fit in.*

Tortilla Flats, 767 Washington St., (@ W. 12th St.), (212) 243-1053, *Bingo & Booze*

Kitsch galore, especially on Bingo Night (Mon)! Elvis memorabilia everywhere, including an original framed check for one of his Caddies . . . Why request the Ernest Borgnine booth? Not sure, but do it anyway! Tex-Mex, music and margaritas. Book in advance for Friday and Saturday night. *Psst . . . in the mood for a Vegas fix?*

Wed's are Vegas Night complete with dice, gambling and the hula-hoop contests between tables to compete for free drinks!

Smalls, 183 W. 10th St. (bet. Sixth & Seventh Aves.), (212) 929-7565, *Live Jazz*

Serious jazz in a teeny tiny subterranean hole in the wall—only in NYC! All-night sessions start heating up about 2 A.M. and sometimes don't end until Rice Krispy Time (8 A.M.) . . . No liquor license so better brown bag it (they do provide setups). Be prepared for the music, promising talents are as serious about their composing and arranging as their playing! Christina Aguilera might get egged here by these hard-core jazz aficionados. No offense, Christina, but you know how jazz fans can get! Definitely a cultural slice of the city. Ten-dollar cover.

Midway, 145 Charles St. (@ Washington St.), (212) 352-1119, *Neighborhood Favorite*

Trendy hangout where the scene is as good as the cuisine. A "very cool" neighborhood haunt jammed to the gills with black-clad babes and hipsters. Belgian fare: mussels, fries, and brews—you can't miss. Wear your titanium shades to avoid the "glare" of pretension. Formerly Waterloo, the same owners have infused this place with new life. We were regulars before, and still pledge our allegiance.

◆ *Not to Miss:*
The Blue Note, 131 W. 3rd St. (@ 6th Avenue), (212) 475-8592, *Musical Institution*

East Village/Lower East Side ·······························

Angel's Share, 9 Stuyvesant St. (bet. 9th St. & Second Ave.), (212) 589-3041, *Secret Hideaway*

Why are there so many hard-to-find joints in this neighborhood? Whatever! Hidden above a violently lit noodle shop, you must enter through the Japanese/Korean BBQ place. Spare(rib) us! Look for the ubiquitous "secret" door behind which all your magical dreams will come true after drinking too much special sake . . . yada yada ya. . . . The bar is exclusive and elegant, with painted murals and luscious upholstery, but for God's sake, sometimes you just need a drink and not a quest for Treasure Island behind a noodle shop!

Arlene Grocery, 95 Stanton St. (bet. Ludlow & Orchard Sts.), (212) 358-1633, *Live Music*

Come discover . . . Lots of great unsigned bands launch here, so get ahead of the trend! There is rarely a cover for this down-and-dirty destination where you can partake in "let it all hang out" fun! A happening place for cheap drinks and loads of activity. *Psst . . . we love Vanessa Carlton.*

B Bar, 40 E. 4th St. (@ Bowery), (212) 475-2220, *Neighborhood Favorite*

So utterly hip you need reservations for cocktails. You'd never guess it was a gas station in its earliest incarnation before upgrading to the Bowery Bar. Its current state of being can be a fun place to convene if you're not turned off by heavy "'tude" from the self-important staff. Twentysomething? Check out weekends. Thirtysomething? Stick to weeknights or get some lipo and glycolic to feel in the game.

Beauty Bar, 231 E. 14th St. (bet. Second & Third Aves.), (212) 539-1389, *Kitsch Cocktail*

Need a manicure and a martini? Never fear, you can get both here!! This former "beauty parlor" (think *Grease:* "Beauty School Dropout") has been converted into a bar. The surroundings have been kept pretty much the same since its salon days. Sit under the old-fashioned dryer as you sip your Cosmo and blow on your nails. The young crowd runs the gamut from German tourists to pink-haired hipsters to uptight career girls letting loose! Sound familiar? *Psst . . . unwind on Thursday and Friday nights with a free cocktail if you get a $10 manicure.*

Brownies, 169 Ave. A (bet. 10th & 11th Sts.), (212) 420-8392, *Live Music*

Catch a rising star at this dark and dingy dive that is mainly for those who want to check out the world of underground music. Don't say we didn't warn you: it's "funky" in the grungy sense of the word, but cheap drinks and fun abound! Everyone in the city knows someone's roommate's boyfriend who has played at Brownies. Maybe you will meet a banker by day and rock star by night! Then again, didn't your mother warn you about musicians?

Decibel, 240 E. 9th St. (@ Second Ave.), (212) 979-2733, *Secret Sake*

Pretends to be invisible but look closely, there *is* a sign. After they check out your "cool quotient" (worth a trip back to your hotel to change into casual chic—Darryl K and Helmut Lang, for example), you glide through the beaded doorway into The Hippest Sake Bar in Manhattan. Premium sakes—hot and cold—and Saketinis of all varieties await. It's dark, even a bit dingy, downtown in a major way. Meet your lover, not your mother.

Drinkland, 399 E. 10th (bet. Aves. A & B), (212) 228-2435, *Fun Galore*

This "Mondrianic" bar is a hang for all who are hip or think they are—fun downtown bar with an edge. Don't forget "Oxygen Wednesdays" when avant-garde bands will breathe new life into your multiculti lungs . . .

Fez @ Time Café, 380 Lafayette St. (@ Great Jones St.), (212) 533-7000, *Live Music*

Enter the Time Café and head past the bar downstairs to this Moroccan salon complete with cushy sofas, velvet (real velvet, by the way) pillows and low arches welcoming you to the night! It's best to go during the week if you are looking to relax and stay awhile because the weekends are packed and rowdy. It's a pretty sexy experience if that's what you are looking for . . . and who isn't? *Psst . . . there is a live-music space at the back that is worth a listen.*

Idlewilde, 141 E. Houston St. (bet. First & Second Aves.), (212) 477-5005, *Trendy concept*

Buckle up, girls, for the ride of the evening! We *hate* theme bars, but we have decided to make an exception . . . Imagine a tricked-out Concorde . . . it's a bar! It's a swanky plane! It's novelty fun for the beautiful and bored! Crowd around the bar before you head to your "bulkhead seat" that reclines and faces your pals. Just don't forget to put on your sexy flight suit—no "coach class" fashion allowed! Don't let the altitude go to your head. Closed on Sunday and Monday nights.

Lansky Lounge, 102 Norfolk St. (bet. Delancey & Rivington Sts.), (212) 677-9489, *Hidden Lounge*

If you have a bad sense of direction, then spare yourself the pain—you will never find it! Here we go: go down the stairs, through the dark alley, up the staircase and thru the green door. Poof! You are transported to a lounge where you sip everything in martini glasses and swing the night away to Frank Sinatra. The crowd is always cool, and the menu is filled with hearty steaks so we suggest late-night cocktails unless you are in the mood for meat and potatoes. Open seven nights a week.

Liquid, 266 E. 10th St. (bet. First Ave. & Ave. A), (212) 677-1717, *Dance The Night Away*

Boogie the night away as hip DJs spin and mix cool tunes five nights a week . . . The only thing that might slow the Dancing Queen down is a sip of the superb house specialty—the Cosmopolitan! You've never had a Cosmo till you've had one of the little pink devils here. The dark and cavernous space is warmed up by a super fireplace in the winter months. Warning: Sunday night is for lovers!

Marion's Continental Restaurant, 354 Bowery (@ 4th St.), (212) 475-7621, *Kitsch Cocktail*

Fantastic kitschy forties-style diner look . . . Great music, happening drinks . . . We'll never grow tired of the easy vibes. Here's the tip: arrive before 7 P.M., order the "yellow plate special" at the bar for an 11-dollar three-course meal.

Mercury Lounge, 217 E. Houston St. (bet. First Ave. & Ave. A), (212) 260-4700, *Live Alternative Music*

Fun low-key music venue for those in search of great local pop/rock bands and national artists just bubbling under mainstream stardom (Lisa Loeb, The Verve, Lucinda Williams, etc.). Don't be surprised to find many a record-label exec patrolling for inspiration. . . . Think positively, they have expense accounts for all those Heinekens you've been guzzling daintily.

Torch, 137 Ludlow St. (bet. Rivington & Stanton Sts.), (212) 228-5151, *Supper Club*

Blast into the past when elegant supper clubs wooed the "in crowd" with A-list talent, ambiance, and fine dining. You'll step through the harlequin-patterned doors and feel transported in body and spirit. After dinner, lush booths and live music will lure you into the Havana-style club area toward the back. Many an aspiring Broadway starlet has sung for her supper at this East Village nightspot.

The Elephant, 58 E. First St. (bet. First & Second Aves.), (212) 505-7739, *Sexy Hot Spot*

Thai-French brunch is served with sexy drinks to hordes of hipsters in Prada pants. It's tiny, so be prepared to sip side by side.

Von, 3 Bleecker St. (@ Bowery), (212) 473-3039, *Quiet Wine Bar*

This lovely little wine bar hideaway will allow you to do just that—hide! Exposed brick walls and a long wooden bar create an inviting yet sophisticated environment. If you're lucky, Karen Von will be behind the bar serving wine by the glass or imported beer (would you really order a Miller Lite here?). Feel free to come back often—regulars rule the roost!

10th Street Lounge, 212 E. 10th St. (bet. First & Second Aves.), (212) 473-5252, *Neighborhood Favorite*

In a city where things change faster than lighting, we are glad some things never change . . . like this neighborhood staple! These guys were way ahead of the "lounge" movement, and they could write the book on how to do it. Come to chill out on one of the couches in this simple but elegant industrial space. There is nothing on the cinder-block walls that are only a match to the cement floor. Mission-style furniture warms it up a bit along with an occasional candle for "mood." People-watching makes the small but annoying cover charge worth it!

✦ *Not to Miss:*
KGB Bar, 85 E. 4th St. (bet. Bowery & Second Ave.), (212) 505-3360, *Underground Hotspot*
Webster Hall, 125 E. 11th St. (bet. Third & Fourth Aves.), (212) 353-1600, *Huge Bar*

SoHo/Nolita/Chinatown/Little Italy

Balthazar, 80 Spring St. (bet. Broadway & Crosby St.), (212) 965-1785, *Neighborhood Favorite*

Paris bistro meets downtown beautiful people scene where oysters are de rigueur! Great lighting, red leather, and cacophony greet you at the door. Wear cool shoes in case he's looking down! Expect to be given the "once-over" by everybody—who said the well-heeled have manners? The "raw bar" menu is excellent. We'd love to pretend that all our evenings here are spent kissing cheeks, sipping gin, and nibbling the occasional Blue Point oysters, but alas we are slaves to the french fries! Great brunch on Sundays.

Bar 89, 89 Mercer St. (bet. Broome & Spring Sts.), (212) 274-0989, *Local Hangout*

If for some God-only-knows reason you would like a peek at those tinkling in the stall next door, come on down! The novelty has worn off for locals, but the coed loo is equipped with see-through glass doors that turn opaque when you close the latch. They also mix a helluva cocktail for those with bladder control. All teasing aside, this is a great little lounge with yummy appetizers and a mischievous crowd!

Barolo, 398 W. Broadway (bet. Spring & Broome Sts.), (212) 226-1102, *Garden Delight*

A delightful spring/summer hideaway! Enter the front of the large façade on this popular street and head straight to the back for the most spacious outdoor patios in SoHo. The trees are lit in the evening making it all seem magical! Could be a great inner-city stress reducer if the staff is in a good mood . . . otherwise, expect them to act out. Don't forget to end the night with a Lemoncello.

Bond Street, 6 Bond Street, (bet. Broadway & Lafayette St.), (212) 677-8487, *Sake Bar*

The doorman might have an attitude if you catch him on one of those nights, and if you do get in, you might notice that you were held at bay only to make way for the celeb couple of the week. But once inside you're sure to enjoy the "less is more" simplicity of this subterranean lounge. Serving a modified version of the restaurant's menu along with plum wine "saketinis." Brought to you by the team behind Indochine—expect a touch of class and make sure you bring yours with you! *Psst . . . the hot chef, Linda Rodriguez, originally at Nobu, was recently rated as one of the city's top chefs!*

 Café Noir, 323 Grand St. (@ Thompson St.), (212) 431-7910, *Chorizo Heaven*

Palm trees give way to the candlelit interior and inviting dark wood bar. Everyone is doing their own thing in this laissez-faire boite. . . . Intimate tête à têtes, cigarette smoking, incense burning, and cocktails are the ticket. Don't miss the French Moroccan tapas menu for late-night munchies or the tangy sangria by the pitcher. Not for the faint of heart or breath, this dark and moody café attracts a fashionable international crowd oozing sex appeal and scintillating conversation.

Canteen, 142 Mercer St. (@ Prince St.), (212) 431-7766, *Neighborhood Newcomer*

The Merc Bar's Marc Newson is tempting fate with this futuristic mod spot that has made quite a splash! People watching at it finest. Sit among the other city dwellers in the orange fluorescent chairs and overlook the sunken dining area. Knowing his track record, we bet this will still be "happening" by the time you read this!

Casa La Femme, 150 Wooster St. (bet. Houston & Prince Sts.), (212) 505-0005, *Romantic Charm*

Rock the Casbah! Walk into the world of plush cushions, Egyptian tobacco in hookas, and curtained "tents" for the romantic Bedouin in all of us! Otherworldly atmosphere for a sizzling second date . . . and the food is dervishly delicious! Winning the See Jane Go prize for the most date-friendly atmosphere. Who else wines and dines you in your own tent? Just don't let him flirt with the belly dancers! *Psst . . . we love the grass floor in the summer months. Also, check out the backgammon boards!*

Cipriani's Downtown, 376 W. Broadway, (bet. Spring & Broome Sts.), (212) 343-099, *Sexy Hot Spot*

Crazy prices, even crazier people make for a festive yet expensive pseudo-Venetian experience. Bellinis are the beverage of choice for the glitterati and Gotham gals. Rooftop terrace dining is great on a balmy summer night. Just sit back and wait for something festive to happen because it will! Smoking is encouraged, so don't flinch if Sarah Jessica Parker brushes your elbow in passing! *Psst . . . there is no sign outside but it is brightly lit enough to ID from the street.*

Double Happiness, 173 Mott St. (bet. Grand & Broome Sts.), (212) 941-1282, *Underground Cool*

The import music scene for the under-thirty set—a very "in" place for the young and uninhibited, with a basement entrance for those in the know. DJs mix, celebutantes hang, nubile flesh haunts the brick cubbyholes in search of . . . whatever. If it seems like everyone but you is on some kind of happy pill, think again—they're just doubly happy! Open seven days, till 4 A.M. on weekends.

Ear Inn, 326 Spring St. (bet. Greenwich & Washington Sts.), (212) 226-9060, *Historic Site*

History lovers, take note! This 1817 federal town house (one of the few left in the city) was fondly named the James Brown House—no, not that James Brown, but an aide to George Washington during the Revolutionary War. The home was Generous George's postwar parting gift to his right-hand man. The liquor license was established in 1898 and the rest is history—a speakeasy/brothel turned cool bar scene in the new millennium. A soulful bartender adds juice to this joint. Open till 4 A.M.; serving food till 3 A.M. on weekends. *Psst . . . cheap eats—the most expensive item is a lobster served on Friday for a whopping $11.95!*

Indochine, 430 Lafayette St. (bet. Astor Place & E. 4th St.), (212) 505-5111, *Neighborhood Favorite*

"Tall and tan and young and lovely"—the girls from Ipanema are using this bar as their clubhouse. Lots of gorgeousness and celebrity cachet—the first time we came, Lauren Hutton was on our right; ten years later she was on our left. This place hit its chic peak years ago but has maintained its popularity and hip factor. The bar is small and dark, with palms that envelop you in an exotic atmosphere perfect for hard-core flirting. Reservations are a must for dinner, or eat hors d'oeuvres at the bar.

Joe's Pub, 425 Lafayette St. (bet. Astor Place & E. 4th St.), (212) 539-8770, *Live Music*

Squeezed into a corner of the Joseph Papp Theater, this hot little bar has a strange yet charming eighties vibe. Multitiered, with a stage in the round, you never know who might burst into song—but don't you even think about it, Tinkerbell! Another fun and lively destination for your Manhattan pub crawl. Open till 4 A.M. daily.

 Lucky Strike, 59 Grand St. (bet. Broadway & Wooster St.), (212) 941-0772, *Late Night*

Keith McNally's virgin restaurateur endeavor is still going strong, and how time flies. Capturing the magic from this American bar/restaurant he has gone on to more fame and fortune with Balthazar (see SoHo) and Pastis (see Chelsea/Meatpacking). Smoky, late-night choice for the delicious penne with asparagus and maybe a little nuzzle from your boy-toy!

M&R Bar, 264 Elizabeth St. (bet. Prince & Houston Sts.), (212) 226-0559, *Casual Chic*

Dive bar chic, total kitsch. The starter kit for up-and-coming Nolita hipsters who sip on silver shakers of magic margaritas. Definitely not a tourist trap, M&R is for those in search of a downtown neighborhood feel with a bit of shine. Great for a late-night snack after you've seen an on-the-rise singer/songwriter at Mercury Lounge (see LES).

Merc Bar, 151 Mercer St. (bet. Prince & Houston Sts.), (212) 966-2727, *Neighborhood Favorite*

The grand dame of the SoHo bar scene, Marc Newson entices urban outdoorsy types with his back-to-nature décor. Gigantic black-and-white photos of waterfalls adorn the walls and a canoe hangs from the ceiling. Meet a friend for drinks—or meet a new friend over drinks! Hint: Can you say, *Looking for Mr. Goodbar?*

N, 33 Crosby St. (bet. Broome & Grand Sts.) (212) 219-8856, *Euro Central*

Perfect for dancing or curling up in a candlelit corner. N (pronounced with a Spanish accent) serves no attitude and no velvet rope, away from the hustle and bustle of SoHo. Keep the sangria and tapas coming and while the night away! *Psst . . . N has one of the most extensive selections of sherry and Spanish wines in the city.*

Pravda, 218 Lafayette St. (bet. Houston & Prince Sts.), (212) 226-4944, *Vodka and Caviar*

From Russia with love by the team that brought you Balthazar! It used to be impossible even for the fabulous to get past this iron curtain: past the KGB, down the steps, through the door, and into the czar's den of inequity for the ultrachic and young . . . Looked like spring break for big-ticket caviar lovers the last time we darkened the doors. The room itself is beautiful as well with a semicircular bar and deep comfy leather club chairs in the middle for panoramic "views" of the hip proletariat.

S.O.B's (Sounds Of Brazil), 204 Varick St. (@ W. Houston St.), (212) 243-4940, *Live Ethnic Music*

Live Brazilian music for those looking to let their hair down! Share a few Caipirinhas at the elevated bar with a handsome stranger (not included with book purchase) and get ready to break in those Sergio Rossi's! Ouch! Dance lessons are offered early in the evening by a scantily clad Brazilian singer. The food is tropical and gives you plenty of energy to rhumba—1, 2 Cha Cha Cha; 3, 4.

Sway, 30 Spring St. (bet. Greenwich & Hudson Sts.), (212) 620-5220, *Lounge*

Grab your camel and take a ride to the middle of nowhere for a Moorish night you won't forget . . . and let's face it, it's cheaper than airfare to Morocco! There's no sign outside—at least, not a sign that says "Sway"—look for "McGovern's Bar" and you'll know you've arrived. Coolness abounds, with a long bar in the front for hanging and chatting. Go to the back for the full experience. Eclectic and fashionable crowd. Gwyneth sightings. *Psst . . . get a recommendation from the bartender for "the drink of the moment"! Last summer it was Stoli Raspberry and Tonic!*

The Mercer Kitchen @ the Mercer Hotel, 147 Mercer (@ Prince St.), (212) 966-6060, *Afternoon Drinks*

This upstairs bar is situated on one of the most centrally located corners in all of downtown. Gorgeous sunsets add to the experience of lounging and sipping Chardonnay with a colleague. Light fare from the downstairs kitchen is served from 6 P.M. until midnight.

The Void, 16 Mercer St. (@ Howard St.), (212) 941-6492, *Late Night*

A unique destination spot for the high-tech and open-minded. Indie film producers and directors come here to use the giant TV screen to preview their latest endeavor in this truly multimedia video lounge. Wednesday nights they play movies from the sixties and seventies. *Sex and the City* meets *Dr. No* in this bizarre bar-cum—entertainment center. Stalk your Indie director crush here. Be careful on weekends because the crowd can lean a little young and restless. Unless, of course, you are that way too!

 23 Watts, 23 Watts St. (bet. Broome St. & W. Broadway), (212) 925-9294, *Dance Club*

Home to models and Euro Trash alike! Formerly known as

Chaos, the name changed but the crowd never left. You're sure to have a ball at this chic multilevel nightclub if you can get in. The bouncers are beyond rude, so arrive with your prettiest friends or hottest boy-toys by your side. Otherwise, expect serious velvet-rope burn! Once inside the gilded cage, expect to be gouged.

✦ *Not to Miss:*

357, 357 W. Broadway (bet. Broome & Grand Sts.), (212) 965-1491, *Champagne Sunday*

Tribeca/Lower Manhattan/Other Boroughs ·····················

Bar Odeon, 136 W. Broadway (bet. Duane & Thomas Sts.), (212) 285-1155, *Neighborhood Newcomer*

Across the street from its more mature sibling, "baby sister bar" is more intimate and funky with a bistro menu that still offers those 2 A.M. Odeon Classics we can't survive a hangover without! Relax in the summer months and enjoy the full "open-door" design effect . . . Just because you've been pruned with a Brazilian bikini wax does not give you license to "flash" passersby.

Divine Bar, 55 Liberty St. (bet. Broadway & Nassau St.), (212) 791-9463, *After-Work Drinks*

After-work spot for the powerful and simply "divine" to meet other young hot-steppers of the New Economy. The candlelit atmosphere will hide any of the flaws your Laura Mercier camouflage couldn't handle! Serving over 65 wines by the glass as well as cocktails. Tapas menu for a nibble while you sip your Shiraz! This "wine and beer only" bar feels like more of a SoHo spot. See other location in MTE.

El Teddy's, 219 W. Broadway (bet. Franklin & White Sts.), (212) 941-7070, *Margarita Cravings*

The Statue of Liberty welcomes you, or at least her head does! Modern, yet timeless, the straight-up margaritas served in martini glasses are deadly, so thank God someone else is driving that yellow car! Authentic Mexican. We are crazy about the Mexican hot chocolate. The bar is the bomb for meeting up with a group of friends!

i, 277 Church St. (bet. Franklin & White Sts.), (212) 431-0965, *Lounge*

The McDonald's on the corner isn't the only one offering supersize portions . . . Sip on a frightening 10-oz. martini from your perch on the velvet banquettes at this little neighborhood newcomer. Getting through the door and down the stairs to the intimate lounge with fantastic DJ is not a problem. Depending on how fast you sip that martini, getting back up the stairs might be! Wow, it's been a long week—wear flats just in case!

Isla, 39 Downing St. (bet. Bedford & Varick Sts.), (212) 352-2822, *Sexy Hot Spot*

Great music, great ceviche trio to kick off the meal, great times in this ultramodern Cuban-style diner that permits dancing in the aisles—in fact expects it! Arrive early before your reservations (a must) and hang at the bar to get in the mood. It's *hot,* it's *cool,* it's *sexy* . . . just try to keep your clothes on! Cha Cha Cha! Open until 1:00 A.M. on weekends and closed on Sundays.

Knitting Factory, 74 Leonard St. (bet. Broadway & Church St.), (212) 219-3006, *Live Music*

Avant-garde jazz and rock featured on two stages/three floors accompanied by phenomenal sound and lighting. Several acts play nightly at varying times—free music at 11 P.M. most nights! Downtown eclectic music types come here for hourly musical mood changes (with or without PMS)—no knitting needles required. Purchase tickets via the general telephone line.

Lush, 110 Duane St. (bet. Church St. & Broadway), (212) 766-1275, *Elegant Lounge*

Tribeca is quite the unproclaimed center for the bubbly. Caviar and champagne are the ticket for you and your compadres of the lush life. An ultramodern lounge that is hard to find but worth an extra trip around the block. The spacious interior is a rarity as is the splendidly gorgeous wood bar. Slink your way into a lovely evening. We miss our John John, Jr., sightings. Open only Wednesday–Sunday, serving until 4 A.M.

The Bubble Lounge, 228 Broadway, (@ White St.), (212) 431-3433, *Lounge*

Blast yourself onto a Bette Davis movie set with luxurious velvet draperies and champagne as the only ticket. Dying to wear Ungaro's latest feather-and-suede Pocahantas coat? Go for it! You will be appreciated and there is a coat check. Your expense account and Platinum Amex by your side, no bottle of bubbly seems out of your reach—but for some you may have to stand on your tiptoes. Don't forget, girlies, champagne is supposedly the least fattening social potion! "Alcofrolics" looking for the total Bubble Lounge experience can add a little Petrossian caviar to the mix, though you may have to phone home for a cash advance. Live jazz on Monday nights sets the mood as the bubbles go straight to your head.

The Screening Room, 54 Varick St. (bet. Canal & Lake Sts.), (212) 334-2100, *www.thescreeningroom.com, Date Place*

Let's do dinner and a movie with a bit of panache. The Screening Room rolls it into one campy and lovely experience complete with evocative cocktails. Enjoy the delectable 30-dollar prix-fixe treat, including movie ticket. Finish the evening with alternative and classic flicks shown in plush art deco surroundings. Don't miss what we call the "Cult Brunch" featuring delicious food and such standards as *Breakfast at Tiffany's* and *Valley of the Dolls.*

Citywide:

www.mojom.com: Log on and find out where your favorite musicians are playing. Full itineraries of artists by city and by category.

Can you keep a secret? The hippest clubs are sponsored by "club organizers" (promoters and urchins for hire who know how to create a party "scene") at secret, changing locations. Look the part while out on the town and you may be slipped an "invite." Policies for admittance can be mysterious and sometimes a bit degrading, so make sure your ego is up to the task. We've had memorable experiences at these exclusive soirees . . .

Tripping

♦ Time Off

The American Musuem of Natural History, CPW (@ W. 79th St.), (212) 769-5100, *www.amnh.org, With Kids*

Discover the wonderment of this world-class facility. The space is grand in scale and with the addition of the Rose Center for Earth & Space, it is hard to find a more otherworldly experience. Housing the most technologically advanced space center on the "planet" and the most powerful virtual reality simulator in the universe. Otherwise, special exhibitions are worthy of a visit on their own. Open 10:00 A.M.–5:45 P.M. every day except Thanksgiving, until 8:45 P.M. on Friday & Saturday. Suggested admission $10 for adults, $7 for kids. *Psst . . . if you are looking for a pleasant and diverse way to spend Friday nights, try the "Starry Nights" events with jazz and cocktails in the Rose Center.*

The Apollo Theater, 253 W. 125th St. (bet. Seventh & Eighth Aves.), (212) 531-5305, *Soul Searching*

Many a star has been born on this stage, long considered the hub of African-American performing arts. We love Wednesday for "Amateur Night" and "Live at the Apollo." Catch a rising star and be seen on national television in the bargain—an affordable $13! Tickets are sold through Ticketmaster or at the theater box office.

The Cathedral of St. John The Divine, 1047 Amsterdam Ave. (bet. 110th & 112th Sts.), (212) 316-7540, *Historic Site*

America's largest Gothic cathedral, patrons claim its grandeur rivals that of its European counterparts. Magnificent stained glass and the wonders of Raphael beckon all of partake of its majesty. While you're in the neighborhood: Columbia University is just a hop, skip, and a jump away. This fortresslike Ivy League campus is "famous" for attracting studly bachelor MBA types. Bring your sexiest specs!

Central Park Tennis Center in Central Park, (West side of park near W. 96th St.), (212) 280-0205, *Outdoor Recreation*

With 26 courts available, chances are pretty good that you can find a place for a "love" match! Permit fee of $50 for the whole season, April through November. And in the "no free lunch" category: in order to separate real tennis freaks from dabblers, passes are not available at the Center itself. Call the permit office for into: (212) 360-8131. Nonmembers can sign up early in the morning by calling the main number and usually get a court the same day for a mere five-dollar charge. *Psst . . . four of the courts are first-class.*

Claremont Riding, 175 W. 89th St. (@ Amsterdam Ave.), (212) 724-5101, *Horseback Riding*

Got that equestrian itch? Rend a faithful steed for a jaunt through Central Park, year-round at $33 per hour (daily, dawn to dusk). Unfortunately, there are no guides, but it's a park, not a maze. There are 4.5 miles of bridle trails to help you along.

The Cloisters @ Fort Tryon Park, (212) 923-3700, *City Respite*

Escape the concrete jungle and head way north to the Met's stash of medieval. Built in Fort Tryon Park from the remnants of five different monastery cloisters, offers stunning views of the Hudson River. Surrounded by trees this is a heavenly place to view fall foliage. Closed on Mondays. Suggested admission is $10. *Psst . . . save your entry "button" for same-day admission to the Met.*

Lincoln Center for the Performing Arts, @ W. 62nd St.–W. 66th St. (bet. Amsterdam Ave. & Broadway), Daily hot line: (212) LINCOLN, *Culture Abound*

The vortex for artistic expression in NYC situated on 15 acres. Here it goes: the Metropolitan Opera, New York Philharmonic, Julliard School, the NYC Ballet, the American Ballet Theatre (ABT/Remember Baryshnikov?), the School of American Ballet, the Film Society of Lincoln Center, the Chamber Music Society, the Lincoln Center Theatre, and the New York Public Library's Collection of the Performing Arts . . . There is something for everyone. *Psst . . . tours of the facility (supergroovy) are given M–F, 10 A.M.–5 P.M. on the hour, $8.25, with students/senior discounts available.*

Lincoln Plaza Cinemas, 1886 Broadway (@ 63rd St.), (212) 757-2280, *Foreign and More*

Turn a favorite pastime into a cultural event! Great art house films in a quasi-new theater setting. Foreign films fresh off the boat, plus gourmet movie treats.

Walter Reade Theater, 165 W. 65th St. (bet. Broadway & Amsterdam Ave.) @ Lincoln Center on the Plaza Level, (212) 875-5600, *Avant Films*

Film as art: undoubtedly the best (and most comfy) place in the city to see the best films, and not just any film. Built in 1991 by the Film Society of Lincoln Center, it specializes in film festivals like Silent Divas of the Italian Film, and the ultimate New York Film Festival held annually in late September/early October. We sat Catherine Deneuve in *Rendezvous* long before it hit mainstream theaters. Get on the mailing list for a nifty monthly "playbill" listing coming attractions—show times included!

◈ Sweet Dreams

Adobe Bed and Breakfast, call for UWS address, (212) 472-2000, *Alternative Housing*

If you have more taste than cash, opt to stay at this circa 1891, fully restored landmark town house. All four rooms are tastefully decorated with inlaid floors and antiques and equipped with kitchenettes. We love the ability to have our own answering machine and own voice on it! Rooms start at $165. No smoking allowed.

Hotel Beacon, 2130 Broadway, (bet. 75th & 76th Sts.), (212) 787-1100, *Neighborhood Favorite*

Take a break here from the throngs of tourists. Situated in a lovely residential area only a short distance from Central Park, Lincoln Center and some great restaurants, the lobby is a happy place to come home to. The rooms are spacious, clean, and get plenty of sunlight. Rates start $135 for a single or $195 for double. Voice mail, hair dryers and comfy robes.

Mayflower, 15 CPW (bet. 61st & 62nd St.), (212) 265-0060, *www.mayflowerhotel.com, Reliable Location*

With this address, we need not tell you any more than the fact that this a nice place to park your Bette Davis eyes. Easy access to Lincoln Center, the Opera or Carnegie Hall, plus a great central location near Central Park for morning runs while on business. It's nothing too fancy but the valet parking, voice mail, and stunning views make it a nice alternative. Rooms are $200 for doubles and $290 for suites.

Trump International Hotel and Tower, 1 CPW (@ 61st St.), (212) 299-1000, *www.trumpintl.com, Pretention Galore*

Stars and stars . . . of both the celebrity and celestial variety! After you spot a few celebs traversing the lobby, check out a few constellations of your own with the convenient telescopes located in every bedroom! Other extras include direct-dial phone and fax, cell phones, a computer and printer. Special perk: they provide personalized stationary and calling cards upon request! Rooms start at $525 with a skyline view. Park views are more.

✦ *Good to Know:*

Audubon Terrace, Broadway (bet. 155th & 156th Sts.), *Bird Watching*

Once the estate of bird enthusiast James Audubon, the "terrace" hasn't changed much since Harlem's heyday in the 1800s. The museums on the terrace (High Beaux Lettres, the Hispanic Society of America @ (212) 926-2234) and The American Numismatic Society (@ (212) 234-3130) are housed in the Beaux Arts buildings with brick-paved courtyards.

Harlem Your Way, (800) 382-9363, *www.harlemourwaytours.com, Uptown Sights*

This Harlem-based company offers customized tours of Harlem, including a gospel tour, a jazz tour—many options to give you "an inside look into the Black capital of the world." While in the neighborhood: lunch at Sylvia's—the most famous restaurant in Harlem, if not NYC.

The *New York City Marathon* is run the first Saturday of every November!

Seeking peace on the West Side? The Shakespeare Garden in Central Park (enter at CPW & 72nd St.) is the place to go. Ramble to the garden and wind your way up to the Belvedere Castle. There are benches to rest on along the way. Bring along your favorite book by the man himself for the complete effect.

Go Fish! Catch a fish in the newly stocked **Harlem Meer** pond at the north end of Central Park—fishing poles provided. Call (212) 794-6564 for details.

New York magazine has flagged the south steps at the Museum of Natural History as "the best place for **al fresco sex**" in the city. But we wouldn't know anything about that!

⏿ Time Off:

The Beekman Theater, 1254 Second Ave. (@ 66th St.), (212) 737-2622, *Neighborhood Favorite*

This is moviegoing at its finest complete with prearranged seating for optimum viewing. The crowd is personally greeted by the manager before the movie starts! Although they show mostly first-run Hollywood films, this theater is an all-around pleasant experience: no escalators and only one showing make it user friendly in a world of multiplex mayhem! Don't be surprised if you run into local residents Woody Allen and Soon Yi.

Central Park Wildlife Center in Central Park, (enter at Fifth Ave. & 65th St.), (212) 861-6030, *Outdoor Activity*

Formerly known as the Zoo, this is one of the best ways to spend an afternoon in the park. The facility includes a rain-forest environment in the Tropic Zone, the Temperate Zone (and a lake complete with island), polar bears, penguins, a new Children's Zoo, and more. Open 365 days a year.

Cooper-Hewitt, National Design Museum, 2 E. 91st St. (bet. Fifth & Madison Aves.), (212) 849-8300, *Dedicated to Design*

The recent 20-million-dollar renovation of this beautiful former home to Andrew Carnegie houses an extensive assortment of architectural drawings, jewelry, prints and special exhibits, such as 1999's Czechoslovakian Cubism. Founded over a century ago by the Hewitt sisters, granddaughters of industrialist Peter Cooper, this museum treasure is worth a peek especially if you are a design aficionado! Free admission Tuesday 5–9 P.M., otherwise $8.

Frick Collection, 1 E. 70th St. (bet. Fifth & Madison Aves.), (212) 288-0700, *Neighborhood Favorite*

This home of former steel tycoon Henry Clay Frick is now home to the likes of Rembrandt, Goya and El Greco. The true enjoyment though is the mansion itself: built in 1914, it occupies an entire city block. Carved ceilings, gorgeous fixtures and a Grecian courtyard oasis make this an opulent retreat amidst the frenzy.

The Jewish Museum, 1109 Fifth Ave. (@ 92nd St.), (212) 423-3200, *Hidden Jewel*

An interesting twist to the Museum Mile, this destination presents 4,000 years of Judaic history in creative ways with ever-changing exhibits. Largest collection in the country of pre-WWII literature and films from Berlin. This is one of the best-curated museums in the city. Open Sunday–Thursday 11:00 A.M.–5:45 P.M., closed on Friday, Saturday and major Jewish holidays. Admission is $8. *Psst . . . kosher café on the premises.*

Kaufmann Concert Hall @ The 92nd Street Y, 1395 Lexington Ave. (@ 92nd St.), (212) 996-1100, www.92ndsty.org, *Alternative Entertainment*

This community resource attracts some of the most interesting authors, lecture series and internationally acclaimed musical artists that push the boundaries of traditional entertainment. The size is perfect—every seat is close to the stage. Season tickets for those in the know.

Loeb Boathouse @ Central Park Lake, (@ 72nd St. & Fifth Ave.), (212) 517-4723, *Outdoor Activity*

It's a sunny fall day . . . what should you do with your new crush? Head to the heart of Central Park for the Boathouse and rent bikes by the hour. Available from 10 A.M.–6 P.M. for $8 per hour or $40 for the full day. Only March–November. *Psst . . . or grab a picnic from the Mark's bar (see Twilight) or opt for a romantic ride in one of the 10 gondolas that cruise the lake May–September.*

The Metropolitan Museum of Art, 1000 Fifth Ave. (bet. 81st & 84th Sts.), (212) 535-7710, *Art Mecca*

If you need to be told why to go here please return our book for a refund. Don't miss the whimsical live-music café experience on Friday and Saturday. L'amour a La Musée! *Psst . . . suggested costs: $10, but you can pay whatever you want. Discounts available for seniors and students.*

Paris Theater, 4 W. 58th St. (bet. Fifth & Sixth Aves.), (212) 688-3800, *Elegant Moviehouse*

It feels like the private theater for guests at The Plaza. This gorgeous big screen shows the Indies destined to be biggies (Roberto Begnini's *Life Is Beautiful* came here first). Arrive early because they always sell out. Be sure to grab some Ghiradelli chocolate drops for a little treat before escaping with your smooching partner to the art deco balcony . . . *Psst . . . time to kill? Visit the Plaza Hotel's Oyster Bar.* Enter on the 58th St. side.

Wollman Rink in Central Park, (enter at Fifth Ave. & 62nd St.), *Outdoor Activity*

The local favorite for ice-skating, this rink offers the unique contrast of gorgeous winter trees and skyscrapers as you whiz around and around and then wipe out. Not to worry, take a hot chocolate and ankle break while you check out the practicing pros. Wheels replace blades when temperatures rise. Admission $8.

✎ *Sweet Dreams*

Barbizon Hotel, 140 E. 63rd St. (@ Lexington Ave.), (212) 838-5700, *www.thebarbizon.com, Reinvented*

Originally a women-only residence, The Barbizon is steeped in women's history even though it's now open to the less fair sex. After a 40-million-dollar renovation, this place offers the same warm feeling as it did in years gone by, but the range of services and amenities has been "updated." The rooms are spacious and the tower suites have tranquil terraces and spectacular panoramic views. *Psst . . . while you are there you can work off last night's dessert from Cafe Boulud (see Eats) at Equinox on the ground floor.*

The Franklin, 164 87th St. (bet. Lexington & Third Aves.), (212) 369-1000 or (800) 600-8787, *Hip & Cool*

This ultrastylish place is an oasis in the small hotel desert. Affordable chic and convenience is what keeps the youthful and fashionable coming back. The tiny rooms are stylish with natural colors and cool black-and-white photos of the City. Gotta love the complimentary beverage service (including espresso and cappuccino) and original cast-iron tubs to soak your tired body after walking around all day. Rates start at $229 for singles and $249 for doubles. *Psst . . . the CD and video library is an added bonus.*

Hotel Wales, 1295 Madison Ave. (bet. 92nd & 93rd Sts.), (212) 876-6000 or (800) 428-5252, *Personality & Convenience*

Room service, please! Built in 1901, this hotel is the perfect mix of the old and new: amenities include modern conveniences like VCRs, CD players, even a sound-therapy machine to help you sleep before you join the madding crowd of Madison Ave. shoppers. Enjoy a complimentary breakfast that includes sumptuous baked goods from Sarabeth's (see Eats) delivered right to your door!

The Lowell Hotel, 28 E. 63rd St., (bet. Madison & Park Aves.), (212) 838-1400, *www.1hw.com, Discreet*

This cozy, elegant hotel has been the temporary home to jet-setters from around the world. It has only 44 suites, which include wood-burning fireplaces and fresh flowers for your neoclassical bedside table. Check out the classics on the bookshelves before giving in to your down pillow. Ask about "theme" suites to suit your fancy! Rooms are $345 for a single and $1,415.00 for a deluxe two-bedroom suite. *Psst . . . the state-of-the-art gym on the second floor overlooks the beautiful tree-lined street.*

The Mark, 25 E. 77th St. (bet. Madison & Park Aves.), (212) 774-4300 or (800) THE-MARK, *www.themarkhotel.com, Privacy*

Classic elegance for the woman on the go who seeks privacy and luxury and has an unlimited T&E. Ask for the Wellness Suite with Cybex Stair-Master, sauna, and steam room. The 120 rooms are stocked with lovely Molton Brown bath products and a direct line to Zitomers (see Treasures) where cosmetic and bath products can be delivered and charged right to your hotel bill. All rooms have king-size beds, and the deluxe suites (60 of them) have elegant foyers and terraces that overlook Central Park. Rates vary seasonally starting at $400. Ask about special weekend packages. *Psst . . . a shuttle is available to Wall St. daily and the theater district on weekends.*

✦ *Not to Miss:*
The Regency Hotel, 540 Park Ave. (bet. 61st & 62nd Sts.), (212) 759-4100, *www.loewshotels.com, Business Plus Luxury*
Four Seasons, 57 E. 57th St. (bet. Park & Madison Aves.), (212) 758-5700, *www.fourseasons.com, Grand Style*
Plaza Athenee, 37 E. 64th St., (bet. Madison & Park Aves.), (212) 734-9100, *www.plaza-athenee.com, European Elegance*

Check out www.ny.com/museums/ for info about all of NYC's museums.

✐ *Time Off*

Bryant Park, bet. 40th & 42nd Sts. (Fifth & Sixth Aves.), (212) 512-5700, *Outdoor Movies*

May through September, grab a blanket and picnic on any Monday night and watch classic films under the stars. *How to Marry a Millionaire* never looked so good as you survey your own prospects from your lawn perch! Arrive early to stake out your turf. It's free.

Kramer's Reality Tours, 432 W. 42nd St. (bet. Ninth & Tenth Aves.), (212) 268-5525, *Seinfeld Diehards*

Seinfeld lives on! At least according to Kenny Kramer. And who better to lead the pack than the inspiration for Michael Richards's cult character "Cosmo Kramer." Every Saturday and Sunday starting at noon, Kenny will escort you through the series' locations. For three hours you can delight in TV seasons past when this was all a reality. Boo-hoo! Costs $37.50, and reservations are a must. Includes cheese pizza (where they ate) and a surprise dessert and soda.

Late Show with David Letterman, 1697 Broadway, (bet. 51st & 52nd Sts.), (212) 975-5853, *Television Taping*

Why freeze your buns off in the studio when you can watch it on TV? We don't know, but the audience is packed each night. Odds are tough unless you are selected by lottery in August, but *some* standby tickets are available the day of the show at 9:15 A.M. sharp at NBC (mezzanine level/49th St. side of Rockefeller Plaza). To participate in the lottery, write: Late Show Tickets, Ed Sullivan Theater, 1697 Broadway, NY, NY 10019.

Liberty Helicopter Tours, W. 30th St. @ Twelfth Ave. (@ PIER 6), Downtown Heliport, (212) 487-4777, *Ariel View*

Experience three different pilot-narrated tours—the shortest in length being the zippedy-do-da four-minute flyby of the Statue of Liberty ("The Statue Express"). Jet helicopters whisk you in and out of the skyscrapers at such close range you can buy some stock on Wall St. from your seat! This company has consistently been awarded for safety by the Helicopter Association International. Reservations requested. Prices range from $53 to $160.

Museum of Television & Radio, 25 W. 52nd St. (bet. Fifth & Sixth Aves.), (212) 621-6600, *Alternative Museum*

A museum dedicated to the medium of TV and radio? How much more American and apple pie can you get? Visit the extensive archives and see historic moments in television and radio history such as Walter Cronkite's commentary of Neil Armstrong landing on the moon. Don't miss the old commercials and old cartoons from TV's inception. Tune in and tune out!

New York Public Library, Fifth Ave. (@ 42nd St.), (212) 869-8089, *Public Facility*

This magnificent Beaux Arts Center is breathtaking, complete with signature lions at the gate. Housing 8.5 million volumes, rare stamps, manuscripts, documents, and other reference material. It's worth a peek even if you think you know it all!

Radio City Music Hall, 1260 Sixth Ave. (@ 50th St.), (212) 247-4777, *Performance Hall*

Not for Rockettes only, this cavernous deco institution hosts everything from Liza Minelli to reggae festivals. This is also a great family destination during the holidays—Ice Capades, concerts, and, of course, those high-kicking babes of yesteryear. Live it, feel it, breathe it . . . You're in the Big Apple, baby! Recent renovations make this worth a walk-by just to see the art deco lobby restored to its grandeur.

The Ziegfeld, 141 W. 54th St. (bet. Sixth & Seventh Aves.), (212) 765-7600, *Historic Movie Theater*

Named after legendary showgirl impresario, Florenz Ziegfeld, this is the last of the old-fashioned cinemas in New York City. Showing mostly "blockbuster" films with all of the modern amenities you expect like Dolby surround sound et al. Popular shows have reserved seating only. Enjoy a retro moment when the occasional "reissue" allows you to see a classic film in its natural habitat!

✒ *Good to Know:*

TKTS, 47th St. @ Broadway, (212) 768-1818, *Broadway Tickets*

Discount theater tix, as much as half off for same-day shows. For Wednesday and Saturday matinees go between 10 A.M. and 2 P.M.; evening performances, 3–8 P.M.; Sunday performances, 11 A.M.–8 P.M. Be forewarned: the lines can be horrific, but not always.

✒ *Sweet Dreams*

Algonquin Hotel, 59 W. 44th St. (bet. Fifth & Sixth Aves.), (212) 840-6800, *www.camberleyhotels.com, Historic*

Visit this legendary hotel of the old New York literati and last bastion of classic style. It's even mentioned in J.D. Salinger's, *Catcher in the Rye*. Like musicals? Alan Jay Lerner wrote *My Fair Lady* in room #908! Each guest is given a copy of *The New Yorker*. Single rooms are $240, two-bedroom suites are $525.

Hotel Modern, 243 W. 55th St. (bet. Broadway & Eighth Ave.), (212) 397-6767, *www.nycityhotel.net, Low-Key Cool*

This mod and funky minimalist hotel offers reasonable rates (for midtown anyway) and relative comfort. The rooms are small but have pizzazz, like wall-sized portraits of Marilyn Monroe! Rates are a steady $245 and they come with a free Continental breakfast. *Pssst . . . the Soup Nazi, made famous by* Seinfeld, *is near by. Delicious sustenance on the go!*

Hudson Hotel, 356 W. 58th St. (bet. Eighth & Ninth Aves.), (212) 554-6000, *www.hudsonhotels.com, Neighborhood Newcomer*

Beautiful people. Ian Schraeger and Phillipe Starck. Beyond spectacular . . . seduced by the ultramod edifice, adventurous "Jane" hops on the industrial-style escalator and is transported into chic oblivion. Let the beauty unravel: a "clubby" bar with a lavender felt-covered pool table, and a main bar with backlit floor and modern mural on the ceiling. Explore a solo dinner at the seats around the exposed kitchen, then wander into the outdoor garden on a starry, starry night. You will think you are dreaming . . . and with a blink up to your room, you can be! There are 1,000 rooms to choose from. Rates start at $95, up to $500.

The Muse, 130 W. 46th St. (bet. Sixth & Seventh Aves.), (212) 485-2400, *Upscale Boutique*

Combining contemporary convenience and comfort, this highly innovative hotel emphasizes personal service. Things to love: a sit-down reception desk, spacious rooms and baths, classic furnishings, toiletries by Philosophy, twice-daily maid service, fitness center/spa services, and the "Midnight Pantry," where you are allowed to raid the "cupboard"—a complimentary buffet of homemade cookies, fruit, cheese, and ice cream. Rates are $300.

New York Hilton, 1335 Sixth Ave. (bet. 53rd & 54th Sts.), (212) 586-7000, *De-Stress*

Book the Stress-Less room equipped with a small fountain, a massage pad, yoga videos, music, and an aromatherapy kit. Or try the Health-Fit rooms that have the Reebok CyclePlus equipment, jogging maps, fitness magazines, and Power Bars. (Just give us the Power Bar and the TV remote.) Best bet: the rates for both specialty rooms are the same as the regular rooms. Rates change depending on availability. Starting at $260.

Paramount, 235 W. 46th St. (bet. Broadway & Eighth Ave.), (212) 764-5500, *See And Be Scene*

Another stylin' success from Ian Schraeger with the assistance of the designer of the millennium, Philippe Starck. Recent renovations have made it even better with computer-driven lighting, a library-style bar (see Twilight) upstairs and a lobby big enough to make you want to hang out. And that's just what you will do when you see the size of your room. Room rates from $220 for a double.

The Shoreham, 33 W. 55th St. (bet. Fifth & Sixth Aves.), (212) 247-6700, *www.shoerhamhotel.com, It's Suite*

This modern hotel with 855 guest rooms and 36 suites is popular with the fashion and entertainment crowd. If you're traveling en masse, take advantage of the Garden Suite, which can accommodate up to 20 people. Many of the penthouses offer private terraces and all bedrooms feature plush down comforters and Belgian linens. Room rates from $295.

Sofitel, 45 W. 44th St. (bet. Fifth & Sixth Aves.), (212) 354-8844 or (800) SOFITEL, *For Grown-Ups*

Opened in summer 2000, this hot hotel attempts to preserve the original architecture of the building amid the ultramodernized backdrop of "Times Square." The interiors were done by Paris-based designer Pierre Rochon, adding his own twist to 1930s art deco Paris meets Manhattan. The  connected traditional brasserie is aptly named Gaby after Picasso's favorite model. Live music adds extra atmosphere for a little unwinding. Rates start at $369 per night. *Psst . . . the bathrooms are the highlight with marble and lizard-print wall coverings, separate audio/TV speakers, and roomy showers!*

The Time, 224 W. 48th St. (bet. Broadway & Eighth Aves.), (212) 320-2925, *www.thetimeny.com, Trendy*

The first luxury boutique hotel, only 192 rooms, to open in the heart of Times Square. Designed by Adam Tihany, the two-story glass façade belies the stark white lobby and guest rooms in the four primary colors. Web TV, Bose Sound Systems, and cell phones upon request at check-in add to the sparkle factor! *Psst . . . the restaurant on the ground floor is the famed NY Coco Pazzo. Delish!*

Webster Apartments, 419 W. 34th St. (bet. Ninth & Tenth Aves.), (212) 967-9000, *Affordable*

Okay, you need short-term housing in NYC to job hunt, relocate, whatever. This is one of the nicer women-only residences in the city. Single rooms, shared baths, two meals a day with room service—application by interview and sliding-scale prices based on income. Chill out in the afternoon between appointments on the leafy private rooftop terrace.

✦ *Not to Miss:*
Royalton, 44 W. 44th St. (bet. Fifth & Sixth Aves.), (212) 869-4400, *Schraeger Mainstay*
Ameritania Hotel, 1701 Broadway (@ 54th St.), (212) 247-5000, *Cheap Yet Chic*

✦ *Good to Know:*
NBC Studios @ Rockefeller Center

What a thrill to see the home of this landmark TV powerhouse in action! Tours depart every fifteen minutes for $10—show up early as they sell out well before departure time. Don't let the ghost of Bryant Gumbel scare you!

Midtown East

♦ Time Off

Mary Boone, 754 Fifth Ave. (bet. 57th & 58th Sts.), (212) 752-2929,
Modern Art

The darling of the art world since the 1980s has made the move uptown
to continue her representation of hot newcomers as well as a stable of the
established and successful (Julian Schnabel and Jean-Michel Basquiat . . .).
She's the Establishment elite of the moment.

Pierpont Morgan Library, 29 E. 36th (bet. Madison & Park Aves.),
(212) 685-0610, *Literary Haunt*

J.P. Morgan, Jr., bequeathed his father's former estate to the city in
1924. Basically a library with books stacked from floor to ceiling (sound like
your house?), the estate plays host to traveling exhibits along with a permanent exhibit of an original manuscript of Dickens's *A Christmas Carol.* Closed
Mondays and holidays. *Psst . . . don't miss the breezy café, but don't get too comfortable because sleepovers aren't allowed.*

Tepper Galleries, 110 E. 25th St. (bet. Park & Lexington Aves.), (212)
677-5300, *www.teppergalleries.com, Antique Auction*

Founded in 1937 this family-owned "country auction" in the city hosts
some of the best and eclectic estate auctions—for the serious antique and
silver collector to those of us in search of wacky vintage Norma Kamali
wallpaper. Even the gal on the prowl will feel at home amidst the local deal-
ers in search of steals to mark up 200 percent in their own galleries. Be sure
to preview on Friday before Saturday sales (9 A.M.–7 P.M.). Inspect before
you bid and bring plenty of cash—no credit cards accepted.

Tour of the United Nations, (First Ave. @ 46th St.), (212) 963-3354,
International Loaping

Take a tour of the center of peacekeeping . . . Besides seeing where the
Security Council meets, the real draw are the amazing "gifts" given by coun-
tries for display throughout the facility. Tours, offered multilingually, start
every half hour. Weird detail: mail a gift or note from the
UN Post Office—complete with their own stamp system
and mailing operations.

✦ *Sweet Dreams*

The Box Tree, 250 E. 49th St. (bet. Second & Third Aves.), (212) 758-8320, *www.theboxtree.com, Romantic*

These two town houses sit side by side and house thirteen romantic rooms, each one luxuriously decorated with antique furniture and working fireplaces. Some of the rooms have canopied beds and the Fabergé Room has hand-painted murals. The ghosts of angels past include Robert De Niro, Steven Spielberg, Barbra Streisand, and Cher. Room rates are $240 on Sunday–Thursday and $340 on weekends.

The Dylan Hotel, 52 E. 41 St. (bet. Madison & Park Aves.), (212) 338-0500, *www.dylanhotel.com, Neighborhood Newcomer*

This is a luxury boutique hotel for those interested in something off the beaten path. A turn-of-the-century town house that formerly was home to the historic Chemist's Club, the hotel's classical architectural details are enhanced by its stylish and modern furnishings. The inviting rooms (only 108) are large but minimalist, and a small but nice gym makes this the perfect place to sleep peacefully. Rates range from $335 to $450.

The Gershwin, 7 E. 27th St. (bet. Fifth & Madison Aves.), (212) 545-8000, *Young & Fun*

Our first thought was "what in the &*%$^ is that!" It's a hostel/hotel funky divey Euro-hip destination for the pierced and poetic, but we like it. Ah to be 23 again. An art gallery, Astroturf roof/sundeck, pop art and red room bar add to the wacky yet festive atmosphere. Think spartan, clean and boheme! Twenty-five dollars per night; first come, first serve; rooms sleep 4–12 people.

Kitano New York, 66 Park Ave. (@ 38th St.), (212) 885-7000 or (800) KITANO.NY, *Geisha Girls*

This is the ideal alternative hotel, perfect for a bridal shower or if you are an executive avoiding the typical upscale New York hotel. Try booking Manhattan's only authentic Tatami Suite featuring a Japanese Tea Ceremony room in the style of *"sukiya-zukuri,"* a centuries-old style of architecture noted for its delicacy, simplicity and use of organic materials. Room service can set everything up for you, but it might be a good idea to consult the front desk regarding the etiquette on what to wear for the event!

Morgan's, 237 Madison Ave. (@ 37th St.), (212) 686-0300, *Discreet*

The most discreet and low key of Ian Schraeger's hotel monopoly. The rooms are small but well-appointed with bathrooms designed by the eternally chic Andrea Putnam and stocked with Kiehl's products—love that cucumber body lotion! Rates start at $420 a night, $925 for a two-room suite. *Psst . . . an overnight stay has its privileges: guaranteed reservations at Asia de Cuba (see Twilight) or the basement bar aptly named Morgan's Bar. Both are highly popular and require jumping over the velvet rope.*

St. Regis, 2 E. 55th St. (bet. Fifth & Madison Aves.), (212) 753-4500, *Grand Dame*

This hotel is as close as you can get to perfection according to our "Jane" instincts. The building's a landmark 1904 structure and frankly, pure heaven! Too bad "heaven" has a heavy price tag! Luscious linens and marble baths, and forget the minibar. Just ask for the maitre d'Etage, an English-style butler on each floor who sees to your requests 24 hours a day. Fitness center and sauna available. Rates start at $590 and go up to $7,000 for the best suite in the house (aptly named the Imperial)! *Psst . . . don't overlook the hotel restaurant Lespinase, which is consistently rated four stars, or the King Cole bar (see Twilight).*

The Waldorf Astoria, 301 Park Ave. (bet. 49th & 50th Sts.), (212) 355-3000, *Classic*

"Meet me in front of the clock inside the Waldorf Astoria!" The landmark oversize bronze clock, bearing small sculptures of winged angels, the Statue of Liberty, Queen Victoria and a few recognized American figures, was built in 1893. The facility is two exquisitely furnished hotels in one: the Astoria and the Towers. The original building (the Astoria) has 1,120 rooms, while the Towers, where every U.S. president since Herbert Hoover has stayed has 118 rooms. Rates at the Astoria are $245 for double rooms and $275 for suites. Waldorf Towers are $375 for double rooms, suites from $635. *Psst . . . don't miss the Steinway baby grand piano given by Cole Porter, who was a permanent resident here from 1937 until his death in 1964. There are stain rings left on the piano by his martini glass.*

Not to Miss:

Fitzpatrick Grand Central, 141 E. 44th St. (bet. Lexington & Third Aves.), (212) 351-6800, *Irish Accommodations*

W Hotel, 541 Lexington Ave. (bet. 49th & 50th Sts.), (212) 755-1200, *www.whotels.com, Spreading Like Bunnies*

Chelsea/Meatpacking

Time Off

Andrea Rosen, 525 W. 24th St. (bet. Tenth & Eleventh Aves.), (212) 627-6000, *Modern Art HQ*

Contemporary art with an edge and attitude. Newly relocated to this daring little art block, this gallery and dealer will not disappoint the collector in search of something just a bit outside the box.

Barbara Gladstone, 515 W. 24th, (bet. Tenth & Eleventh Aves.), (212) 206-9300, *It Gallery Girl*

The "of-the-moment" contemporary art dealer in town . . . and her moment doesn't seem to be ending anytime soon, though it began in the 1980s. If you have limited time to catch the best and the brightest in the world of contempo art, this is your destination. Expect the unusual from Europe and the U.S.

Chelsea Piers, Pier 59-62 @ the Hudson River, (212) 336-6666, *Fitness Fanatic*

Oh, the games people play! Since 1985, this complex has provided a great outlet for all girls who get island fever from time to time. Ice Skating (@ Pier 61, (212) 336-6500) for $10.50 (plus $5 for skate rentals), Golf (@ Pier 59, (212) 336-6400) $15 for 100 balls, Sports Center (@ Pier 60, (212) 446-6000) and let's not forget bowling, gymnastics, baseball cages, and more. Call the main number for all of the other activities. *Psst . . . they offer three kinds of day passes ranging from $25 to $50.*

Dia Center for the Arts, 548 W. 22nd St. (bet. Tenth & Eleventh Aves.), (212) 989-5566, *www.diacenter.org, Wide-Open Space*

Touted as the catalyst to the burgeoning Chelsea art scene, the Dia opened its doors back in 1987 when most of us were still mastering the "art" of aerobic dance! The main focus remains minimalism and conceptualism housed within four gigantic stories of warehouse space including a glass gazebo. Visit the one-of-a-kind printed matter bookstore, home to one of the country's most important offerings of "artist-made" books. Visit Dia once and you'll be hooked.

Paula Cooper, 534 W. 21st St. (bet. Tenth & Eleventh Aves.), (212) 255-1105, *Art Leader*

Originally located in SoHo, Paula Cooper is credited for launching the first commercial art gallery in that neighborhood in 1968. She had the first commercial art gallery in SoHo so for her to jump the fence is a big deal— this gal is still playing art-world hardball after 30 years in the game. With the 1976 Jennifer Bartlett installation of *Rhapsody,* Paula arrived on the 'hood fling in your kitchen!

The Garage Flea Market 112 W. 25th St. (bet. Sixth & Seventh Aves.), (212) 647-0707 or **Sixth Avenue Flea Market,** Sixth Ave. (bet. 24th & 25th Sts.), (212) 243-5343, *Flea Market*

Hands down the biggest, best and most popular flea market in Gotham City. Anything goes—imagine a garage sale/chachki convention in Heaven! Furniture, loads of vintage clothing, antiques (closer to the 26th St. side), and tons of miscellaneous "junk."

☞ *Sweet Dreams*

Chelsea Hotel, 222 W. 23rd St. (bet. Eighth & Ninth Sts.), (212) 243-3700, *www.hotelchelsea.com, Landmark Building*

If these walls could talk! This classic New York institution of a hotel has been the home away from of many writers, artists, composers and performers throughout the century. Built in 1882, once it was the tallest building in the city. The high ceilings, thick walls. The cool artwork is the work of past  guests. What's good enough for onetime guest Mark Twain is good enough for us! Ambiance galore for the artist in you. Most of the rooms are equipped with kitchenettes but don't expect a minibar. Rates start at $165.

Union Square/Gramercy/Flatiron

♦ Time Off

De La Guarda, 20 Union Square East (@ 15th St.), (212) 239-6200, (telecharge for tickets), *Performance Art*

This off-Broadway show originated in Argentina as a reaction to the end of dictatorship twelve years ago. It's a once-in-a-lifetime experience (and we're dying to see it again!). Most of the action takes place above your head, and beware, it is somewhat interactive. Synthetic storms shower the audience, flying, rope ballet, and bare-chested primal screaming add up to an event "dripping" in sensuality. At one point during the evening a quasi-nude human bird swoops down and takes an audience member into the sky. The show evolves into a full-blown dancing, singing, kissing "free for all" with minitrinket animals falling from the heavens.

Union Square Greenmarket, @ Union Square, (14th St. & Broadway), *Outdoor Market*

Country meets city in the greatest open-air greengrocer since Mr. Green Jeans. (We are showing our age!) Starting at 8 A.M. on Mondays, Wednesdays, and Fridays. It's worth a visit even if Martha Stewart leaves you cold and your kitchen has not been used in weeks. Top chefs poke and prod Amish-grown veggies that will be four-starred tonight.

♦ Sweet Dreams

The Inn at Irving Place, 56 Irving Pl. (bet. 17th & 18th Sts.), (212) 533-4600, *www.innatirving.com, Worthy*

This exquisite landmark town house offers 12 private guest rooms and suites that are furnished with Edith Wharton-esque antiques. But modern comforts have not been forsaken, so this gem was included in the exclusive group of Small Luxury Hotels of the World. Rooms offer climate control as well as the latest cyber amenities. Rates are $300 to $500.

The Giraffe Park, 365 Park Ave. (@ 26th St.), (212) 685-7700, *www.hotelgiraffe.com, Beauty Abounds*

Bring a favorite CD when you book a room at this small but chic hotel. Its 73 rooms are all well appointed with special high-speed Internet access, cordless phones, CD players, and more! This place screams of elegance and sophistication without any of the pretension usually associated. Mosey between the health club and the lobby for a gratis selection of wine and cheese served each weekday evening. Rates are $325 to $2,500 for the Piano Suite. *Psst . . . includes a continental breakfast as well!*

Gramercy Park Hotel, 2 Lexington Ave. (@ 21st St.), (212) 475-4320, *www.gramercyparkhotel.com, Neighborhood Staple*
  This funky hotel is located on NYC's one and only private park. Guests will have access to a the very valuable gate key that the hotel porter keeps for guests of the hotel. Think of the romantic sunset strolls with the handsome European thing you met at the happening lobby bar (see Twilight). Some of the "oversize rooms" (by New York standards) have a park view. Singles from $150, doubles from $170.

Greenwich Village

⚘ *Time Off*

Angelica Film Center, 18 W. Houston St. (@ Mercer St.), (212) 955-2000, *Ultra Art Films*
  The spacious café and grand foyer is the perfect setting for the style-conscious to linger over cappuccino regardless of the films at hand. Be that as it may, the film selection is stellar—all the "up-to-the-moment" art films with major backing (think Miramax and Begnini).

Film Forum, 209 W. Houston St. (@ 6th St. & Varick St.), (212) 727-8110, *Art Films*
  Best place to see old classics and newer alternative films in a cozy neighborhood setting. The local crowd mirrors the artsy nature of the theater. Where else could you see Juliette Binoche in *Lovers on the Bridge* on the big screen? Seating is limited, so arrive early to avoid front-row neck cramps.

Forbes Magazine Galleries, 62 Fifth Ave. (@ 12th & 13th Sts.), (212) 206-5549, *Unique Collection*

  Enter the world of the late Malcolm Forbes and experience the richness of his personal art and memorabilia collection. With a dozen Fabergé eggs on display, second

only to The Hermitage in St. Petersburg, the gallery also boasts an incredible selection of moving toy soldiers and trains, and an unparalleled collection of presidential papers and correspondence. The gallery is located on the ground floor of the magazine offices, and admission is free!

Greenwich Village Literary Pub Crawl, 567 Hudson St., (@ W. 11th St.), (212) 613-5796, *Literary Afternoon*

Led by actors from the New Ensemble Theatre Co., this wacky excursion is actually a fascinating walking tour for the intellectual alcofrolic: literary-minded and very thirsty! The tour includes visits to places where famous writers met and drank, including speakeasys such as Chumley's (see Twilight), the Cornelia Street Café, and Cedar Tavern (see Twilight). Who knows when inspiration might strike! Every Saturday at 2 P.M. from the Whitehorse Tavern. Reservations recommended.

⸎ Sweet Dreams

Abingdon Guest House, 13 Eighth Ave. (bet. 12th & Jane Sts.), (212) 243-5384, *www.abingdonguesthouse.com, Classic B & B*

Got more panache than cash? This New England–style brownstone has two separate guesthouses with nine rooms outfitted with items collected from the owner's world travels. They also provide such necessary amenities as private phone lines, cable TV, and A/C for those August visits! Its unique charm and one-of-a-kind décor make this a special find. There is no sign outside so call ahead for specific directions. Rates are $200.

Bed and Breakfast on Downing Street, 30 Downing St. (bet. Sixth Ave. & Bedford St.), (212) 627-9087, *Rooms To Rent*

The French know how to run hotels and make great croissants. Here the two collide! Run by the owners of the highly successful and arty Le Gamin cafés (see Eats), this charming tiny two-room hideaway includes breakfast at any of their cafés. Word of mouth is all that is needed to keep this place occupied, so don't be too frustrated to find their phone constantly busy! Nonsmokers preferred. How very un-French of them! Room rates are $100. No credit cards accepted.

Larchmont Hotel, 27 W. 11th St. (bet. Fifth & Sixth Aves.), (212) 989-9333, www.larchmonthotel.com, *Simple But True*

Beauty on a budget. Situated in a quiet brownstone on a tree-lined street, the welcoming and elegant entrance sets the stage for this cozy "European-style" hotel (some rooms have to shave a bath). The rooms cost so little that you won't balk at waiting for the "toilette"! Terry-cloth robes and slippers are included. Rates are from $69 to $99. Includes a Continental breakfast.

Washington Square Hotel, 103 Waverly Pl. (bet. Fifth & Sixth Aves.), (212) 777-9515, *Sleep Here, www.wshotel.com*

Do we have the "inn-formation" for you: 180 rooms, many of which face Washington Square Park! Take note of the small fitness facility which is rare for such low rates in this prime location. Rates are $165–$199. *Pssst . . . the money you save staying here can be put to good use across the street at our favorite Italian eatery, Babbo (see Eats!). Get out your comfy Tod's and explore the neighborhood.*

East Village/Lower East Side ···

⚘ Time Off

Anthology Film Archives, 32 Second Ave. (@ 2nd St.), (212) 505-5181, *Ultra Art Films*

No Kevin Costner flicks here. Arty Arty Arty. Even Fellini might be too mainstream. Bring a pillow for your tush and some snacks in your purse. You'll get much more than indigestion for your time and money. Perhaps creative enlightenment?

Lower East Side Tenement Museum, 90 Orchard St. (@ Broome St.), (212) 431-0233, *www.tenement.org, Historic Site*

Experience the American immigrant life in this unique 1863 tenement interactive/building/museum. Step into the world of the turn-of-the-century ethnic New Yorker by visiting this fully restored tenement. Tues–Fri. @ 1,2,3,4 P.M. plus Thurs. @ 6,7 P.M. Sat. and Sun. every 30 minutes between 11 A.M. and 4:30 P.M. Suggested eight-dollar donation. Gallery 90, at 90 Orchard St., serves as the visitor center.

P.S. 122, 150 First Ave. (@ E. 9th St.), (212) 477-5288, *Avant Art*

A performance space with two theaters, a gallery and a day-care center all rolled into one. In the East Village, this is the preeminent alternative cultural center committed to encouraging new artists (and some not too new, like Spalding Grey) for almost 20 years. Pushing the boundaries is the goal in this "performance" space where that could mean anything from opera to DJ-ing. Support your local starving artist.

Sweet Dreams

Off SoHo Suites, 11 Rivington St. (bet. Bowery & Chrystie St.), (212) 979-9651, *Groups*

This all-suite hotel is not quite in SoHo, so rates are reasonable, ($199–$259). Every suite has room enough for four people. While the décor leaves a bit to be desired, the downtown location can't be beat, and they offer a fitness center, laundry, and kitchen on-premises.

Good to Know:

Tompkins Square Dog Run

Dogs run free and look so happy doing it. Let your pet experience "life without the leash"!

Free shopping tours by the Orchard Street Shopping District Center leave from Katz's Deli (Ludlow & E. Houston Sts.) every Sunday @ 11:00 A.M. from April–December. Call (212) 226-9010 for more info!

SoHo/Nolita/Chinatown/Little Italy

Time Off

The Broken Kilometer, (1979), 393 W. Broadway (bet. Spring & Broome Sts.), no phone, *It's Free*

Sculpture with a twist. Viewing is a must at this loft space in SoHo that contains 500 highly polished, round solid brass rods, each measuring two meters in length and five centimeters in diameter. They have been placed precisely in five parallel rows of 100 rods each and are illuminated by stadium lights; together they weigh 18¾ tons and would measure 3,280 feet if laid end to end. Get a peek at this true New York treasure, which has been on view to the public since 1979. Open Wed.–Sat. 12–3 P.M., 3:30–6 P.M., September–June.

Deitch Projects, 76 Grand St. (bet. Wooster & Greene Sts.), (212) 966-9074, *Seriously Mod Art*

"Projects" is an apt title for this inventive and provocative home to large-scale installations and performance art concealed behind an unassuming small door. The entire gallery was once transformed into a "cavernous and light blue swimming pool," giving the viewer the unique sensation of standing on the drain—literally and figuratively. Rumor has it Yoko Ono shows here, but regardless of star power, Deitch is an artistic adventure for the mind and spirit and a champion of the emerging artist—Vanessa Beecroft, Teresita Fernandez.

Phyllis Kind Gallery, 136 Greene St. (bet. Houston & Prince Sts.), (212) 925-1200, *Neighborhood Find*

Starting in Chicago in 1967 and moving to New York in 1975, Phyllis Kind has always been in the business of promoting modern artists and their work—both the well schooled as well as the "art brut," outsider art. The first to show Howard Finster in 1977, she also helped to make the careers of Jim Niett and Roger Brown. *Psst . . . she always has a presence at January's Outsider Art Fair in the historic Puck Building.*

Poets House, 72 Spring St. (bet. Broadway & Lafayette Sts.), (212) 431-7920, *Relax & Read*

Picture this: a cozy living room with slipcovered chairs inviting you to relax in bohemian style, a book of poetry in your lap. Housing over 35,000 volumes of poetry from the obscure to the famous, the space is bathed in sunlight via floor-to-ceiling windows. T.S. Eliot has never been so invigorating! No membership required.

◢ *Sweet Dreams*

Bevy's SoHo Loft, 70 Mercer St. (bet. Spring and Broome Sts.), (212) 431-8214, *Budget & Style*

Can't swing the high-end ticket of the SoHo Grand? Never fear, Bevy's fits the bill as the only bed-and-breakfast in the neighborhood. There are three large rooms available within the loft, which has a working fireplace area, high ceilings and a picnic-style table for breakfast. Single with shared bath for $75, double with private bath $170. Funky but fun and functional!

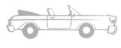

The Mercer, 147 Mercer St. (@ Prince St.), (212) 966-6060, *Rich & Famous*

Enter off the brick-lined streets into a chic and sleek haven that was many years in the making. Originally built by John Astor in 1890 as an office building, it has been fully restored by internationally renowned designer Christian Liagiare into luxurious "artist loft" spaces. No detail has been overlooked: 15-foot ceilings, oversize windows, and gigantic bathrooms with plush bathrobes and FACE Stockholm products. Rooms are stocked with full bottles of wine. Rates from $325 for single up to $1,850 for the penthouse suite.

Sixty Thompson Hotel, 60 Thompson St. (bet. Spring & Broome Sts.), (212) 431-0400, *www.60thompson.com, Neighborhood Newcomer*

This boutique is stylish, friendly, and ultra accommodating for all of your downtown "sleeping beauty" needs! Boasting only 100 rooms, 24-hour service, DVD players, and cell phone in each room, a 1,000-CD library and access to nearby Crunch and New York Sports Clubs are just a few of the extras. We love the Thompson Loft Suite with a fireplace and terrace for al fresco dining on a fall evening, or rent the whole top floor for a private affair. Rates start at around $370 and suites at $500–$650, $1500 for the Thompson Loft.

SoHo Grand, 310 West Broadway (bet. Grand St. & Canal Sts.), (212) 965-3000, *www.sohogrand.com, Star Studded*

Minimalist chic makes this ultrahip hotel *the* place to stay downtown for aesthetically and artistically inclined gals. Enter the upstairs lobby via the grand staircase, and while you're registering, request a special meal for your pet mink. The third floor is reserved for pet lovers who can't bear to travel without their animals. Room rates from $279 for a double.

♦ Time Off

Brooklyn Museum of Art, 200 Eastern Parkway, (718) 638-5000, *Cutting-Edge*

Always pushing the envelope, this avant-garde home to some of the country's most controversial exhibits (like 1999's SINSATION) is a great place to "educate" yourself on the latest and greatest in modern art. BAM is great for the young and not-so-young. *Psst . . . the first Saturday of each month you can mingle with 5,000 other art-hungry festive types with curator-led tours, films, live music, and dancing. You are bound to know somebody, or . . . meet somebody!*

Downtown Boathouse, Hudson River @ Pier 26 (N. Moore St.), (212) 966-1852, *Afternoon Outing*

This organization volunteers their time and boats to introduce the sport of kayaking to beginners. Visitors are encouraged to try out the sport free of charge provided they sign a release form. Stroke to the Statue of Liberty and back. However, before you become addicted be aware: there is a long wait list for cheap boat storage. The boathouse allows people with their own equipment to use the launch site gratis.

Off & Around the Beaten Path, (718) 562-4735), *Take A Break*

Getting "island fever?" See how the other half lives via this festive and touristy jaunt through three of the burroughs: Brooklyn, Queens, and the Bronx at your fingertips for $40 a head. Bronx only? Thirty dollars gets you the Botanical Gardens, Yankee Stadium, City Island, and Wave Hill. They'll even fetch you at your hotel for free . . . whoopee!

Isamu Noguchi Garden Museum, Long Island City, Queens, 32-27 Vernon Blvd. (@ 33rd Road), (718) 204-7088, *www.noguchi.org, Sculpture Garden*

This Japanese-American artist (1904–1988) had a career that spanned seventy years and two continents. A naturalist at heart, Noguchi used stone, irregular form, and chiseled surfaces as "a metaphor for one's experience and knowledge of the world"—the smooth and rough, separate but together, symbolizing the human condition. The most comprehensive Noguchi collection in the world, this museum is more of a living tribute to his genius, taking you through the sprawling Queens space where he worked and into the exterior gardens. Even the café has tables designed by the sculptor and produced by Knoll. Akari still manufactures its Noguchi "light sculpture" collaborations available by mail order . . . Open seasonally, free tour daily at 2 P.M. *Psst . . . and don't miss the funky collection of abstract art up the street along the edge of the water overlooking the city!*

P.S.1 Contemporary, 22-25 Jackson Ave. (@ 46th Ave.), Long Island City, Queens, (718) 784-2084, *www.PS1.org, Cutting-Edge Art*

The globally influential Museum of Modern Art has teamed up with P.S.1 to create a mecca for cutting-edge contemporary art. Drawing crowds of Manhattan's most adventurously dressed culture-seekers, this nouveau museum relies on an energetic throng of young curators to pursue the best of the hypercurrent art world.

New York Stock Exchange Interactive Education Center, 20 Broad St. (@ Liberty St.), (212) 656-5165, *www.nyse.com, Classic Site*

Get a glimpse of the center of the financial universe in action. You must go early (in a power suit, of course!) but once you are in the gallery, it looks like a cross between a majestic ballroom and a scene out of *Leaving Las Vegas.* And the best part is it's free!

Wave Hill, 675 W. 49th St. (@ Henry Hudson Pkwy.), the Bronx, (718) 549-3200, *www.wavehill.org, Peaceful Hideaway*

Overlooking the Hudson River and the Palisades, this 28-acre estate was a former home to Teddy Roosevelt and Mark Twain (no, they didn't cohabit). This peaceful getaway has been transformed into a cultural and educational center complete with sculpture garden and reflecting pool. We haven't been this relaxed since Dr. Dan gave us gas before a filling!

✦ Sweet Dreams

Bed & Breakfast on the Park, 113 Prospect Park West (bet. 6th & 7th Sts.), Brooklyn, (718) 499-6115, *www.bbnyc.com, Off The Beaten Path*

Situated across the street from lovely Prospect Park, this period brownstone is only a 20-minute subway ride from Manhattan. The owner is a former antique dealer who managed to stash some of her "jewels" for display in this home away from home for the aesthetic traveler! Rates start at $110 for singles, $250 for doubles.

Regent Wall Street, 55 Wall St. (bet. William & Hannover Sts.), (212) 845-8600, *www.regenthotels.com, Power Trip*

Set to take over the world, or at least your own "fund"? We have your number—this 144-room property is housed in a circa 1842 landmark that once hosted the New York Stock Exchange. The rooms are oversize and combine perfectly Old-World grandeur (deep tubs for long bubble baths) and New World technology (DVD players and Web TV). Rates are $600, $800 for a suite.

Tribeca Grand Hotel, 2 Sixth Ave. (bet. White & Walker Sts.), (212) 519-6600 or (877) 519-6600, *www.tribecagrand.com, High Tech*

This eight-story hotel opened in May 2000 with a high-tech bang! Designed to be technologically savvy without being antiseptic. The Church Lounge is a great place to hang with the young and the beautiful in a cozy living room atmosphere. The rooms come equipped with broadband Internet connectivity via high-speed ports, wireless keyboards, and Herman Miller ergonomic chairs. Best of all: local calls are free! Rates range from $399 to $649 for a suite.

✦ *Good to Know:*
Battery Park—Grab a blanket and some snacks for a peaceful and harmonious evening on the green green grass of Battery Park. Take the 1,9 to South Ferry.

✦ *Citywide:*
Call *NYC/On Stage* at (212) 768-1818 for theater tix, times, locations and plot previews including Broadway, off-Broadway, Off-Off, dance, classical concerts, and opera. A distant second is the Broadway Line (888-411-BWAY) which sticks exclusively to the Great White Way and you must know which show you are looking for before you dial.

City Pass: www.citypass.net: Buy this 28-dollar "passport" to the city's major attraction's. This nine-day pass will gain you entry to half a dozen sights for one low price. Choose from: **Empire State Building Observatory,**

the *Intrepid* **Sea-Air-Space Museum, Metropolitan Museum of Art, American Museum of Natural History,** and more. Purchase passes at the first attraction you visit or at local visitor bureaus.

TV's Channel NY1 is dedicated to 24 hours of New York news and weather. Segments run in 10-minute increments.

Taking the subway just got easier. Now you can purchase *MetroCards* from any HSBC bank machine instead of standing in line underground.

Cultural Pass: Offering unlimited admission to a number of NY museums as well as discounts to Broadway and off-Broadway shows. Purchase at the **NYC Official Visitor Info Center** @ 810 Seventh Ave. (@ 53rd St.), (212) 484-1222, or **American Express** offices.

Urban Ventures, (212) 594-5650, *Alternative Housing*
    Started by two women, this B&B concept has grown to offer over 600 residences around the city. There is something for every taste and budget—prices can be as low as $35 a night. Rooms available on a daily, weekly, or monthly basis.

In *hotel hell?* Call the **Hotel Reservation Network,** (800) 964-6835, with affiliations with more than 400 hotels in 14 cities. You might save time and money!

The **Staten Island Ferry** is free (but it does cost 40¢ to get back) to get an up-close view of the Statue of Liberty! Depart from Battery Park.

◆ Planes, Trains, Automobiles
John F. Kennedy International, (718) 533-3400, 15 miles to midtown, 1 hour travel time, taxi costs $30.
LaGuardia, (718) 533-3400, eight miles to midtown, 45 minutes travel time, taxi costs; $15–$27 plus tip.
Newark International Airport, (973) 961-6000, 16 miles to midtown, 1 hour travel time, $40–$60 plus tip.

Long Island Railroad (LIRR), (718) 217-5477, trains to Long Island and back from Penn Station.

New Jersey Path, (800) 234-7284.

Port Authority Bus Terminal, (bet. 40th & 42nd Sts.) (718) 330-1234.

Taxi alternative? Call **212 Blue-Van** for a ride to any of the airports. They will pick you up at your door and take you to your airline of choice with only three other stops for a mere $15. Book two hours in advance from your home or your hotel.

Rental car alternatives: **New York Rent-a-Car,** (888) 329-0189, has several locations in the city and offers "hometown equivalent" of the majors. Leeway on rates makes this a great place to show up near closing time and get a deal. Non–bargain hunters can go for the Ferraris ($1,100 for three days) or a new VW Beetle ($329 for three days).

Be a Star: At least for one night! **Silver Star Limousine Service,** (800) 640-ASTAR, rents Rolls Royces for $100 an hour. Or you can get the regular "status" limo for six or seven friends for $65 per hour plus the standard 20 percent gratuity.

✧ Getaways

New Age Health Spa, Neversink, New York, (914) 985-7600, *www.newagehealthspa.com, Detox Headquarters*

If the thought of soaking in a hot tub, getting exotic massages and facials, doing yoga in the outdoors, meditating in the fall foliage, and losing a few pounds sounds enticing, then do we have the place for you. And you won't blow your whole savings account to do it. Sharing a room ensures an even better bargain! Remember this is a smoking-, alcohol-, and caffeine-free environment, so make sure you can make it without your morning latte and nighttime champagne!

How to get there: They offer a minivan pickup and return service from Manhattan, so leave the driving to them. The ride is about 90 minutes. Pickups are available at the southeast corner of Madison Ave. and 72nd St. Call for info.

The Castle at Tarrytown, (400) Benedict Ave., Tarrytown, NY (914) 631-1980, *www.castleattarrytown.com, Princess Dreams*

Located on a hilltop, the Castle at Tarrytown is exactly what you'd think—a fairy-tale setting for a weekend getaway! Reminiscent of Norman fortifications, the building has historic landmark status. With such luxury amenities as state-of-the-art fitness center and heated indoor pool, the Castle is a nice mix of old-fashioned and up-to-date. Rooms book fast in the summer, as it is a popular wedding location. In other seasons, however, this place is an accessible gem. Rooms are $285 to $625.

Old Drover's Inn, Old Route 22, Dover Plains, New York, (914) 832-9311, *East Coast Cool*

This 1750 colonial farmhouse is perfectly restored and preserved. (The name comes from "drovers," which are New England cowboys). Four enchanting rooms, three with fireplaces, and the best breakfast on the East Coast. It's no wonder they have been rated so highly in several travel magazines and made an exclusive member of the Relais and Chateaux Group. Weekend rates for 2 people, including breakfast and dinner, start at $290.

Woodbury Common Premium Outlets, Exit 16, NYS Thruway, Central Valley, New York, (914) 928-4000, *Shopping Bonanza*

Need to satisfy a true shopping craving? Easy to do for $22.45, the cost of a round-trip bus ticket on Shoreline from Port Authority, (212) 736-4700. Call ahead to see if your favorite store is having a sale, and ask to get on their mailing list so that you know when their seasonal sales are. Knock yourself out at all 200 stores.

Skinny-Dipping . . . Where to take it all off:

Point O' Woods, Fire Island: Head to the Fire Island Hotel and Resort. Walk through the hotel lobby (clothes on, of course), turn left, and walk for about 15 minutes until you see your fellow nudists!